Hagi Kenaan • Ilit Ferber
Editors

Philosophy's Moods: The Affective Grounds of Thinking

D1872103

Springer

Editors
Hagi Kenaan
Department of Philosophy
Tel-Aviv University
Ramat Aviv
Israel
kenaan@post.tau.ac.il

Ilit Ferber
Department of Philosophy
Tel-Aviv University
Ramat Aviv
Israel
iferber@post.tau.ac.il

ISSN 0923-9545
ISBN 978-94-007-3825-6 ISBN 978-94-007-1503-5 (eBook)
DOI 10.1007/978-94-007-1503-5
Springer Dordrecht Heidelberg London New York

Softcover reprint of the hardcover 1st edition 2011

Printed on acid-free paper

Springer is part of Springer Science+Business Media (www.springer.com)

Contents

Philosophy's Moods: Biographical Notes

Bettina Bergo is Associate Professor at Université de Montréal and author of *Levinas between Ethics and Politics* and co-editor of several collections, notably *Levinas and Nietzsche: After the Death of a Certain God* (Columbia, 2008), *Trauma: Reflections on Experience and Its Other* (SUNY, 2009), *Levinas's Contribution to Contemporary Thought* (double issue of the New School for Social Research *Graduate Faculty Philosophy Journal*, 1999). She translated three works of Levinas, Marlène Zarader's *The Unthought Debt: Heidegger and the Hebraic Heritage* (Stanford), co-translated and edited *Judeities: Questions for Jacques Derrida* (Fordham 2007), and Didier Franck's *Nietzsche and the Shadow of God* (forthcoming, Northwestern).

Shlomo Cohen received his MD and Ph.D. in philosophy from the Hebrew University in Jerusalem. He is a practicing physician and has taught philosophy, especially moral theory, at Hebrew University, Tel-Aviv University, and at UCLA. He is currently completing a manuscript on the ethics of shame.

Ilit Ferber is Assistant Professor in the Philosophy Department at Tel-Aviv University. She has published articles on Benjamin, Freud, Brecht and Herder. She recently completed a book manuscript entitled *Melancholy and Philosophy: Walter Benjamin's Early Writings*, and her current research deals with the relationship between pain and theories of the origin of language in Rousseau, Herder, Freud, Benjamin and Wittgenstein.

Eli Friedlander is professor of philosophy at Tel Aviv University. He is the author of *Signs of Sense: Reading Wittgenstein's Tractatus* (Harvard University Press, 2000) and *J.J. Rousseau: An Afterlife of Words* (Harvard University Press, 2004), *Walter Benjamin: A Philosophical Portrait* (Harvard, 2011).

Wayne J. Froman teaches philosophy at George Mason University, where he was department chair, 1989–1999. His extensive publications, largely in phenomenology, include: "Heidegger and the Essence of Technology" in *Metaphysik der praktischen Welt* (Festgabe für Otto Pöggeler), edited by A. Grossmann and C. Jamme, "Merleau-Ponty and Phenomenological Philosophy," in *Études Phénoménologiques*, edition edited by J. Taminiaux, "The Strangeness in the Ethical Discourse of Emmanuel Levinas" in *Addressing Levinas*, edited by E. Nelson, A. Kapust and K. Still, and the book *Merleau-Ponty: Language and the Act of Speech.* During 1995–1996, he held a Fulbright Research Professorship at the Hegel-Archiv, Ruhr Universität/Bochum.

Ido Geiger teaches philosophy at Ben-Gurion University of the Negev, Israel. His principal research interests lie in German Idealism, especially Kant and Hegel. He is the author of *The Founding Act of Modern Ethical Life: Hegel's Critique of Kant's Moral and Political Philosophy* (Stanford University Press, 2007).

Lewis R. Gordon is the Laura H. Carnell Professor of Philosophy and Jewish Studies at Temple University and Visiting Professor at the University of the West Indies at Mona, Jamaica. His books include, more recently, *Disciplinary Decadence* (Paradigm Publishers), *An Introduction to Africana Philosophy* (Cambridge UP), and, with Jane Anna Gordon, *Of Divine Warning: Reading Disaster in the Modern Age* (Paradigm Publishers). He is past president of the Caribbean Philosophical Association.

Vered Lev Kenaan teaches classics and comparative literature at the University of Haifa. She is the author of *Pandora's Senses: The Feminine Origins of the Ancient Text* (Wisconsin University Press, 2008).

Hagi Kenaan teaches philosophy at Tel-Aviv University. In addition to studies in phenomenology, aesthetics and the philosophy of art, he is the author of *The Present Personal: Philosophy and the Hidden Face of Language* (Columbia University Press, 2005) and *Emmanuel Levinas: Ethics as an Optics* (Tel-Aviv, 2008).

Jeff Malpas is Professor of Philosophy at the University of Tasmania and Distinguished Visiting Professor at La Trobe University, Melbourne. He is the author of *Heidegger's Topology* (Cambridge, 2006) and co-editor of *Perspectives on Human Dignity* (Springer, 2006).

Stephen Mulhall is Professor of Philosophy at New College, Oxford. His work on Heidegger includes *Inheritance and Originality: Wittgenstein, Heidegger, Kierkegaard* (Oxford University Press, 2001), and *Heidegger and "Being and Time" – Second Edition* (Routledge, 2005). He is currently working on themes in Nietzsche and Sartre.

Yaron Senderowicz is a senior lecturer and the former chairman of the department of philosophy, Tel-Aviv University. His main research areas include Kant and German idealism, philosophy of mind and phenomenology. His books include *The Coherence of Kant's Transcendental Idealism* (Springer, 2005), *Controversies and the Metaphysics of Mind* (Forthcoming in John Benjamin Publishing Company). He is the associated editor of *Pragmatics & Cognition.*

Daniel Strassberg studied medicine and philosophy at the University of Zurich and psychoanalysis at the Psychonanalytisches Seminar Zürich. Since 1985 he practices psychoanalysis in private practice and teaches philosophy and psychoanalysis. Among his publications is *Das poietische Subjekt. Giambattista Vicos Wissenschaft vom Singulären* (Fink, 2007).

Ben-Ami Scharfstein is Emeritus Professor of Philosophy at Tel-Aviv University. After teaching philosophy in several American universities, he emigrated to Israel in 1955. There he established what was to become the Department of Philosophy in what was to become the University of Tel-Aviv. He has written books mainly in the field of comparative culture in religion, politics, philosophy and art. His books include *The Need to Believe* (with Mortimer Ostow) (1954); *Mystical Experience* (1974); *The Philosophers: Their Lives and the Nature of Their Thought* (1980); *The Dilemma of Context* (1989); *Ineffability: The Failure of Words in Philosophy and Religion* (1993); *Amoral Politics: The Persistent Truth of Machiavellism* (1995); *A Comparative History of World Philosophy: From the Upanishads to Kant* (1998); and *Art without Boundaries: An Exploration in Art and Humanity* (2009).

Contributors

Bettina Bergo Université de Montréal, FAS-Philosophie, CP 6128 Succ. Centre-ville, Montréal, Québec H3C 3J7, Canada, bettina.bergo@umontreal.ca

Shlomo Cohen Department of Philosophy, The Hebrew University, Mt Scopus, Jerusalem 91905, shlomo_inc@yahoo.com

Ilit Ferber Department of Philosophy, Tel-Aviv University, P.O. Box 39040, Ramat Aviv, Tel-Aviv 69978, Israel, iferber@post.tau.ac.il

Eli Friedlander Department of Philosophy, Tel-Aviv University, P.O. Box 39040, Ramat Aviv, Tel-Aviv 69978, Israel, frieli@post.tau.ac.il

Wayne J. Froman Department of Philosophy, George Mason University, Fairfax, VA 22030, USA, wfroman@gmu.edu

Ido Geiger Department of Philosophy, Ben-Gurion University of the Negev, P.O. Box 653, Beer-Sheva 84105, Israel, geigeri@bgu.ac.il

Lewis R. Gordon Department of Philosophy, Temple University, Philadelphia, PA 19122, USA, gordonl@temple.edu

Hagi Kenaan Department of Philosophy, Tel-Aviv University, P.O. Box 39040, Ramat Aviv, Tel-Aviv 69978, Israel, kenaan@post.tau.ac.il

Vered Lev Kenaan Department of Hebrew and Comparative Literature, University of Haifa, Mount Carmel, Haifa, 31905, Israel, vered.lev.kenaan@gmail.com

Jeff Malpas School of Philosophy, University of Tasmania, Private Bag 41, Hobart, TAS 7001, Australia, Jeff.Malpas@utas.edu.au

Stephen Mulhall New College, Oxford, UK, stephen.mulhall@new.ox.ac.uk

Yaron Senderowicz Department of Philosophy, Tel-Aviv University, P.O. Box 39040, Ramat Aviv, Tel-Aviv 69978, Israel, yaron.senderowicz@gmail.com

Daniel Strassberg Weinberg Street 145, CH-8006, Zürich, Switzerland, dastrass@swissonline.ch

Ben-Ami Scharfstein Department of Philosophy, Tel-Aviv University, P.O. Box 39040, Ramat Aviv, Tel-Aviv 69978, Israel, sbenami@post.tau.ac.il

Part I
Introduction

Moods and Philosophy

Hagi Kenaan and Ilit Ferber

I. Toward a Phenomenology of Moods

Jean-Paul Sartre's novel *Nausea*, presented as the journal of Antoine Roquentin, opens with the narrator's statement of an unexplained change that has pervaded his world. Roquentin's need to examine this disturbing sense of change is the explicit reason why he begins writing.

> The best thing would be to write down events from day to day. Keep a diary to see clearly—let none of the nuances or small happenings escape even though they might seem to mean nothing. And above all, classify them. I must tell how I see this table, this street, the people, my packet of tobacco, since *those* are the things which have changed. I must determine the exact extent and nature of this change. (Sartre 2007: 1)

Roquentin searches for an understanding by attending to the manifestations of the ordinary. Through close attention to the ordinary, he seeks to articulate the manner in which his whole being-in-the-world has changed.

> For instance, there is something new about my hands, a certain way of picking up my pipe or fork. Or else it's the fork which now has a certain way of having itself picked up, I don't know. A little while ago, just as I was coming into my room, I stopped short because I felt in my hand a cold object which held my attention through a sort of personality. I opened my hand, looked: I was simply holding the door-knob. (Sartre 2007: 4)

Roquentin is unaware of the phenomenological resonance and philosophical potential of his detailed daily descriptions. He is thus somewhat surprised when, his inspection of experience reveals to him the world itself, the world of which he is part, rather than a private mental domain. The unmistakable presence of a new quality acquired by the world – or, perhaps, the new absence of a dimension that has

H. Kenaan (✉) • I. Ferber
Department of Philosophy, Tel-Aviv University, P.O. Box 39040, Ramat Aviv, Tel-Aviv 69978, Israel
e-mail: kenaan@post.tau.ac.il; iferber@post.tau.ac.il

H. Kenaan and I. Ferber (eds.), *Philosophy's Moods: The Affective Grounds of Thinking*, Contributions To Phenomenology 63, DOI 10.1007/978-94-007-1503-5_1,

unexpectedly vanished from the world – makes it difficult for Roquentin to find the terms to pinpoint the change he has experienced.

> So a change *has* taken place during these last few weeks. But where? It is an abstract change without object. Am I the one who has changed? If not, then it is this room, this city and this nature; I must choose. (Sartre 2007: 4)

Yet, despite his intentions, Roquentin is ultimately unable to choose between the internal and external, since the very opposition between the two realms cannot do justice to his experience. Roquentin's world has changed in a manner that does not lend itself to an understanding in terms of a mere subjective occurrence. At the same time, however, Roquentin is unable to frame the change in terms of the objective state of things, e.g., in terms of objects and their properties. "It is an abstract change without object," one that cannot register within the objective order of facts. Roquentin's difficulty is, in itself, revealing.

Roquentin is ultimately concerned only with the specificity of his own situation, i.e., with a mood that reveals the bare "such-ness" of the world and bears a distinctive affect of nausea. Yet, despite his focus on a specific mood, Roquentin's explorations inadvertently provide a few important insights into the more general structure of moods. His ability to identify a transformation in the quality and form of his experience of the world, together with the inability to explain this transformation in terms of the common opposition between the subjective and the objective, is indeed indicative of the unique manner in which moods are present in our lives.

As a corollary we may say, with Heidegger, that moods are world revealing. For Heidegger, a central figure in this collection and clearly the most important twentieth-century advocate for moods, Dasein always belongs to a world; but this world is neither the totality of objective facts nor a merely subjective experience. World is rather the human realm of meaningfulness that precedes the distinction between the subjective and the objective. Our embeddedness in the world, our basic attachment to meaning, finds its primary expression in the experience of the world as that which matters to us: in moods.

With a new friend around, the city that seemed so gloomy now appears joyful and vibrant. Indeed, the world matters to us in different ways, at different times – revealed through the changes of moods that are, concomitantly, a disclosure of moods' dynamic infrastructure. Like Roquentin, we know that moods change, but their constant flux indicates more than their plurality and transitional nature. Change is the primary manner in which moods or the spectrum of moods is revealed to us. What their constant movement signifies is that moods are always already there, operative – in this form or another – in structuring our encounter with the world. As Heidegger puts it, "We are never free of moods .... A state-of-mind always has its understanding ... understanding always has its mood" (Heidegger 1962: 182 [143]).

According to Heidegger, moods precede any form of cognition and, moreover, they condition it. "Mood is a primordial kind of Being for Dasein, in which Dasein is disclosed to itself prior to all cognition and volition, and beyond their range of disclosure" (Heidegger 1962: 175 [136]). Or as he puts it elsewhere: "The possibilities of disclosure that belong to cognition reach far too short a way compared with the primordial disclosure belonging to moods, in which Dasein is brought before its Being as 'there'" (Heidegger 1962: 173 [134]). The totality in which moods allow us to experience the world is therefore more comprehensive and immediate than any form of cognitive comprehension, or even sensual perception, can ever be. Moreover, the wholeness of this totality stands in stark opposition to the traditional conception of rationality as a constant attempt to "seize" and, in some ways, confiscate what is opposite it. Mood offers an alternative approach in which absorption in, and captivation with, the world ground the possibility of thinking and the constitution of meaning. This special configuration of moods has a distinctly unintentional structure, as is famously analyzed by Heidegger in his discussion of the difference between fear and anxiety. Anxiety, for Heidegger, does not disclose a single object *in* the world that threatens us; it is rather the world as totality that comes to matter to us: "That about which anxiety is anxious is none of the inner worldly things at hand.... What anxiety is about is the world as such" (Heidegger 1962: 232, H187).

Moods are crucial for an understanding of our being-in-the-world; however, are moods also pertinent to an understanding of the distinctly philosophical openness to the world? What is it about moods that makes them specifically important to phenomenology?

Since Husserl, phenomenology has consistently singled itself out by making a point of its point of entry into reflection. Phenomenological reflection is dependent on, and cannot begin without, an essential transformation of our ordinary gaze. This transformation or alteration of the "natural attitude" is not a trivial aspect but constitutes a "moment" wherein resides much of the difficulty of practicing the phenomenological method. For Husserl, "The phenomenological *epoché* lays open ... *an infinite realm of being of a new kind*, as the sphere of a new kind of experience: transcendental experience" (Husserl 1999: 27). The question of the full significance of the Husserlian *epoché* and the transcendental field it lays open lies beyond the scope of this introduction. What is, nevertheless, important to notice is that the *epoché's* cognitive value stems from a unique transformative experience. With the phenomenological *epoché*, "the whole concrete surrounding life-world" changes and shows itself as "only a phenomenon of being instead of something that is." This happens through "the philosophically reflective Ego's abstention from position-takings, his depriving them of acceptance" that thereby modifies the given into a "mere phenomenon" (Husserl 1999: 20).

What the phenomenologist acquires by "this universal depriving of "acceptance", "inhibiting" or "putting out of play" of all positions taken toward the already given objective world is the universe of phenomena in the... phenomenological sense" (Husserl 1999: 20–21). Phenomenology, in other words, not only begins with a crucial shift away from our ordinary immersion in the world; it is, moreover, dependent on the possibility we have as humans of dodging or disconnecting ourselves from the claims of the ordinary world to which we are typically riveted. The *epoché* is a constitutive "moment" in the phenomenological response to the world, one that opens up the world as a phenomenological field by finding a new distance within our ordinary proximity to things. This distancing is of course different in many ways from the new experience, the transformation, that Sartre's

Roquentin seeks to account for. But, at the same time, the *epoché*, read against the background of Roquentin's insights, raises the question whether the possibility of the *epoché* and thus of phenomenology in general is not couched in the very structure of mood.

In *The Transcendence of the Ego*, Sartre addresses a similar question when he criticizes Husserl for neglecting the presence of a specific mood constitutive of the *epoché.* While making extensive use of Husserl's phenomenology in developing his "theory of consciousness," Sartre is nevertheless critical of the manner in which Husserl, in his emphasis on scientific value, blurs the existential motivations pulsating in the *epoché.* He writes that

> as long as one remains in the "natural" attitude, there is no reason, no motive for exercising the *epoché*. In fact, this natural attitude is perfectly coherent. There one will find none of those contradictions which, according to Plato, lead the philosopher to effect a philosophical conversion. Thus, the *epoché* appears in the phenomenology of Husserl as a miracle. (Sartre 1987: 102–103)

For Sartre, the *epoché's* radical transformation of experience calls for a more coherent explanation–one that emerges from his analysis of the relationship between consciousness and Ego.

> If the natural attitude appears wholly as an effort made by consciousness to escape from itself by projecting itself into the *me* and becoming absorbed there ... and if this effort is never completely rewarded, and if a simple act of reflection suffices to tear itself abruptly away from the *I* and be given as independent, then the *epoché* is no longer a miracle, an intellectual method, an erudite procedure: it is an anxiety which is imposed on us and which we cannot avoid: it is both pure event of transcendental origin and ever possible accident of our daily life. (Sartre 1987: 102–103)

What Husserl ultimately fails to see, according to Sartre, is the connection between the transformative possibility opened by the *epoché* and the unavoidable and everlasting presence of anxiety, a mood that reflects in the most fundamental way the self's difficulty in facing its own constitution. For our purposes, the question of the specificity of the mood motivating the *epoché* is less important. What is at stake, rather, is the more general understanding that mood grounds the reflective turn by which philosophy releases itself from the grip of the ordinary so as to return to the ordinary with a transformed way of seeing.

II. Wonder, Melancholy and Anxiety

Philosophy's Moods questions how philosophical thought operates within and through moods, exploring the different roles moods play in the history of philosophy: In what ways do moods constitute philosophy's reflective turn? What do moods teach us about philosophy's encounter with the world? Can we identify certain moods that are predominant in philosophical thinking?

Our premise in exploring these questions is that certain clusters of moods can be identified as central in and for the history of philosophy. In this book, we focus on what we take to be three fundamental categories of moods, which reveal different dimensions of the presence of moods in philosophy's encounter with the world. We take as fundamental moods the states of wonder, melancholy, and anxiety: each opens up a complex and nuanced domain of corresponding philosophical states of mind.

The ascendancy of *wonder* in ancient philosophy poses an interesting challenge to what we take to be the traditional attempt to separate reason from affectivity. In wonder, we find not only what the Greeks understood as the beginning of philosophy or its underlying drive, but also the kind of engagement with meaning that remains open to the mystery of being, to that which resists explanation and cannot be fully conceptualized. Plato's evocation of wonder in connection with the appearance of the rainbow points at a perplexity that cannot be exhausted by physical description. The rainbow is a natural phenomenon that calls for an explanation. Its striking appearance and unexpected beauty arouse the desire to understand the underlying conditions that make this appearance possible. However, when we look at a rainbow, the availability of a physical explanation does not do away with our initial sense of an enigma, and our fascination with the rainbow seems to reveal to us a dimension of reality which escapes rational explanation. Wonder echoes the essential lack felt in the presence of the world's unreachable beauty and thus marks the beginning of philosophizing.

Wonder, consequently, is not a monolithic mood, but grounds philosophy by resonating the twofold structure of its response to the mystery of the world. It causes our fascination and captivation with the world to resonate while concomitantly responding to a fundamental discontent vis-a-vis what escapes explanation. Another way to put this is to say that wonder harbors both proximity and distance, both a passionate attraction and a resistance to the powers of fascination.

The movement from wonder to *melancholy* may suggest a historical paradigm shift that occurred, roughly, in the seventeenth century, when the philosophical desire to know, exemplified by the ancient Aristotelean wonder, gradually dissolves into an entirely different commitment. The inability to know is no longer linked with wonder and its accompanying forms of desire but with melancholy and doubt. Philosophy's confrontation with its own limits apropos the impossibility of knowing the world no longer finds its expression in passionate wonder but now takes the form of a deep melancholic recognition of what lies outside the scope of knowledge. Descartes' doubt is a paradigmatic example of this crisis, whose resolution is undertaken by a radical withdrawal into a domain of disinterested inquiry. With Descartes, doubt overshadows fascination, and thus the systematic purging of passion and the deliverance from the attractions of unjustified belief become the only way to overcome this melancholic predicament.

The gaze's turn from the enthralling world into the skeptic, dejected self is also a movement from great yearning and attraction to closure and self-sufficiency. As means of coping with melancholy, the formation of Descartes' *cogito* is thus a symptom of a withdrawal which seeks to resist the allure of the world. When melancholic scrutiny conditions the disclosure of the world, the *self* becomes formative for the appearance of meaning and the disclosure of the world. In this respect, melancholy can be said to gather a special class of moods in which detachment from the world and absorption in the self become essential.

Responding to the seventeenth century's melancholic disappointment with the world, the enlightenment sought ways to re-secure, through the power of reason, the grounds of thinking. In the nineteenth century, the affective dimension of philosophy seems to shift away from the optimism of the enlightenment into a new philosophical state of mind: the mood of anxiety. Anxiety challenges, in many senses, both ancient wonder and baroque melancholy: in it, neither the world nor the self are encountered, but we are faced with nothingness – modernity's response to the insufficiency of both wonder and melancholy. Anxiety altogether challenges the intentional structure of consciousness and the understanding of meaning in terms of "content" and opens up, rather, the possibility of philosophizing from within a void.

Anxiety is not a desire for the world (as in wonder) or the self (as in melancholy) but rather brings about a complete transformation of desire into its modern version. With its essentially non-intentional structure, the space of anxiety allows meaning to show itself in a new way that is in constant reference – not simply to that which is-not, but to radical nothingness. Anxiety might lack the attraction toward the world that echoes in wonder, but in its reverberation of nothingness it can grant access to that dimension of the meaningful which was forbidden to thought by Parmenides and to which ancient Greek wonder could not be responsive.

III. Philosophy's Moods

The articles in this volume have been divided into four thematic sections. The first three align with the aforementioned clusters of moods: Wonder, Melancholy, and Anxiety. The last section centers on what we take to be starkly missing in those clusters, namely, philosophy's relation to the other or to alterity. This last section questions the relationship between moods and morals and explores the way in which moods not only determine philosophy's relation to the world or self but also to the other.

The book's first section discusses the role of wonder in the history of philosophy and the implications of some of the complexities it entails. Lev-Kenaan discusses the phenomenon of wonder at the intersection of ancient Greek philosophy and the cosmological epic. Reading Plato and Aristotle together with Hesiod, Lev-Kenaan uncovers the underpinnings of the philosophical thematization of wonder in the mythical imagination. She shows that, for the ancients, the affect of wonder is uniquely philosophical because of its intimate correspondence with the experience of origin. Froman underscores the philosophical importance of wonder by attending to mood's undermining of the "metaphysics of presence" characteristic of the philosophical tradition from Greece to the modern age. Through a dialogue with Heidegger, Merleau-Ponty, and Levinas, Froman offers a phenomenological account of a double movement – toward and away from the world – that is always operative in philosophy's moods. Friedlander attends to wonder through a reading of Walter Benjamin's writings on childhood and his account of the child's view of colors. Opening up the possibility of articulating the experience of color as a mood, Friedlander shows how this special attunement can bring out the texture of experience as an interrelated totality that grounds the unity of one's being in the world.

Part II fleshes out the distinguishing traits of melancholy's special inverted structure and contemplates the implications of the structure of an inward-turned gaze for the kinds of openness facilitated by mood. Ferber explores the senses in which the structure of Leibniz's fundamental metaphysical entity, the Monad, should be understood as melancholic. In challenging the basic contradiction between utter closure and expression, Ferber shows how the Monad exemplifies the productive relationship between melancholia's essential closure and its philosophical openness to the world. Strassberg discusses the history of shame in philosophical thought, describing shame as a gateway to philosophical truth. The paper regards Plato, Rousseau, and Nietzsche as offering three different paradigms to articulate the intimate relationship between truth and shame, models based on the different ways that shame structures selfhood. Nostalgia is the center of Malpas's essay, which discusses the uniqueness of this mood in the context of the disclosive character of moods in general. Nostalgia, for Malpas, is not merely the desire to return to the past. Following its Greek etymology, it is a longing for the return home whose philosophical implication is a new understanding of homesickness as a form of disorientation, forcing us to question our own being in the world.

The articles in the third part of the book discuss the distinctive structure of anxiety and its implications for an understanding of the modern condition of philosophy's reflexivity. Bergo explores the emergence of the Kierkegaardian notion of "anxiety" by tracing its origins in Schelling's conception of *Sehnsucht* – an objectless yearning. Bergo shows that the concept of anxiety develops as an outcome of Kierkegaard's repositioning of Schelling's philosophy of freedom within an existentialist framework and underscores the importance of the physicality and corporeality of mood over and against its psychological essence. Mulhall revisits Heidegger's analysis of moods in order to evaluate its significance to the philosophical understanding achieved in the phenomenological tradition. By focusing on perplexity, anxiety and shame, Mulhall argues that Heidegger's texts are informed throughout by moods and explores their implications to the phenomenological tradition. Concentrating on the role of anxiety in *Being and Time*, Mulhall shows how this mood determines the very structure of Heidegger's text and its implications on the movement from the book's first division to the second. Senderowicz focuses on Heidegger's conception of anxiety in the context of Heidegger's understanding of subjectivity and selfhood. Showing how Heidegger's treatment of anxiety responds to a fundamental problem in Husserl's conception of the transcendental "I," Senderowicz points to a blind spot in the Heideggerian understanding of the relationship between self-awareness and selfhood.

In the last section, both Geiger's and Cohen's articles discuss the crucial relation between moods and moral sentiments. Geiger reconsiders Kant's moral theory, arguing for the central presence of feeling and emotion in it, thereby challenging what is usually conceived of as Kant's conviction regarding the separation of feeling and passion from reason. He thus shows that according to Kant, reason is not itself sufficient for grounding the moral act which necessarily depends on the possibility of turning to our affective inner life. Cohen focuses on a dimension of mood he calls the "Proto-Ethical," which he understands as constitutive of the possibility of morals. He argues that the intelligibility of ethics is necessarily dependent on this aspect of mood. Gordon offers a re-evaluation of the impact of racism on philosophical reasoning through a reading of Fanon as a philosopher of mood. Gordon argues that Fanon's thinking emerges from a constant confrontation with the moral foundations of philosophy which, in turn, is intrinsically related to Fanon's preoccupation with the mood of his own thinking. The book's closing article by Scharfstein offers a personal evaluation of the manner in which the philosopher's thought is influenced by the imminent presence of death. Against the background of an autobiographical reflection, Scharfstein gives a reading of the affect of death in the writings of Hume and Kant.

This volume aspires to open up a prism through which the continuous and unremitting presence of moods in the history of philosophy can be traced and explored. We hope that the intertwining perspectives offered here can create a stepping stone for further philosophical explorations of the crucial role moods play in philosophical thought.

References

Heidegger, Martin. 1962. *Being and Time*. Trans. John Macquarrie and Edward Robinson. New York: Harper & Row.

Husserl, Edmund. 1999. *Cartesian Meditations: An introduction to phenomenology*. Trans. Dorion Cairns. Dordrecht: Kluwer.

Sartre, Jean-Paul. 1987. *The Transcendence of the Ego*. Trans. F. Williams and R. Kirkpatrick. New York: Farrar, Strauss and Giroux.

Sartre, Jean-Paul. 2007. *Nausea*. Trans. Lloyd Alexander. New York: New Directions Books.

Part II
Wonder

Thauma Idesthai: The Mythical Origins of Philosophical Wonder

Vered Lev Kenaan

I. Philosophy's Beginning in Wonder

> For it is owing to their wonder (*to thaumazein*) that men both now begin and at first began to philosophize; they wondered originally at the obvious difficulties, then advanced little by little and stated difficulties about the greater matters, e.g., about the phenomena of the moon and those of the sun and of the stars, and about the genesis of the universe. And a man who is puzzled (*aporon*) and wonders (*thaumazon*) thinks himself ignorant (whence even the lover of myth is in a sense a lover of Wisdom, for the myth is composed of wonders); therefore since they philosophized in order to escape from ignorance, evidently they were pursuing science in order to know, and not for any utilitarian end. (*Metaphysics* I, 982b)[1]

In this known passage, a *locus classicus* in the history of philosophy, Aristotle turns to unravel the mystery surrounding a philosophical awakening.[2] It is a commonplace that for Aristotle philosophy is born out of wonder – and we should emphasize that it is not a substantive, *thauma,* indicating an object's form which he uses, but, a verbal noun, *to thaumazein* with its implication that wonder is a mode of engagement, an experience. Is wonder a mood for Aristotle? And, if so, what kind of experience does it build upon?

"It is owing to their wonder that men both now begin and at first began to philosophize." Wonder triggers men to begin to philosophize. Its affective state seems to call for a response that, in its rational sublimation of the instinctual, has a cognitive

[1] All translations are by Richard Mckeon, *The Basic Works of Aristotle*, New-York: Random House, 1941. Hereafter mentioned by text title and pagination.

[2] Aristotle's insights regarding wonder and philosophy are inspired by Plato in the *Theaetetus* 155d.

V.L. Kenaan (✉)
Department of Hebrew and Comparative Literature, University of Haifa, Mount Carmel, Haifa, 31905, Israel
e-mail: vered.lev.kenaan@gmail.com

H. Kenaan and I. Ferber (eds.), *Philosophy's Moods: The Affective Grounds of Thinking*, Contributions To Phenomenology 63, DOI 10.1007/978-94-007-1503-5_2,

or even metaphysical potential. Aristotle describes this potential in terms of the crystallization of a human will to defy ignorance and to search for knowledge that, for him, is typical of a free mind seeking after meaning. Can we hear in Aristotle's wonder the reverberation of Plato's *eros*?[3] Despite the clear differences between these two concepts, Aristotle follows Plato's treatment of *eros* in presenting wonder as constitutive to the human search for understanding. Unlike Plato's understanding of *eros*, Aristotle's wonder does not seem to be tied to humanity's desire for immortality.[4] And yet, Aristotle nevertheless ascribes to wonder the capacity to make the divine present for humans.[5] Wonder, according to him, enables us to encounter the enigmatic dimension of the world whose comprehensive decipherment is "justly regarded as beyond human power" (*Metaphysics* I, 982b). In wondering, we experience the limits of our human knowledge and thereby the presence of the transcendent.

Wonder creates a beginning for philosophy. What kind of beginning is involved here? Aristotle refers to both ancient and contemporary beginnings, to men who "now begin and at first began to philosophize." As such, he may ultimately seem concerned with a structural condition rather than a temporal form of beginning, that is, with a constitutive stage by which philosophy can be said to emerge into its own form. This is the way Hannah Arendt, for example, reads Aristotle. For her, an understanding of what he means by the "starting-point of thinking" should be achieved in terms of the question "what makes us think?" (Arendt 1977: 141, 143).

While generally following such a reading, I also think that it may too easily blur the presence of a specific temporal dimension that is at play in Aristotle's framing of wonder. Appearing at the opening of *Metaphysics,* the theme of wonder is formative in shaping Aristotle's discussion of the early historical stages of philosophy. As such, wonder marks not only the inner inceptive form of philosophy, but primarily connotes an archaic point in time, in which a new form of desire has presented itself: the desire to understand. At the beginning of *Metaphysics,* wonder functions as a trope in creating a biography for philosophy, one that has a mythical aura, evoking a mythical notion of time. In the context of his discussion of the early stages of philosophy, wonder marks an experience of an *arche*, a primordial beginning. And, as Aristotle reflects on the manner in which philosophers and poets alike begin their cosmological inquiries, the backdrop for his discussion is created by the structural analogy between *to thaumazein* and *arche* (*Metaphysics* I, 983b). In this essay, the relationship between these two concepts will be explored through a comparative reading of Book One of Aristotle's *Metaphysics* and Hesiod's *Theogony*.

[3]Clearly, this question should be preceded by the question whether we hear in Plato's wonder the reverberation of his *eros*.

[4]Plato's Symposium, 208A–B.

[5]This is also Plato's view on wonder, *Theaetetus* 155d.

II. Wonder and the Search for *Arche*

Aristotle

In Greek thought wonder is understood as that which exposes the beholder to the hidden presence of the *arche*, the source and the beginning of things. With wonder, a path of inquiry is opened into the origin of things – a theme that shapes the beginning of such cosmological works as Hesiod's *Theogony*. In this respect, Aristotle's discussion of *arche* develops in a manner that still bears the mark of the mythopoetic concerns that characterize Hesiod's quest for origins.

In the philosophical lexicon that Aristotle creates in *Metaphysics* book 5, the first term to be discussed is *arche*:

> 'Beginning' means (1) that part of a thing from which one would start first... (2) That from which each thing would best be originated... (3) That from which as an immanent part, a thing first comes to be...(4) That from which, *not* as an immanent part, a thing first comes to be, and from which the movement or the change naturally first begins...(5) That at whose will that which is moved is moved and that which changes changes...(6) That from which a thing can first be known – this also is called the beginning of the thing. (*Metaphysics* 5.1. 1012b–1013a)

Aristotle furnishes each of the above subcategories with examples that manifest the different significances and functions that *arche* has in relating to and in determining the nature of things. Thus, whereas in linear constructs such as a road, *arche* signifies a starting point that is immanent in the thing itself (1), the *arche* of a genealogical line (4) is not immanent in the offspring. Examples of material or intellectual kinds of *arche* underscore its position as the source of things and as a cause constitutive of their possibility of developing into what they are. Articulating the meaning of *arche* as a driving force, Aristotle thus credits Hesiod for being the first to do so in his *Theogony*. The significance of Hesiod's *arche* as a driving force is especially evident, Aristotle argues, in the role Eros has in the poet's cosmogony:

> One might suspect that Hesiod was the first to look for such a thing -- or some one else who put love or desire among existing things as a principle (*arche*), as Parmenides, too does; for he, in constructing the genesis of the universe, says: "Love first of all (*protiston*) the Gods: she planned." And Hesiod says: "First of all things (*protista*) was chaos made, and then broad-breasted earth... And love, 'mid all the gods pre-eminent,"[6] which implies that among existing things there must be from the first a cause (*aitia*) which will move things and bring them together. (*Metaphysics* 1.4. 984b)

---

[6]Aristotle is inaccurate. Hesiod says in *Theogony* 116–122: "In truth, first of all Chasm came to be, and then broad-breasted Earth ... and Eros, who is the most beautiful among the immortal gods, the limb-melter – he overpowers the mind and the thoughtful counsel of all the gods and of all human beings in their breasts" (Hesiod, *Theogony*). Hereafter: Hesiod: *Theogony.* All translations of Hesiod are taken from Glenn Most, *Hesiod* I, Loeb Classical series, 2006.

Aristotle reads Hesiod as an originator, the first to search for the cause of things. Yet, in emphasizing Hesiod's originality as a cosmological thinker, Aristotle seems to forget, or rather strangely omits, an essential dimension of Hesiod's first principle. For Hesiod, Eros "pre-eminency" among the gods is tied to his mode of being as the most beautiful and most destructive power. But for Aristotle Eros's beauty and destructiveness cannot coincide: as a cosmological first principle, Eros needs a clear and distinct – a coherent and unified – identity which he lacks in Hesiod. Hesiod does not think of *arche* in this manner. On the contrary, it is precisely the inner complexity, the incoherence of Eros as a principle of beginning that generates the world's phenomenality as a site of wonder. This takes place, as I shall shortly show, with the transubstantiation of the paradoxical nature of Hesiod's *arche*-figure of Eros in the first female figure, the first Woman whose appearance is inseparable from a dimension of wonder that she brings to the world through her ability to reverberate the world's *arche*.

For Aristotle, the sense of *arche* is intertwined with that of cause, *aition*: "for all causes (*aitia*) are beginnings (*archae*)" (*Metaphysics* 1.4. 984b). And, while he clearly makes a point of distinguishing between the different meanings of *arche* and *aition* (*Metaphysics,* 5.1–2), the inner connection between these two terms is nevertheless made evident as he examines the four types of *aitia*.[7] In fact, *arche* is an integral part of Aristotle's explanation of three of his four causes. Corresponding to the "why" of a thing, *ousia* is both a "cause (*aition*) and principle (*arche*)" (*Metaphysics,* 5.1–2). The second cause, matter (*hule*) or substratum (*upokeimenon*), identified by the Pre-Socratic philosophers as an *arche (i.e.,* Thales' water, or Anaximenes' air) is defined by Aristotle as "a principle of all things" (*arche panton Metaphysics* 1.3.983b). But, similarly to a cause, the principle is said to be the source "from which they come to be."[8] *Arche* also appears in the definition of the third cause as *he arche tes kineseos*, the source of movement or the driving force (*Metaphysics* 1.3.983a).

In both Greek and Latin, the concept of beginning is tied to an idea of regulation. The Greek *arche* is thus connected to the word *archon* meaning a king, a ruler,[9] and in Latin, *principium* is a beginning whose meaning is intrinsically tied to the word *princeps*, a leader, and hence, *principium* means a beginning which is also a ruling principle. This aspect of *arche* is something that Aristotle identifies as echoing in early Greek thinking. That is, he recognizes and underscores the importance of the accomplishment of these thinkers in envisioning beyond the

[7]For example, after referring to matter as an *aition*, Aristotle relates to the source of motion as the other type of cause: *hetera arche*. *Metaphisics* 1.3.984a.

[8]"Of the first philosophers, then, most thought the principles which were of the nature of matter were the only principles (*archas*) of all things. That of which all things that are consist, the first from which they come to be, the last into which they are resolved (the substance remaining, but changing in its modifications), this they say is the element and this the principle (*archen*) of things." *Metaphysics* 1.3.983b.

[9]Aristotle explains that "the magistracies in cities, and oligarchies and monarchies and tyrannies, are called *archai* and so are the arts, and of these especially the architectonic arts." *Metaphysics* 5.1.

temporal and spatial appearances of *arche* an autonomous conception of beginning and origin. Yet, Aristotle's genuine homage to the radical turning point brought about by the first philosophers is, at the same time, deeply critical of their naivety and scientific immaturity. The limited character of the thinking of these proto-philosophers (among whom Hesiod is considered a major contributor) is particularly made manifest in Aristotle's discussion of the prototypical senses of the notion of "cause" that he takes to be operative in these early stages of thinking. According to him, the first philosophers were not able to grasp more than two kinds of "causes" whose explanation they could provide only in a limited, vague and scientifically unsatisfying way:

> These thinkers, as we say, evidently grasped, and to this extent, two of the causes which we distinguished in our work on nature – the matter and the source of the movement – vaguely, however, and with no clearness, but as untrained men behave in fights; for they go round their opponents and often strike fine blows, but they do not fight on scientific principles; and so too these thinkers do not seem to know what they say; for it is evident that, as a rule, they make no use of their causes except to a small extent. (*Metaphysics* 1.4.85a)

The Pre-Socratic philosophers and the cosmological poets express, at times, deep intuitions about the nature of things. But, they cannot be said to know what they speak of, since their utterances are singular – free floating – events that have no grounding in a systematic framework of understanding. The first philosophers speak in the same manner that "untrained men behave in fights." They may occasionally "strike a fine blow" but this would ultimately be deficient since they are, in principle, barred from achieving any comprehensive view on what they are doing. In this context, however, wonder seems to play no significant philosophical role. In itself, it seems unable to serve a source of enlightenment. It cannot, in itself, illuminate the mind. In other words, as long as the mind lacks the regulating principles of *episteme*, ignorance will continue to rule in the face of wonder.

Aristotle's criticism of the beginnings taken by the first cosmological thinkers is reminiscent of Plato's criticism of the place of divine inspiration in the creation of the poets. Driven by the Muses' magnetic power, the poets, according to Plato, say things that they cannot explain. Analogously, the wonder motivating the first philosophers may have inspired them to articulating certain truths, but these cannot be justified because they do not belong to a systematic space of reasons and explanation. Wonder has turned the first philosophers into fighters, active agents but, lacking the grounding of reason, their activity ineluctably remains arbitrary and, for Aristotle, ultimately disappointing. In this respect, the experience of wonder can be philosophically operative only through an epistemic response that aims at the overcoming of that wonder.

> Yet the acquisition of it [i.e., knowledge] must in a sense end in something which is the opposite of our original inquiries. For all men begin, as we said by wondering that things are as they are, as they do about self-moving marionettes, or about the solstices or the incommensurability of the diagonal of a square with the side; for it is seems wonderful to all who have not yet seen the reason, that there is a thing which can not be measured even by the smallest unit. But we must end in the contrary and, according to the proverb, the better state, as is the case in these instances too when men learn the cause; for there is nothing which would surprise a geometer so much as if diagonal turned out to be commensurable. (*Met.* 1.2.983a)

The philosopher does not dwell in wonder, but, once touched by wonder, moves in the opposite direction toward a better state of understanding. Scientific thinking is a movement initiated by perplexity, which directs itself away from the initial perplexing experience, the *arche*, from which it began. In developing, it should thus free itself from the initial affect – e.g., the bafflement, the shock – of wonder. It must grow as "second thoughts" and become part, as Aristotle recommends, of a cognitive domain of a "second-order."[10]

Hesiod

While Aristotle hears in Hesiod's cosmology the first resonance of a philosophical notion of *arche*, in the Greek mythic mind, *arche* nevertheless primarily presents itself as a lost point in time that the cosmological poet aspires to recover in his search for an understanding of the nature of Gods and the universe. For Hesiod, the notion of *arche* cannot be extracted from the visibility of the world but appears as an essentially absent sign whose re-presentation is the goal of his poetry. In *Theogony,* which is both a genealogy of the Greek gods and a cosmological epic, this aspiration is manifest in the address to the Muses:

> Tell how in the first place gods and earth were born, and rivers and boundless sea seething with its swell, and the shining stars and the broad sky above, and those who were born from them, the gods givers of good things; and how they divided their wealth and distributed their honors, and also how they first took possession of many-folded Olympus. These things tell me **from the beginning** (*ex arches*) [my emphasis]; Muses who have your mansions on Olympus, and which one of them was born first. (*proton*) (*Theogony* 108–115)

As Hesiod begins his genealogical account, his aim is not so much to capture the essence of the universe beyond its phenomena, but rather to see and represent the world as yet empty of things. However, since this is precisely what cannot be done by mortals and he finds himself riveted to the sights of the world – rivers, sea, sky and stars – Hesiod turns to the Muses for help. Aided by their divine knowledge, Hesiod attempts to reconstruct a lost picture of an absolute beginning (*arche*) that is otherwise beyond our grasp. This beginning consists of four primordial entities or dimensions of being: Chaos, Gaia, Tartaros and Eros. Other entities soon join them, but the four cosmic principles do not disappear. Their primordiality makes them invaluable to the cosmic genealogy and their constitutive qualities are thus lent to the process of formation by which the world at large, the Olympian gods, and human beings come into being. As such, the four primordial beings are the source and ultimate point of access for any inquiry into the meaning of the world. For Hesiod, in other words, the inner form of a representation of the ultimate beginning consists in these four primordial elements, which reflect the birth of meaning. For mythical thinking, beginning is a genetic mark, a physiognomic signature inscribed by the

[10] The proverb Aristotle refers to is "second thoughts are better." See the note in Aristotle (1980).

four elements on the face of things. Hesiod's preoccupation with the question of arche makes him, as Aristotle reads him, an important figure among the early cosmologists. Yet, the uniqueness of the manner in which his poetry deals with *arche* lies in its actual attempts to provide a picture, a re-presentation of that *arche*. In this sense, Hesiod's poetry is not only a response to an originary sense of wonder in the face of a lost *arche,* but should be read as a work that, in itself, aims to evoke wonder. As such, wonder never leaves the thinking of the poet. Unlike the Aristotlean philosopher, the development of the poet's thinking is dependent on its ability to continually resonate wonder.

III. Thauma Idesthai

In returning to Aristotle's understanding of wonder, it is interesting to notice that very little is said about the affective dimension of wonder, its being as a mood or as an actual experience. If wonder is philosophy's essential mood, how does the philosopher experience it? How exactly is wonder transformed into reflection, philosophical thought or speech? How is a philosopher born? Aristotle leaves these questions unanswered.

A possible starting point for reconstructing his position would be to notice the visual context in which wonder typically appears. Considering Aristotle's paradigm of wonder apropos his description of a man puzzled by the phenomena of the moon and the stars, the intimate connection between wonder and the visual becomes clear. Furthermore, the gaze operative in Aristotle's philosophical wonder is one that is specifically directed upwards, towards the sky. "They wondered originally at the obvious difficulties, then advanced little by little and stated difficulties about the greater matters, e.g., about the phenomena of the moon and those of the sun and of the stars" (*Metaphysics* I, 982b). The connection Aristotle makes between wonder and the visual appearance of the celestial bodies is indicative of the philosopher's desire to uncover the invisible order of things. Does the brightness and sensual impact of these luminaries also play a role in the beholder's reflective turn?

In *The Life of the Mind*, Hannah Arendt analyzes the ancient conception of philosophical wonder as deriving from a specific experience of beauty, one that tempts the viewer into a position of contemplation. According to Arendt who examines the Homeric wonder, the appearance of godlike men, or of gods disguised as mortals, discloses an important feature of this visual experience: in wonder, one admires the invisible as it appears in the guise of the familiar. Hence, for her, "the wonder that is the starting–point of thinking is neither puzzlement nor surprise nor perplexity; it is an admiring wonder" (Arendt 1977: 143). It is the appreciation of a beauty that reveals itself slowly, or even softly, with neither fear nor anxiety. Arendt locates wonder at the moment in which the invisible presence of a harmonious order is revealed. Reflecting on Anaxagoras' words that "the appearances are a glimpse of the non-revealed" (*Opsis gar ton adelon ta phainomena.* B21a), Arendt develops the idea that the visual experience of the invisible conditions a new philosophical awareness:

> Philosophy begins with an awareness of this invisible harmonious order of the *kosmos*, which is manifest in the midst of the familiar visibilities as though these had become transparent. (Arendt 1977: 144)

The eye's encounter with beauty generates a process of a growing awareness towards the invisible order of the *kosmos*. As she fills in the outlines of this ancient philosophical experience of wonder, Arendt's account nevertheless remains one sided in the manner it refuses to make a place for the more disturbing or disruptive ways in which the mysterious and unintelligible character of things affect us. For Arendt, "admiring wonder conceived as the starting-point of philosophy leaves no place for the factual existence of disharmony, of ugliness, and finally of evil" (Arendt 1977: 150). Arendt's insistence on severing wonder's harmonious, beautiful and tranquil constitution from other senses of radical perplexity seems to miss a certain richness and complexity that, in my view, were an integral part of the ancient experience of wonder. This richness can be partly reconstructed by turning to archaic poetry in which wonder figures eminently. In this context, poetry should be regarded as an important companion to philosophy, and I shall try to elaborate the significance of philosophy's wonder by illuminating its relationship with its origins in archaic poetry. Indeed, in archaic poetry, the experience of wonder is depicted in a wide spectrum of scenes of spectatorship. Wonder is typically tied to the experience of seeing. But although it, indeed, has a strong visual dimension, it can also take an acoustic form. Moreover, while beauty is a common paradigm for wonder, in mythical imagery it is not solely associated with beauty, and can also emanate from the encounter with the ugly, or even the monstrous. Furthermore, wonder is not simply a pleasant experience, but might involve a shocking effect. Wonder does not leave the spectator calm or indifferent. The appearance of wonder touches us in a manner that forces the beholder to respond emotionally and intellectually. And finally, the appearance of wonder is not limited to our encounter with natural phenomena, but can be part of the world of culture and artifacts.

As Arendt explains, *to thaumazein* is indeed tied to a mode of perception that involves recognition of the hidden, invisible, and the divine, dimension of appearances. In Greek archaic poetry, the glimmering appearance of the solar bodies, the presence of gods, charismatic heroes, the manifestation of the arms of war, woven fabrics, architectonic structures, powerful speech, portents, terrible sights, are all examples of the formulaic expression *thauma idesthai* – a wonder to behold.

In the mythic imagination, however, wonder is often associated with an irregular, dramatic, even shocking visual experience. And as such, it never leaves the beholder comfortable and secure. In archaic poetry, wonder is accompanied by a sense of danger stirred by the beholder's new self-awareness to his or her fragility. Beholding a great light, for example, is experienced as an unexpected appearance of a shining divinity. Such singular and irregular visual experience leaves the beholder with a deep sense of gratitude for remaining alive after being exposed to the forbidden, inaccessible, hidden, or transcendental vision.

How can these mythical aspects of wonder contribute to our understanding of the formation of philosophy's wonder? I shall attempt to answer this question by turning again to Hesiod's *Theogony* which, in its thematization of wonder as the divinity of *Thauma*, serves as a point of reference for Aristotle and, before him, for Plato (*Theogony*: 237,265,780). Facing, in *Theaetetus* (*Theaetetus*: 155d), the state of perplexity of his young interlocutor, Plato's Socrates explains to him that his "sense of wonder is the mark of the philosopher." For Socrates, "Philosophy indeed has no other origin." And, this is also where the mythical presence of Hesiod surfaces:"He was a good genealogist who made Iris the daughter of Thaumas." Thaumas, the divine figure of wonder, is the father of Iris. And so, for Plato, Iris, the vision of the rainbow, is the embodiment of wonder in the domain of the visual. The rainbow is a natural phenomenon that not only strikes the eye with its beauty, but calls for an explanation as well. And yet, even when an explanation is at hand, and we understand how the rainbow is created, there remains a sense of wonder, of the unexplainable. Wonder is the appearance of a world whose mystery cannot be reduced to our (human) understanding.[11]

Hesiod, however, merely names *Thauma*, and leaves the specification of his divine function and role in the cosmological order obscure. At the same time, the effect of wonder is central to Hesiod's *Theogony* and I shall focus here on what I not only take to be a paradigmatic Hesiodic example but moreover an example that illuminates the mythical pre-figuration of the philosophical concept of wonder.

IV. The First Woman: Wonder at the Birth of Meaning

> Immediately he contrived an evil for human beings in exchange for fire. For the much-renowned Lame One forged from earth the semblance of a reverend maiden by the plans of Cronus' son; and the goddess, bright eyed Athena, girdled and adorned her with silvery clothing, and with her hands she hung a highly wrought veil from her head, **a wonder to see (*thauma idesthai*)**; and around her head Pallas Athena placed freshly budding garlands that arouse desire, the flowers of the meadow; and around her head she placed a golden head-band, which the much-renowned Lame One made himself, working it with his skilled hands, to do a favor for Zeus the father. On his were contrived many designs, highly wrought, **wonderful to see (*thauma idesthai*)**, all the terrible monsters the land and the sea nourish; he put many of these into it, **wondrous (*thaumasia*)**, similar to living animals endowed with speech, and gracefulness breathed upon them all. Then, when he had contrived this beautiful evil thing in exchange for that good one, he led her out to where the other gods and human beings were, while she exulted in the adornment of the mighty father's bright-eyed daughter; and **wonder (*thauma*)** gripped the immortal gods and the mortal human beings when they saw the steep deception, intractable for human beings. (*Theogony* 570–589; my emphases.)

[11]But even if the mystery of sight remains, it does not quench the quest for meaning that wonder incites. Hanna Arendt comments that "what we marvel at is confirmed and affirmed by admiration which breaks out into speech, the gift of Iris, the rainbow, the messenger from above." Her interpretation relies on the *Cratylus* where Plato suggests that "Iris" derives from the verb to tell (*eirein.*) (Arendt 1977: 142–3).

The "Shock of the New"

While *Theogony* addresses the divine origins of the world of phenomena, Hesiod does not explicitly tie his poetic investigation to an experience of wonder.[12] Unlike Plato and Aristotle who stage the birth of the philosophical mind as the moment of facing heavenly luminaries, Hesiod's awakening as a cosmological poet is tied to a revelation scene, an act of deliverance from a dark state of being.[13] Wonder arises in Hesiod only at a second stage, one that incorporates the move from *phusis* to *techne.*

Following the establishment of Zeus's rule after the maturation of the physical world with its divine forces and the rise of the human race, the creation of the first woman takes place as a radically new event. Unlike the preceding series of natural births, the appearance of the first woman marks a new era: she is the first product of a scheme and craftsmanship. The first woman is thus a wonder for Hesiod, as she is also the first artificial creation.

The first woman is the first work of art, the first product of manufacture and the first manifestation of *techne* in a world of natural births, a world lacking a creator. Although *techne* is paradigmatically opposed to *phusis*, Hesiod presents the artificial as that which surprisingly bears the sign of nature. The appearance of the first woman is a source of wonder. It leads men to see the world as they have never seen it before. The first woman is an *arche* figure which, in being the first of her kind, bears the effect of novelty. The first woman is contrived as the gods' gift to mankind.[14] And, in receiving this gift, the already established community of men encounter a completely new phenomenon.

The depiction of an archetype necessarily involves the birth of a stereotype. And, indeed, Hesiod's depiction of the first woman consists in one of the harshest misogynist stereotypes in ancient poetry:

> For from her comes the race of female women: for of her is the deadly race and tribe of women, a great woe for mortals, dwelling with men, no companions of baneful poverty but only of luxury. (*Theogony:* 590–3)

---

[12]Hesiod, however, depicts the encounter with the Muses on Mount Helicon as wonderful to gaze on (*theeton Th.* 30–31). For a further discussion of the transformative encounter with the Muses, see Lev Kenaan (2008: 44–46).

[13]"One time, they taught Hesiod beautiful song while he was pasturing lambs under holy Helicon. And this speech the goddesses spoke first of all to me, the Olympian Muses, the daughters of aegis-holding Zeus: "Field–dwelling shepherds, ignoble disgraces, mere bellies: we know how to say many false things similar to genuine ones, but we know, when we wish, how to proclaim true things" (*Theogony*: 22–28).

[14]The significance of the first woman as an artifice carries heavy misogynist connotations. The narrative presents her as a cunning device and a divine punishment contrived by Zeus as a retribution for Prometheus' theft of the fire. The Greek imagination makes the first woman's secondariness an unnecessary addendum, an afterthought that means punishment, catastrophe, *pema*, for mankind. This misogynist framework does not overshadow, however, the illuminating force that the wonder of the first woman bestows on mankind.

The first woman strikes her beholders with wonder. In the context of the text's misogynism, the effect of wonder created by the first woman is clearly violent. Furthermore, it is connected to a dangerous form of beauty. The first woman is not simply beautiful, but rather a "beautiful evil," *kalon kakon*. The significance of this twofold nature for the cultural construction of the feminine is well known. Interpreting beauty as a cultural scheme and the wonder of this beauty as a deluding mask goes hand in hand with the text's anti-feminine ideology. And yet, the wonder aroused by the first woman operates in another important way that needs clarification.

In *Theogony*, the cardinal moment in which the first woman is identified with evil occurs once the female image is gazed upon. Evil is not part, however, of the actual process of the woman's creation by the divine artists, Athena and Hephaestus. It acquires its signification only once the feminine model is completed and its image revealed to the divine and human assembly. The audience's first response is fear. This fear is directed towards the future and is tied to the threatening possibility of a fatal deceit. For men, charming beauty is a recognized source of danger. Yet, why is this beauty dangerous? In Hesiod, this is primarily due to its novelty. The feminine *arche*-figure marks a break with routine; it announces an end to old times.

Bracketing the misogynist context, we may say that wonder is tied to an experience of seeing things for the first time. Or better put, the affect of wonder is one by which the gaze is experienced as new. In Hesiod, the fear, which the sight of the first woman instigates is indicative of the "shock of the new." The anxiety and hatred toward the change that Woman brings about, is thus also reflective of the structure of wonder as a transformative experience. The first kind of transformation that wonder opens up is the overcoming of fear. This is made possible since there is a dimension of distance inherent in wonder, one that allows us to experience the "shock of the new" without suffering its fatal and destructive consequences. Unlike the encounter with the monstrosity of Medusa, the experience of wonder allows us to endure what we see. Whereas the sight of Medusa petrifies and immediately kills, the sight of the first woman allows the gaze to change and become reflective. Here, the centrality of the visual paradigm for the articulation of wonder becomes more apparent. It is not so much that wonder must consist of a visual experience, but that wonder is couched in a kind of distance for which vision can serve as a trope. Unlike taste, smell and touch, "eye contact" presupposes a structure of distance.

Wondering at a Lost Beginning

This leads us to the deeper sense of wonder that I find so crucial for the reading of Hesiod. In Hesiod, the seeing of the first woman cannot simply be understood as an encounter with an object in the visual field. Instead, what the first woman brings to the world of men is the very condition of the visual; the first woman is that which makes things visible for the first time. This is the deeper sense of the Hesiodic *thauma*, which brings the beholder into a mode of self-recognition: 'here I see for the first time,' or, 'now I see differently.' In *Theogony*, this kind of recognition is made possible through the artificial wonder created by the first work of art. This is, in my view, the reason for Hesiod's preference in articulating wonder through an artificial rather than a natural phenomenon. It is only at the world's second stage, when language and *techne* establish their centrality, that the means are provided for recovering the world's cosmological origins. Hesiod does not attribute to nature the impact of wonder since for him nature is already structured through various processes of disguised and disguising entities.

As Hesiod describes the creation of the first work of art, it has still not been revealed to the human eye. As the first woman is presented to the assembly and evokes wonder, this wonder is strongly connected to the question of the unknown origins of the new phenomenon. In this sense, wonder becomes that which invites the beholder to reflect upon the origins of an enigmatic appearance. But, once a specific question of origins is opened up by the artwork (who created that artwork?), it can find no satisfaction and continues to echo in an amplified manner, evoking, in turn, the ultimate metaphysical question of the universe's origins. The wonder at the first woman reverberates the lost beginning of the cosmological event of creation, and involves an experience of retracting a memory of *arche*.[15]

The Teleological Wonder

Hesiodic wonder provokes the question concerning "the purpose and the good" of the new appearance of the woman. The reflection concerning the significance of the new creation is motivated by the teleological concern that Aristotle maps as the fourth *aition* (*Metaphysics* 1.3.983a). This type of cause that according to Aristotle has not been acknowledged by the first philosophers in their cosmological inquiries (*Metaphsics* 1.4.985a) is central for Hesiod, however. In contrast to the physical world, the first woman has a creator, and her creation is teleological. She is, first of all, the product of Zeus's thoughts, who is otherwise not directly responsible for forming the cosmic elements. Once the artwork opens up the question of its *telos*, it, in fact, provokes a whole series of teleological questions leading to the ultimate question regarding the *telos* of the world's coming into being.[16]

---

[15] In the case of the first woman, this specifically involves the recovering of one of the first cosmological principles. As the final link in the erotic development of the cosmos, the creation of the first woman manifests a family resemblance to the cosmos's erotic forces. Beginning with the primordial erotic principle, continuing with its concretization in the divine Aphrodite, the creation of the Woman is a human embodiment of both the divine Aphrodite and the abstract Eros. Her striking appearance is a visual reminder of the hidden existence of Eros as a cosmological *arche*.

[16] In *Theogony*, the intrinsic connection between the *telos* of the first artwork and that of the universe is couched in the image of the first woman as a miniature of the world. The first woman is composed of earth, her head wreathed in grass and flowers. Her clothing and adornments shine by virtue of the earth's golds and silvers. The creatures represented on her diadem not only populate the world, but are themselves metonymic of earth, sea, and sky. Eros, the fourth primordial element, is represented by a reference to first woman's erotic qualities of charm (*charis*).

Transformative Wonder

What is the gift of the first woman's wonder? In what way does the wonder of the first woman foreshadow the origin of philosophy? The world begins in a state of total darkness, murkiness, and invisibility. Not only is the beginning dark: its general outlook upon the world is no less gloomy. Life is lived in the dimness of night. The first woman is the first figure to endow men with a perspective allowing them a reflective distance from the world. Wonder in this sense predicates thought on visibility. Wonder then preconditions visibility marking the distance between man and world. This distance is a prerequisite for seeing. With the first woman visibility becomes an indispensable element of being in the world. Her crucial role in determining the experience of seeing can be understood in relation to the figure of Eros. Incorporating one of the principles of visibility in an early stage of *Theogony*, Eros is said to be "the most beautiful (*kallistos*) of the immortal gods" (120). However, such beauty is senseless in the dark being of the primordial world. Because the first woman's beauty shines in brightness it liberates men from their primordial condition of blindness. Accentuating the visibility of the first woman by means of her erotic charm and beauty, the gods open men to their senses.

The world described in *Theogony* is a godly realm, for its nature is the creation of the gods and is indistinguishable from them. Prior to the first woman's appearance, humanity's primordial existence led persons to perceive of themselves as a natural continuation of the anthropomorphic cosmology. The first woman's sight strikes the human mind with the realization that men are to be found outside of, in front of, or in the world. Men can no longer solely think of themselves as indistinguishable from the world. According to Hesiod, cosmic beauty is what allows us to return to the world from which the first woman's wondrous appearance separated us. The wonder of the first work of art is shocking. Surprised by the sensual discovery, men can no longer perceive themselves as intrinsic part and extension of the world. They can no longer perceive the world as a given. In wondering about the nature of their world through the first woman's estranging effect, they also become desiring subjects, and in this sense, they become open to philosophy's quest.

Seen as a miniature of the world, the significance of the wonder of the first woman becomes obvious. Nowhere else does the text of *Theogony* present the world to the reader as an object of admiration, or meditation. Only with the appearance of the first woman is it possible for us to break from the flux of phenomena. Her appearance therefore marks a crucial turning point in the cosmogony. It undergirds a provisional substitute, functioning as a visual reflection of the untitled cosmos. For further discussion of how the appearance of the first woman incorporates the cosmological picture, see Lev Kenaan (2008: 39–47).

References

Arendt, Hannah. 1977. *The Life of the Mind*. Orlando: Harcourt.
Aristotle. 1941. *The Basic Works of Aristotle*. Trans. Richard Mckeon. New-York: Random House.
Aristotle. 1980. *The Metaphysics I-IX*. Trans. H. Trendennick. Cambridge: Harvard University Press, Loeb Classical Library.
Hesiod. 2006. *Hesiod* I. Trans. Glenn Most. Cambridge: Harvard University Press, Loeb Classical Library.
Lev Kenaan, Vered. 2008. *Pandora's Senses: The Feminine Character of the Ancient Text*. Madison: Wisconsin University Press.
Plato. 1980. *Symposium*, ed. Kenneth Dover. Cambridge: Cambridge University Press.

Attentiveness: A Phenomenological Study of the Relation of Memory to Mood

Wayne J. Froman

Mood is a topic that figures prominently in Martin Heidegger's 1927 *Being and Time* (Heidegger 1996). Mood is a clue to the limitations of the philosophical tradition where a "metaphysics of presence" has governed since the Greek age. My first task is to specify how it is that the topic of mood marks those limitations. Heidegger made the point that a certain understanding of perception has served all along as the model for philosophy's "metaphysics of presence." Maurice Merleau-Ponty's phenomenological analysis of perception will demonstrate why this model is untenable, and precisely in so doing, will bring us back to the topic of mood. My next task is to specify how this takes place in Merleau-Ponty's work. At the heart of perception, Merleau-Ponty finds a movement away as well as a movement toward, and this finding is indicative of a sense of self that is decisively at odds with philosophy's "metaphysics of presence." Such movement is crucial in Heidegger's analysis of mood. I will illustrate this by way of Heidegger's analyses of several moods, including fear, anxiety and boredom. The movement away, which Heidegger identifies with forgetting, always comes first. Ultimately, Heidegger finds in the resultant enigma an intimation of a way of thinking that would be other than philosophy's metaphysics of presence. All of this helps to establish mood's philosophic import.

The precedence of the movement away intrinsic to mood is accentuated in the phenomenological work of Emmanuel Levinas. Levinas identifies the movement away with a non-perdurance in "the Same," where "the Same" is understood as the ultimate standard in traditional metaphysics. My task now will be to specify the implications as understood by Levinas. Importantly, Levinas finds here memory's role in our current living of life. The final step will be to probe how forgetting and memory are, in Merleau-Ponty's terms, made to go together in life everyday, and to

W.J. Froman (✉)
Department of Philosophy, George Mason University, Fairfax, VA 22030, USA
e-mail: wfroman@gmu.edu

H. Kenaan and I. Ferber (eds.), *Philosophy's Moods: The Affective Grounds of Thinking*, Contributions To Phenomenology 63, DOI 10.1007/978-94-007-1503-5_3,

ask what mood is most indicative of what happens here. In order to do so, I will follow the lead of phenomenologists such as Heidegger and Merleau-Ponty who find that philosophy has traditionally obscured art's truth in much the same way as it has obscured the importance of mood. I will turn to the literary work of Franz Kafka with the help of Walter Benjamin's exceptional analysis. What I find of crucial import here is, in Benjamin's terms, how Kafka "touches ground."

Turning first, then, to Heidegger's *Being and Time*, mood is specified in the first division of this text as one of three *existentialia*, features of one's own "to-be-in-the-world," or "being-in-the-world" [in-der-welt-sein]. The other two are understanding and discourse, and the three are "equiprimordial." In order to explore how Heidegger understands mood, it is indispensable, in all of this, to emphasize the phenomenological sense of world, one of the most enduring of phenomenological precepts, I think.

In the initial development of phenomenology, in Edmund Husserl's middle period work, where the aim is to provide means for exploring the vast and very largely taken for granted content of one's awareness, world is specified in association with the horizontal structure of this content. World is, in this context, the horizon of horizons of the content of my awareness. In Husserl's later work, particularly the 1929 *Crisis of European Sciences and Transcendental Phenomenology* (Husserl 1970), we find the development of the sense of the "life-world," *die Lebenswelt*, the pre-predicative or pre-reflective context within which all of our reflections, our projects, and our actions go on. The point has been made that Husserl was, in fact, responding to Heidegger here. My purpose here is not to adjudicate that matter. Rather, my interest lies in pointing up the distinction between Husserl and Heidegger with regard to world. On Husserl's account, in *The Crisis of European Sciences and Transcendental Phenomenology*, the life-world remains a transcendentally grounded context. Ultimately, for Heidegger, the transcendental would amount to a primary modern variant of the "philosophy of presence," developed first in Greek thought. This philosophy of presence, although anticipated by Plato, is established in Aristotle's work in a form that will turn out to be decisive. In brief, this takes place when the issue of individuality is submerged within the philosophy of substance. Individuality is generated within substance. When the aporia of individuality, in effect, is lost, the philosophy of presence takes hold. Being gets effectively equated with presence. The mode of thinking that this entails is basically one of "making present," which is to say, "knowing." When Kant works out the fundamentals of the modern variant, namely, transcendental philosophy, philosophy of presence operates there by means of Kant's stipulation of the transcendental unity of apperception. Already, the prevailing concern with conditions of experience signals that the phenomenality of world has been obscured. Heidegger writes in *Being and Time* that Kant did not see the phenomenon of world (Heidegger 1996: 295). One finds, as a consequence, a reversion to an account of the "I" that is, in effect, congruent with substance metaphysics, or in other words, a form of the philosophy of presence.

The issue pertaining to world would show up if we come back to Husserl's middle period work and we ask how it is that with world understood as the horizon of horizons of the content of my awareness, I am nevertheless aware of my being in it. Husserl was certainly aware of this issue. Heidegger finds that I find myself always already in-the-world, and thus ahead of myself, in effect, and my mode of being is "to-be-in-the-world," or "being in the world." Knowing is a way of comporting oneself toward entities or beings encountered in the world, founded upon that "to-be-in-the-world," which is prior. No doubt there are rejoinders available on behalf of Kant, and on behalf of Aristotle as well. The fact is that Heidegger articulated such rejoinders to a further extent than others because this was of the character of the de-structive retrieval at work in his readings of such pre-eminent thinkers in the philosophical tradition, a retrieval, specifically, of the questioning that first underlies the philosophy of presence. The question as to whether in Husserl's work one finds at least an analogue of the transcendental unity of apperception is one that I will not address directly here.

Mood, Heidegger specifies, as a feature of my to-be-in-the-world, brings me to a direct encounter with the enigmatic character of this mode of being, that is, my to-be-in-the-world. In his lecture course *Basic Problems of Phenomenology* (Heidegger 1982), which dates from the time of *Being and Time*, Heidegger specifies that what has served all along as a model, in effect, for the philosophy of presence is the standard way of understanding perception, which is to say, the understanding of perception as a bringing together of a concept with a sensory manifold, or in a word, as adequation. The task of undoing or of de-structing this sense of perception fell to Maurice Merleau-Ponty. In the book *Phenomenology of Perception* (Merleau-Ponty 1962), Merleau-Ponty describes how the long-standing accounts of perception, both empiricist and intellectualist, rely on the element of units of sensation, which we never do actually encounter. They are ex post facto constructs employed in order to reconstruct the perceptual field. The idea that there is "a little person within the person" who is constantly ordering the units of sensation is undermined as well. By the time that Merleau-Ponty's description of the dynamic of perception concludes in his *Phenomenology of Perception*, we find ourselves facing the following enigma: the dynamic that he is describing is the source of the vantage point from which this description proceeds. In his later work, unfinished when he died, and published under the title *Le Visible et l'invisible*, *The Visible and the Invisible* (Merleau-Ponty 1968), Merleau-Ponty puts the philosophical point as follows: perception gives us access to the world, but at one and the same time, removes us to a margin of the world. In perception everyday, we make these two go together. When philosophy then comes to explain this, it finds itself caught up in contradictions of one type or another. The enigma, which *The Visible and the Invisible* probes is that everyday we do what we do not understand, and for which, moreover, we are hard pressed indeed to give an account.

With the movement away and the movement toward that pertains to perception, Merleau-Ponty uncovers an affective quality of perception that the tradition has long obscured. At the same time, such movement is indicative of self, which Merleau-Ponty explicitly characterizes as "the original of an elsewhere." It is in terms of this "elsewhere" that I am to understand my opening upon a world. This sense of selfhood is decidedly at odds with any sense of selfhood that involves an over-stepping or an over-riding of whatever might have come before it, and breaks, decisively, with any metaphysics of presence.

At one point in *The Visible and the* Invisible, Merleau-Ponty quotes from Claudel's work *Art poétique*: "From time to time, a [person] lifts his [or her] head, sniffs, listens, considers, recognizes his [or her] position: he [or she] thinks, he [or she] sighs, and, drawing [a] watch from [his or her] pocket…, looks at the time. *Where am I*? and, *What time is it?* such is the inexhaustible question turning from us to the world…"

Merleau-Ponty then comments:

> The watch and the map give here only a semblance of an answer: they indicate to us how what we are living is situated in relation to the course of the stars or to the course of a human day, or in relation to places that have a name. But where are these reference events and these landmarks themselves? They refer us to others, and the answer satisfies us only because we do not attend to it, because we think we are "at home." The question would arise again and indeed would be inexhaustible, almost insane, if we were to ask: but where is the world itself? And why am I myself? How old am I really? Am I really alone to be me? Have I not somewhere a double, a twin? These questions, which the sick [person] puts to himself or [to herself] in a moment of respite—or simply that glance at his [or her] watch, as if it were of great importance that the torment take place at a given inclination of the sun, at such or such hour in the life of the world—expose, at the moment that life is threatened, the underlying movement through which we have installed ourselves in the world and which recommences yet a little more time for itself. (Merleau-Ponty 1968: 103–104).

The torment, then the moment of respite, and the movement whereby we have installed ourselves in the world return us to mood. Mood, Heidegger observes, brings me to a direct encounter with the enigma of my to-be-in-the-world, and mood does so by virtue of disclosing a "how" of the to-be-in-the-world that I am and must be, in a word, of my facticity. Each of the existentialia is a way in which I am my to-be-in-the-world. Heidegger's word translated as "mood" is *Befindlichkeit*, to which the specific moods, *die Stimmungen*, belong. *Wie befinden Sie sich*? In English we ask: how are you doing? We cannot just be being. There is always a "how." This is disclosed by way of the turning away from and the turning toward that are intrinsic to mood. *Being and Time* provides analyses of both fear and anxiety. Here is the description of the turning away from and the turning toward intrinsic to fear:

> Taking care of things which fears for itself leaps from one thing to the other, because it forgets itself and thus cannot *grasp* any *definite* possibility All "possible" possibilities offer themselves, and that means impossible ones, too. He who fears for himself stops at none of these—the "surrounding world" does not disappear—but he encounters it in the mode of no longer knowing his way around in *it*. This *confused making present* of the nearest best thing belongs to forgetting oneself in fear. That, for example, the inhabitants of a burning house often "save" the most unimportant things nearby is known. When one has forgotten oneself and makes present a jumble of unattached possibilities, one thus makes possible the confusion that constitutes the nature of the mood of fear. (Heidegger 1996: 314).

In anxiety, unlike fear, what one is anxious in the face of, and what one anxious about, are the same, specifically, the to-be-in-the-world that I am and that I have to be, in a word, my *Da-sein*, my being-there, itself. Here is the description of the turning toward and the turning away from that characterize anxiety:

> Beings in the surrounding world are no longer relevant. The world in which I exist has sunk into insignificance, and the world thus disclosed can set free only beings that are not relevant. The nothingness of the world in the face of which *Angst* is anxious does not mean that an

> absence of innerworldly things objectively present is experienced in *Angst*. They must be encountered in just such a way that they are of *no relevance at all*, but can show themselves in a barren mercilessness. However, this means that our heedful awaiting finds nothing in terms of which it could understand itself, it grasps at the nothingness of the world. (Heidegger 1996: 315).

Heidegger makes the point that anxiety is extraordinarily rare. It holds one on the verge of a decisive moment.

In the lecture course *The Fundamental Concepts of Metaphysics* (Heidegger 1995), dating from several years after *Being and Time*, Heidegger provides a very extensive analysis of boredom. Unlike anxiety, which is extraordinarily rare, boredom, Heidegger finds, is the prevailing mood of the times. Ultimately, in what Heidegger characterizes as "deep boredom," one becomes entranced by the temporal horizon per se as this stretches itself out, in effect, as the movement whereby we have installed ourselves in the world recommences, in Merleau-Ponty's words, yet a little more time for itself. In boredom, time, in effect, passes too slowly. The German word for boredom, *Langeweile*, says as much. What we do then is to fill in the time in order to pass the time. At one stage of his step by step approach moving from more superficial boredom to "deep boredom," Heidegger describes how one's looking at one's watch (the gesture that figures in Merleau-Ponty's description of a disclosure of the movement whereby we have installed ourselves in the world) marks a passing of time by filling in the time. It is in such a passing the time in filling in the time that the movement away from and the movement toward characteristic of boredom lie. With such passing the time in filling in the time, what we do, in effect, is to put boredom to sleep. What Heidegger's analysis aims at is awakening that sense of deep boredom, awakening the mood, as he puts it, and this in anticipation of another prevailing mood.

This movement away from and this movement toward are indicative of selfhood.

Heidegger specifies that in each case the to-be-in-the-world is *mine*. Merleau-Ponty will characterize selfhood as "the original of an elsewhere," and he will specify that it is precisely by way of this "original of an elsewhere" that we are to understand my opening upon a world.

Every mood involves both a turning away from and a turning toward. What mood returns me to is my "having-been," and therefore of the three "temporal ecstasies" of past, present, and future, mood is most closely associated with past. Still, *Da-sein*, there-being, per se, is primarily futural. My having-been actually comes out of the future, and this pertains to the sense in which, as *Da-sein*, there- being, I am always ahead of myself. Importantly, having-bee does not pertain to something left behind. I *am*, as Heidegger puts this, "in the process of having-been." What this points up is that the movement away from, disclosed by mood, or, as Heidegger also puts it, a "backing away," is, in fact, the first movement. How can this be? That I first back away actually means, in effect, that I am not anywhere before that. Heidegger identifies the backing away with forgetting and he stipulates unequivocally that a forgetting happens before any remembering, and not the other way around. How can that be? The answer cannot be that what is forgotten is nothing in a sense where such nothing would fill the role, so to speak, of a forgotten something. This is precisely where no philosophy of presence will hold. We are brought closer to the heart of the enigmatic character of the underlying movement whereby I have installed myself in the world.

While being in the process of having-been will figure again importantly in Heidegger's initial approach to the issue of historicity, just before the published text of *Being and Time* breaks off, never to be followed by another projected section of Part I and a projected Part II, it is actually in Heidegger's later work that the implications of the precedence of the "backing away," the forgetting, or the withdrawal will loom very large. In a greeting that Heidegger sent in 1976 to participants in an annual meeting in the United States of the Heidegger Circle, a few days before his death, and thought to be his last written document, he makes the point that all that he had done in regard to thinking Being in a manner that does not fall into the mode of the philosophy of presence had been aimed, in fact, at thinking, ultimately, what the Greeks had called *aletheia*, and that we translate as "*die Wahrheit*," or as "truth" (Heidegger 1978). In his essay on the topic of *aletheia* in Heracleitus, Heidegger had made the point directly that what takes place first is the "lethic," which is to say, the forgetting (Heidegger 1975). As Heidegger understood matters, the predominant mood in the period of Greek thought was one of wonderment, specifically, a wonderment at the gathering coming to presence of beings in the wake of an inaugurating event, or in other words, at the fact of world. In our time, when the prevailing mode of the philosophy of presence comes from the identification of subjectivity as the *hypokeimenon* or ground, culminating when Hegel specifies the Absolute precisely as Idea, the obscuring of a precedent forgetting or withdrawal reaches an extreme point. The prevailing mood now becomes one of deep boredom, again, an entrancement with the temporal horizon as this stretches itself out, an entrancement that Heidegger distinguishes from the "captivation" that operates here where different animals are concerned. In *The Fundamental Problems of Metaphysics*, Heidegger writes that this means that we have become bored with ourselves. He writes elsewhere that today, wherever we turn, we find, again and again, only ourselves. When in the mid-1930s important unfinished text, published in 1989, *Beiträge zur Philosophie: Vom Ereignis*, where the issue of "another beginning" becomes a critical one, Heidegger indicates that the prevailing mood of such a beginning would be *die Scheu*, a word for a type of awe that involves a timidity, consistent with the sense of an initial forgetting or withdrawal (Heidegger 1999).

We find another phenomenological variant of the precedence of forgetting or of withdrawal in the work of Emannuel Levinas. Levinas understands the means Husserl developed for gaining access to the very largely taken for granted content of awareness as an awakening, in effect, from the sleep of what Husserl called "the natural attitude," where "taken-for-grantedness" reigns, basically, taken-for-grantedness of world. But, on Levinas's account, this awakening aims always, for Husserl, at a superior knowing. The analysis, Levinas finds, must be pushed beyond the letter of Husserl's text. This radicalizing of what Husserl called the transcendental phenomenological reduction is comparable to Heidegger's understanding of being-in-the-world as a radicalizing of Husserl's sense of the intentionality of consciousness, how consciousness is never bare or empty but rather is always consciousness-of this, or consciousness-of that. In the 1974 essay called "From Consciousness to Wakefulness: Starting with Husserl" Levinas writes:

> At the level of the Ego—where subjectivity is at its most alive—there intervene, in Husserl, the terms "sleep" and "sleeplessness" [*veille*]. The Ego is situated outside of immanence while belonging to it—as "transcendence in immanence"— which must signify the following: a *difference* in relation to the "remaining-the-same" or to "finding oneself-the-same-anew," which is the duration (or the temporalization, as one says today) of immanent time or the flow of lived experience. But this is a difference other than that which separates the intentional object from this flow.
>
> What might this exteriority signify, which tears at the innermost of the intimate? What is the meaning of this "soul within the soul," this alterity, there where everything is nevertheless coincident with self or rediscoveries of self, this unreality at the heart of lived experience? What might this exteriority—which would not be an intentional ecstasy—signify? A retro-cendence: that which is identified in immanence and recovered there, detaches itself from itself or comes to its senses, like the instant at which sleep gives way and where, in awakening, the lived experience before us discolors as a dream that is past and may only be remembered. (Levinas 1998a: 23–24).

In the book that he wrote on Michel Foucault's work (Deleuze 1988), Gilles Deleuze wrote that it was Merleau-Ponty that taught all of us how an exteriority, more external than any externality, turns on itself and results in an interiority more internal than any internality. Merleau-Ponty cited the painter Cézanne approvingly: "Nature is on the inside." The forgetting or the withdrawal, on Levinas's understanding, marks my relatedness to the other, and that relation, he specifies, is actually not a relation, by virtue of the fact that the other cannot be assimilated and so the relation remains untotalizable. The untotalizable character of this relation that is not a relation marks, for Levinas, the priority of a peace that is not merely the absence of war driven by the intent to reduce the other to the Same.

At the extremity of this relation that is not a relation, and that challenges Egoity, where I am responsible to the other, even unto the death of the other, comes what Levinas calls "the one-for-the-other," my coming to the aid of the other, and here it is that I am most myself, in that no one else can do what I do. In a text first published in 1977, called "Questions and Answers," Levinas responds to questions put to him by other philosophers at a meeting in 1975 celebrating the 400th anniversary of the University of Leyden in Holland. In one response, Levinas, mindful always of Heidegger's early 1930s politics, describes how it is on the basis of this sense of responsibility that he could understand better a point pertaining to selfhood that Heidegger makes in *Being and Time*. Here is part of that response:

> It is from this idea that I have even understood better certain pages of Heidegger. (You know, when I pay homage to Heidegger, it is always costly to me, not because of his incontestable brilliance, as you also know). In Section 9 of *Sein und Zeit*, the *Dasein* is posited in its *Jemeinigkeit* ("Mineness"). What does this *Jemeinigkeit* signify? *Dasein* signifies that the *Dasein* has to be. But this "obligation" to be, this manner of being, is an exposition to being that is so direct that it thereby becomes mine! It is the emphasis of this rectitude that is expressed by a notion of *first property*, which is *Jemeinigkeit*. *Jemeinigkeit* is the extreme measure of the way in which *Dasein* is subject to ess*a*nce [essence in a verbal sense]. Heidegger says a few lines below: it is because the *Dasein* is *Jemeinigkeit* that it is an

> *Ich* [an I}. He does not at all say that the *Dasein* is *Jemeinigkeit* because it is an *Ich*; on the contrary, he goes toward the *Ich* from the *Jemeinigkeit*, toward I [*moi*] from the "superlative" or the emphasis of this subjection, from this being-delivered-over-to being [être-livré-à-être], of this *Ausgeliefertheit*. (Levinas 1998b: 92).

This is how Levinas understands Heidegger's specification that *Da-sein*, there-being, which is always *my* there-being, is ahead of itself, always. This is consistent with Merleau-Ponty's characterization of the self as the original of an elsewhere. The self is not to be found in first over-stepping or over-riding what comes before it.[1]

What now of the awakening, this "non-rest or non-perdurance in the Same" that Levinas describes as "the *living* of life—an incessant bursting of identification"? In "From Consciousness to Wakefulness," Levinas writes: "Awakening is the I sleeping and not sleeping, *for whom* takes place all that comesto pass in immanence itself: an awakened heart, a nonbeing, a nonstate *in the depth of moods* [my emphasis] slumbering in their identity, an insomnia or a throbbing in the ultimate recess of the subjective atom" (Levinas 1998a: 24). This awakening, this insomnia, marks that forgetting or that turning away that is intrinsic to mood and that always happens first. We recall Levinas's description of how in the instant at which sleep gives way, in awakening, the lived experience before us discolors as a dream that is past and may only be remembered. Forgetting or withdrawal, in its turning away, indeed has turned us now toward memory.

At this point, I turn for illumination to the literary art of Franz Kafka, one of whose most widely appreciated works, *Metamorphosis*, is about someone who "awakened one morning from a troubled sleep." We do know, at least, that at one point Kafka attended meetings of a Philosopher's Club, along with his friend Hugo Bergmann, who wrote *Untersuchungen Zum Problem der Evidenz der inneren Wahrnehmung* (Bergmann 1908), a text addressing Husserl's early work, and who eventually found his way to the land of Israel. Max Brod, the executor of Kafka's literary estate, wrote of Kafka: "The world of those realities that were important for him was invisible." On this, in his essay "Franz Kafka: On the Tenth Anniversary of His Death," Walter Benjamin, of whom Hannah Arendt wrote in her Introduction to the collection of Benjamin's essays called *Illuminations* that he regarded himself as closer to Kafka than to any other contemporary writer, with only one exception, namely Marcel Proust (who was himself no stranger to questions pertaining to forgetting and memory), wrote:

> What Kafka could see least of all was the *gestus*. Each gesture is an event—one might even say, a drama—in itself. The stage on which this drama takes place is the *World* Theater [my emphasis] which opens up toward heaven. On the other hand, this heaven is only background; to explore it according to its own laws would be like framing the painted backdrop of the stage and hanging it in a picture gallery. Like El Greco, Kafka tears open the sky behind every gesture; but as with El Greco—who was the patron saint of the Expressionists—the gesture remains the decisive thing, the center of the event. (Benjamin 1969: 121).

---

[1] Concerning the comparison between Levinas's thought and Heidegger's thought see my "Levinas and Heidegger: A Strange Conversation" in Froman (2011).

In his essay, Benjamin takes note of a desire that Kafka once expressed as follows: "to hammer a table together with painstaking craftsmanship and, at the same time, to do nothing—not in such a way that someone could say 'Hammering is nothing to him' but 'To him, hammering is real hammering and at the same time nothing,' which would have made the hammering even bolder, more determined, more real, and, if you like, more insane." This would amount, in effect, to a gesture where there is no forgetting.

But this was a desire, perhaps a dream. Kafka, Benjamin observes, would definitely not consider himself one to whom forgetting is alien. His own clan, as Walter Benjamin puts this, comprised those who, in effect, represented forgetting, those who were pre-historic and the animals appearing in Kafka's work. Apart from the clan, but closely related, were "the assistants" who recur throughout Kafka's work. Benjamin writes of these assistants that "[t]hey have not yet been completely released from the womb of nature, and that is why they have [quoting Kafka] 'settled down on two old women's skirts on the floor in the corner. It was…their ambition…to use up as little space as possible. To that end they kept making various experiments, folding their arms and legs, huddling close together; in the darkness all one could see in their corner was one big ball'" (Benjamin 1969: 116–117).

These assistants, then, are constantly backing away, constantly withdrawing. Then there is Odradek in Kafka's text "The Cares of a Family Man." Odradek, Benjamin observes, is the "form which things assume in oblivion" (Benjamin 1969: 133). Here, from the story "The Cares of a Familyman," is Kafka's description:

> One is tempted to believe that the creature once had some sort of intelligible shape and is now only a broken-down remnant. Yet this does not seem to be the case; at least there is no sign of it; nowhere is there an unfinished or unbroken [sic] surface to suggest anything of this kind; the whole thing looks senseless enough, but in its own way perfectly finished. In any case, closer scrutiny is impossible, since Odradek is extraordinarily nimble and can never`be laid hold of. (Kafka 1993: 184).

Of all the figures in his work who signal a forgetting, one who was evidently of special significance for Kafka was the figure of "the little hunchback." In her Introduction to *Illuminations*, Hannah Arendt tells us that "the little hunchback," a German fairy-tale figure out of *Des Knaben Wunderhorn*, the famous collection of German folk poetry, figured not only in Kafka's writings but in his conversation as well. Several stanzas of the folk poetry go as follows:

> When I go down to the cellar
> There to draw some wine,
> A little hunchback who's in there
> Grabs that jug of mine.
>
> When I go into my kitchen,
> There my soup to make,
> A little hunchback who's in there
> My little pot did break. (Benjamin 1969: 6).

> When I come into my room,
> My little bed to make,
> A little hunchback is in there,
> With laughter does he shake.
>
> When I kneel upon my stool
> And I want to pray,
> A hunchback man is in the room
> And he starts to say:
> My dear child, I beg of you,
> Pray for the little hunchback too. (Benjamin 1969: 134).

Children's fairy-tales are surely not without a share of the enigmatic, the strange, or the uncanny. "The little hunchback" is a figure of being burdened, or recalling language invoked earlier on, a figure of facticity. Throughout his life, Benjamin observes, Kafka tried to get the burden off his back. One is here reminded of the point in Merleau-Ponty's *Phenomenology of Perception* where he writes: "One day, once and for all, something was set in motion which, even during sleep, can no longer cease to see or not to see, to feel or not to feel, to suffer or be happy, to think or rest from thinking, in a word to 'have it out' with the world."[2] Regarding "the little hunchback," Walter Benjamin writes:

> In his depth Kafka touches the ground which neither "mythical divination" nor "existential theology" supplied him with. It is the core of folk tradition, the German as well as the Jewish. Even if Kafka did not pray and this we do not know—he still possessed in the highest degree what Malebranche called "the natural prayer of the soul": attentiveness. And in this attentiveness he included all living creatures, as saints include them in their prayers. (Benjamin 1969: 134).

Such "attentiveness," or such "wakefulness," signals a return, a memory, in a present, of the forgetting that nevertheless remains prior, or in Benjamin's terms, a point where Kafka "touches ground." In Kafka's writings we find gestures that perform what they say. Here is a little text where this "attentiveness" or "wakefulness" takes place, a return or a memory, in a present, of a turning away from that nevertheless remains prior:

> I ran past the first watchman. Then I was horrified, ran back again and said to the watchman: "I ran through here while you were looking the other way." The watchman gazed ahead of him and said nothing. "I suppose I really oughtn't to have done it," I said. The watchman still said nothing. "Does your silence indicate permission to pass?" (Kafka 1993: xxxiv).

In the 1993 English collection of Kafka's stories that he edited, Gabriel Josipovici, in his Introduction, notes in regard to this text that "[w]e would, of course destroy the story…if we were to substitute for it some generalizing comment, such as 'to hesitate is to be lost,' or 'human self-awareness will not allow us to act naturally'." I agree. My question is this: if moods, as Heidegger specified in *Being and Time*, are only displaced by moods, with their turning this way and that way, what mood is it that pertains to this "attentiveness," or this "wakefulness"? In what mood does the

---

[2] Froman (2011), pp. 406–407.

basic relation between forgetting and memory lie? The answer lies, I find, in the mood that is strongest of all, as indicated in Heidegger's characterization in *The Basic Concepts of Metaphysics*, although when we take notice of mood we tend to regard first such evident ones as grief or joy. This strongest of moods is the mood that goes unnoticed in the midst of everyday life's coming and going.[3] In the turning away from and the turning toward of life in the everyday, in it's everyday character, and how that can return, even when broken into from an outside, there lies a basic memory, in a present, of the forgetting that has always, and still, happens first.

My interest here has been in mood and memory. The question of futurity is one that I will leave open largely, except to note that by virtue of how, with an awakening within the mood that characterizes everydayness, such that the forgetting still remains prior, there is a sense of looking back from an anticipated future at what happened here. Whatever did, remains, and here I close with a characterization found with no elaboration in the discussion of everydayness in Heidegger's *Being and Time*, "inextinguishable" (Heidegger 1996: 339).

References

Benjamin, Walter. 1969. "Franz Kafka: On the Tenth Anniversary of His Death." In *Illuminations*. Trans. H. Zohn, Hannah Arendt (Editor and Introduction). New York: Schocken Books.

Bergmann, Hugo. 1908. *Untersuchungen zum Problem der Evidenz der Inneren Wahrnehmung*. Halle: Niemeyer.

Deleuze, Gilles. 1988. *Foucault*. Trans. Sean Hand. Introduction by Paul Bove. Minneapolis: University of Minnesota Press.

Froman, Wayne. 2011. "Levinas and Heidegger: A Strange Conversation." In *Interpreting Heidegger: Critical Essays*, ed. Daniel Dahlstrom. Cambridge: Cambridge University Press.

Heidegger, Martin. 1975. "Aletheia (Heraclitus, Fragment B16)." In *Early Greek Thought*. Trans. David F. Krell, and Frank Capuzzi. New York: Harper and Row.

---

[3] Here is the pertinent passage:

And precisely those attunements [Stimmungen] to which we pay no heed at all, the attunements we least observe, those attunements which attune us in such a way that we feel as though there is no attunement there at all, as though we were not attuned in any way at all—these attunements are the most powerful. At first and for the most part we are affected only by particular attunements that tend toward "extremes," like joy or grief. A faint apprehensiveness or a buoyant contentment are less noticeable. Apparently not there at all, and yet there, is precisely that lack of attunement in which we are neither out of sorts, nor in a "good" mood. Yet even in this "neither/nor" we are never without an attunement. The reason we take lack of attunement as not being attuned at all, however, has grounds of a quite essential nature. When we say that a human being who is good-humoured brings a lively atmosphere with him, this means only that an elated or lively attunement is brought about. It does not mean, however, that there was no attunement there before. A lack of attunement prevailed there which is seemingly hard to grasp, which seems to be something apathetic and indifferent, yet is not like this at all. We can see once more that attunements never emerge in the empty space of the soul and then disappear again; rather, Dasein as Dasein is always already attuned in its very grounds. There is only ever a change of attunement. (Heidegger 1995: 68)

Heidegger, Martin. 1978. "Neuzeitliche Naturwissenschaft und Moderne Technik." In *Radical Phenomenology: Essays in Honor of Martin Heidegger*, ed. J. Sallis. Atlantic Highlands: Humanities Press.

Heidegger, Martin. 1982. *Basic Problems of Phenomenology.* Trans. Albert Hofstadter. Bloomington: Indiana University Press.

Heidegger, Martin. 1995. *Fundamental Concepts of Metaphysics: World, Finitude, Solitude.* Trans. William McNeill and Nicholas Walker. Bloomington: Indiana University Press.

Heidegger, Martin. 1996. *Being and Time.* Trans. Joan Stambaugh. Albany: University of New York Press.

Heidegger, Martin. 1999. *Contributions to Philosophy (From Enowning).* Trans. Parvis Emad, and Kenneth Maly. Bloomington: Indiana University Press.

Husserl, Edmund. 1970. *The Crisis of European Philosophy and Transcendental Philosophy.* Trans. David Carr. Evanston: Northwestern University Press.

Kafka, Franz. 1993. *Collected Stories.* Trans. Willa and Edwin Muir , Gabriel Josipovici (Editor and Introduction). London: Everyman's Library.

Levinas, Emmanuel. 1998a. "From Consciousness to Wakefulness: Starting with Husserl." In *Of God Who Comes to Mind.* Trans. Bettina Bergo. Stanford: Stanford University Press.

Levinas, Emmanuel. 1998b. "Questions and Answers." In *Of God Who Comes to Mind.* Trans. Bettina Bergo. Stanford: Stanford University Press.

Merleau-Ponty, Maurice. 1962. *Phenomenology of Perception.* Trans. Colin Smith. London: Routledge & Kegan Paul.

Merleau-Ponty, Maurice. 1968. *The Visible and the Invisible.* Trans. Alphonso Lingus. Evanston: Northwestern University Press.

A Mood of Childhood in Benjamin

Eli Friedlander

To memory, at least, childhood can appear, more than other ages of life, to be traversed by moods. This is maybe why some images of it awaken intense homesickness for no explicable reason. Such homesickness frames Walter Benjamin's autobiographical *Berlin Childhood around 1900.* The text was mostly composed, as Benjamin left the continent and its cities for the rural surroundings of the island of Ibiza, off the coast of Spain. An introductory passage recounts the circumstances of, and set the affective tonality for, the inception of writing: "In 1932, when I was abroad, it became clear to me that I would soon have to bid a long, perhaps lasting farewell to the city of my birth" (SWIII: 344).[1] To face the impending loss Benjamin engages in a process of inoculation, deliberately calling to mind "those images which, in exile, are most apt to waken homesickness (*Sehnsucht*): images of childhood". His autobiographical writing initially presents itself as a strategy of defense, something of a cathartic practice, with the help of which "the feeling of longing would no more gain mastery over [his] spirit than a vaccine does over a healthy body" (SWIII: 344).

But controlling the outpour of sentiment further seems to depend for him on achieving insight or understanding. Specifically, Benjamin puts forth the puzzling claim that it is not recalling the images as such, but the insight achieved through them into what he calls the *irretrievability* of the past that would limit the melancholic potential of memory. But why wouldn't recalling images of childhood precisely *be*

[1]"Berlin Childhood around 1900" in Benjamin (2002: 344). Throughout this essay I will refer to Benjamin's writings immediately following the quote by way of the following abbreviations: SW (followed by the volume number) – *Selected Writings of Walter Benjamin* Cambridge: Harvard University Press. *C – Complete Correspondence* (Benjamin 1994), *O – The Origin of German Tragic Drama* (Benjamin 1977), *A – The Arcades Project* (Benjamin 1999b).

E. Friedlander (✉)
Department of Philosophy, Tel-Aviv University, P.O. Box 39040, Ramat Aviv,
Tel-Aviv 69978, Israel
e-mail: frieli@post.tau.ac.il

H. Kenaan and I. Ferber (eds.), *Philosophy's Moods: The Affective Grounds of Thinking*,
Contributions To Phenomenology 63, DOI 10.1007/978-94-007-1503-5_4,

a retrieval of the past? Is it that we would then be able to embed them in a historical context and thus achieve objective understanding to replace the subjective early impressions? This reality check, opposing as it does the mature knowledge of reality to the illusory perspective of childhood, might explain why one would feel the early relation to the world to be irretrievably lost, but it would hardly be of help to the melancholic, whose devotion to his memories knows no bound. Another possibility of being true to the attachment to the past, without giving up on the mature insight into its meaning, suggests itself as Benjamin writes "The images of my metropolitan childhood perhaps are capable at their core, of pre-forming later historical experience." (SWIII: 344) This would imply that images of childhood can transform and open from *within* the medium of memory the present in which that past is realized.

The title of Benjamin's work, "Berlin Childhood around 1900" can offer an entry point into this problematic of memory. It brings together time, space and a particular experiential world: Childhood, in that city, around that time. Such a title structure, not untypical in Benjamin, would suggest the incorporation of the environment of living in the individual's space of experience. It would moreover point to the possibility of finding a level, or dimension of the individual's memory in which those surroundings themselves are refracted. Since surroundings are not your usual kind of "middle sized dry goods", one might wonder whether a child would pay attention to them at all. Indeed, what would it be for us to do so? For thought or perception needs an object, and surroundings would just be too diffuse to get a hold of. Moreover, the deeper the level of experience conjured, the more independent of faces, names, events and stories, the less it would seem up to us to deliberately bring it to mind.

Note then that Benjamin is not saying that he is reminded of various images perceived in childhood, as though recalling the things he has seen. He speaks of how "the experience of the big city is precipitated in a child of the middle class". In other words, an image, as the term is used here, is not the correlate of a past perception, but rather something emerging only in memory, standing for and gathering surroundings that may not have been intentional objects of consciousness. The term Benjamin uses to characterize the emergence of the images, "precipitation", suggests that when experience accumulates and memory is saturated, that mass can condense, undergo a change of state, or precipitate into an image. "Precipitation" brings to mind the weather and in particular those rainy days whose importance has in part to do with the all-over quality that rain brings to the city. It makes it a uniform grey with no shading and brings it out *as* an environment, in a mood that transforms even one's sense of time (In rainy weather, as Benjamin puts it "from morning until evening one can do the same thing" (A: 104)). But the image in which that whole environment is precipitated bears no obvious similarity to it. It is the otter in the zoo. For the child, the otter is the "sacred animal of the rainwater": "… when I gazed into the water" Benjamin writes "it always seemed as though the rain poured down into all the street drains of the city only to end up in this one basin and nourish its inhabitant… whether it was formed in this runoff of the rains, or only fed from arriving streams and rivulets, is something I could not have decided." The child would endlessly wait to catch a glimpse of the "glistening inmate of the cistern", which after briefly darting up to the surface, would immediately "hurry back to urgent affairs below" (SWIII: 366). Waiting, boredom and expectation are condensed in that memory image, which at the same time serves as an image of the necessity of waiting for the weight of the past to manifest itself.

Take another image of memory and of what memory is, the image of the butterfly hunt: "Between us, now" Benjamin writes, "the old law of the hunt took hold: the more I strove to conform, in all the fibers of my being, to the animal – the more the butterfly itself, in everything it did, took on the color of human volition; and in the end, it was as if its capture was the price I had to pay to regain my human existence" (SWIII: 351). Not only does the metamorphic creature *par excellence* become the object of the mimetic transformation of the child, but that identification itself is the support for a deeper, more formless, absorbing of the surroundings. The flight of the butterflies is governed by "the conspiring elements – winds and scents, foliage and sun" (SWIII: 350). The word 'conspiracy' suggests that the elements come together through some secret plan, of which the butterfly becomes the image. The ephemeral creature can become a gathering point for those diverse intangible dimensions, and through its flight, allow them to enter the child. It is possible for sure to describe the movement of the butterfly in terms of the various factors causally affecting it in space and time, but image-space, (as Benjamin calls it in his essay on Surrealism) is opened by the image being a confluence of what might neither be physically nor psychologically related. The imagination casts a net over a single colorful object but the threads of that net are tied to a large and disparate mass of materials. Their relationships are not a matter of similarity, association or metaphorical displacement, but go through the image at their center. Because of that implicit environment of meaning, the image would appear particularly significant and attractive. It would don, what Benjamin calls in a different context, an aura, and would return to us a gaze, rewarding us with meaning for the attention we pay it, just like the butterfly would seem to "take the color of human volition" when the child tracks it.

I would like now to focus my attention on a specific feature of the images of memory I described, namely their color. One is gray. In the other not only do we find colored butterflies, but even the name of the place in which the hunt took place, "Brewery Hill", "has lost all heaviness ... and is, at most, a blue-misted hill" "It lies in air so blue" that Benjamin compares the image to "those glistening Limoges enamels, on which the ramparts and battlements of Jerusalem stand out against a dark blue ground" (SWIII: 351). What are those colors in memory and what is their relation to the memory of color in childhood?

"The concern with color", Benjamin writes in an early fragment entitled 'A Child's View of Color', "cancels out intellectual cross references of the soul and creates a pure mood" (SWI: 51). I take moods to be distinguished from feelings or other emotional states in part by being affective manifestations of one's surroundings and one's being in them. To create a mood, color must then bring out the texture of experience as an interrelated totality, and should not appear as a property of isolated objects. This is not to say that to enter such a mood would require concentrating on the subjective space of one's sense impressions. Such an artificial and complicated attitude would, if anything, serve only to cover up the mood one might find oneself in. Moods neither are objects of attentiveness, nor do they demand concentration to manifest themselves. Just as being in a state of daydreaming does not involve concentrating on one's reveries, the child can find himself in tune with color absent mindedly, lost or immersed in it, through his numerous occupations and distractions.

Consider briefly, by way of comparison and contrast the place of color in Kant's account of aesthetic judgment and beauty. For Kant beauty is a field in which the discriminations we made, not by way of determinations of properties of an object, but rather by relating back the object to its condition of possibility, reflecting its form. This leads Kant to argue that color in itself cannot be judged beautiful, for it is lacking form. It is mere matter of sensation, and therefore can be effective but would open no space for reflection. One could find a color agreeable, but not demand agreement over that feeling. Yet, Kant adds, the association physics discovered between colors and vibrations of the ether would hint at the possibility of also *perceiving* color as form.[2] Color phenomena that make manifest such a space of possibilities can themselves become objects of a proper aesthetic judgment. I will argue later that this is not quite the way to save color phenomena for aesthetics, but consider here a further, particularly significant, elaboration of the relation of color and feeling in Kant. He takes colorful beings, such as flowers and butterflies, as well as the whimsical play of light in nature, to hint at the possibility of an attunement of man to nature as a whole.[3] Indeed, it would not be the form, but the very existence of such colorful beings that would be of significance. As opposed to the presence of beauty in art, their multiple dispersed existence in our surroundings is a sign nature gives, of itself, for the possibility of its attunement to our human faculties. *That* there is color would induce an affective state that reveals our position in the world in what can be called a mood of hope.

This is, for sure, a peculiar case of second order aesthetic experience, rather than a paradigmatic disinterested aesthetic judgment, for the pleasure in color would involve an intellectual interest in there actually being beauty in nature at all. The presence of such an interest (i.e. of an idea of reason) further makes clear that for Kant the susceptibility to the very existence of colors in their relation to the idea of morality presupposes a degree of cultivation we will not expect in children.

Trying then to find another way into the mood of color, we note that the world of childhood is, even if only implicitly, present in Kant's famous characterization of aesthetic judgment as a free play of the faculties. Beauty engages the faculties of the mind, imagination and understanding, in a purposive movement. That free activity of the imagination is a mode of responsiveness that opens the space of form common to the mind and the object in which the object now appears pleasantly significant. By this somewhat unorthodox reformulation of Kant I mean to form a bridge to the human capacity to respond to the form in things which Benjamin calls the mimetic faculty Benjamin (1999a). The play of childhood is for him one of its clearest mani-

[2] See Kant (2001): § 14.

[3] Kant (2001): § 42.

festations: "Children's play is everywhere permeated by mimetic modes of behavior, and its realm is by no means limited to what one person can imitate in another. The child plays at being not only a shopkeeper or teacher, but also a windmill and a train" (SWII: 720). We speak in such contexts of the power of children's imagination. But then, the child cannot play at being a color: "All form, every outline man perceives, corresponds to something in him that enables him to reproduce it... But this ability finds its limit in the world of color. The human body cannot produce color. It does relate to it not creatively but receptively: through the shimmering colors of vision" (SWI: 442).

Perhaps to separate the receptivity of color from active forms of imaginary identification, Benjamin recounts, in a passage of the *Berlin Childhood* entitled 'Colors', a chameleonic transformation, as the child wanders inside an abandoned summerhouse with stained-glass windows: "passing from one colored pane to the next, I was transformed; I took on the colors of the landscape that – Now flaming and now dusty, now smoldering and now sumptuous – lay before me in the window" (SWIII: 380). The image of immersion in color brings out a fundamental difference between the place of color in the child's world and its appearance in art. One can be absorbed in contemplation facing a painting, but the child absorbs color, as though it is his environment. Something similar to that immersion occurs with the experience of watercolors "when things would take me to their bosom as soon as I overcame them in a moist cloud" (SWIII: 380). Note the peculiar logic of this description. The child acts upon the linear design in his coloring book so as to conquer it with color. But a moist cloud spreads as soon as the brush touches the paper and it absorbs the watercolor. Color instead of functioning as the extension of the action of the child, expands, opens up and, so to speak, surrenders itself. And it is this surprising deflection of the action into a mere gesture that captures the gaze of the imagination and takes the child in.

Considering the "resplendent, self-sufficient world of colors" in children's books (of which Benjamin was himself a passionate collector) is a further occasion to develop the contrast to painting. In painting colors are part of the form, constitutive of the medium or cannon. They are not experienced as covering anything, not a background or even one another, but rather belong to the work in the same way as blushing or paling belong to the expression of a state of mind. With illustrations of old children's books on the other hand, the graphic design is first printed and the coloring, often through its imperfections, is experienced as superimposed or hovering over the line. One can be full of wonder at the colors of such illustrations, whereas to say of a painting that it has beautiful colors would sound not just as lacking taste, but also as a grammatical error. In painting to detach color from design or form would risk making it a mere effect. But in illustration color runs no risk of taking over. Since illustrations in children's book share with writing the horizontal plane, to look at them as one views a painting, vertically, as something to be displayed, would conflict with their meaning. They thus escape the whole problematic of the theatrical effect. They are, moreover, experienced as unpretentious *coloring* and makes no claim to draw our interest or sole attention. Coloring-in makes color the *content* of the object, what brings it alive. But its flatness stops short of introducing the object into its isolated existence in space, for this would depends to a large extent on light and shading.

Now, one might of course argue that all this ignores the main difference between coloring and painting, namely that the one is a mechanical task of reproduction according to a model whereas the other is a creative activity. This is of course correct but such an emphasis on creativity might hide the distinctive function of the imagination in the world of children. Indeed precisely the understanding that one cannot be active in relation to color distinguishes those modes of imaginative receptivity from adult creativity and makes them valuable. For Benjamin "… coloring in has a purer pedagogical function than painting" (SW1: 51). We are yet to see what it is.

Just like watercolors, soap bubbles, pieces of jewelry, decals and the magic lantern, all provide an opportunity for what Benjamin calls "pure imaginative contemplation" (note the expression). "Their magic lies … in the colored glow, the color brilliance, the ray of colored light" (SWI: 443). Among such phenomena he singles the rainbow as a "pure childlike image". It is an image of boundaries solely defined by color: "In it color is wholly contour" (SWI: 50). The distinct colors of the rainbow and its geometrical shape might tempt us to think of the order of color on the model of harmony (and Newton did try to form an analogy between the seven colors he thought he perceived in his prismatic experiments and the octave in music). But, the existence of rainbows makes all the more evident the obvious: that whereas color is so much part of the space of experience, the sounds we hear do not form the harmonies of music. This is why music can often feel out of this world. Moreover, the possibility of arranging colors on a wheel or a solid need not imply that they form a quasi-mathematical order. "Color" Benjamin writes "does not relate to optics the way line relates to geometry" (SWI: 49). Contrary to what Kant argued, the experience of color does not reflect for the most part in its appearance the mathematical armature of its description by way of physics. (more generally it does not feel like a symptom of something else: sounds or smells lead back to an independently characterized source, tastes and tactile qualities can hardly be separated from the substances they are qualities of.) But color can retain the quality of a pure appearance, thereby forming "an order consisting of an infinite range of nuances" (SWI: 50). Harmony demands separation, but color allows countless continuous transitions. Nevertheless, its nuances, even when minimal, can be immediately and utterly clear. This is why color *can* be experienced as a fluid medium of delicate change occurring of itself. It is not so much the mixing of saturated colors but rather the contemplation of transparent colors that often provide the occasion to experience differences of intensity, shimmering light, subtle and shifting nuances and continuous merging. "In their illumination and their obscurity" Goethe writes "the transparent colors are without limits, just as fire and water can be regarded as their zenith and nadir…." (Quoted in Benjamin, SWII: 443)

One might speak here of an effortless dissolution of boundaries, of a dimension of experience in which change is felt to be eminently possible. But it is change without destruction. "Painless change" Benjamin would call it, very different from the anxious, sublime or ecstatic emotional states in which we imagine ourselves experiencing the world in its boundless totality. With color the experience of merging is one of endless dissolution with no temptation to transcendence. The mood of color is created, Benjamin writes "without thereby sacrificing the world" (SWI: 51).

There is pleasure in color, involvement with experience, but its appearance is not seductive as it promises nothing beyond itself. Color can intoxicate in a most ordinary and prosaic manner without occasioning any display of emotion, hinting thereby at its spiritual nature. Benjamin recounts one such 'profane illumination' with color in the second part of the passage 'Colors' in which a contest is established between the higher and lower senses on the occasion of the child untying a gold string that held together a packet of chocolates. Every square was wrapped separately in colorful tinfoil of green and gold, blue and orange, silver and red and the whole formed a resplendent edifice in which the order was purely a matter of color constituted by the principle that no "bricks" of the same color would be allowed to touch. The contest between mouth and eye is decided as the desire stimulated by the chocolate is purified, one might say redeemed, by being taken up into the experience of color. Its sweetness as it dissolves in the mouth becomes part of the memory image of the dazzling dissolution of color in the child's hearth.

Let me, at this point, briefly turn to discoloration and its attendant mood. It too depends on everyday matters: That there is day and then there is night. But the shift of mood that I want here to characterize is not merely the result of darkness, of night falling. For not to see things is different than seeing them discolored. Discoloration requires seeing them in another light. If the mood of color is most apparent as the sense of transparency of color, the passage entitled "The Moon" in the *Berlin Childhood* can be seen as laying out of the imaginary implications of the fact that white can be opaque or cloudy, but there is no such thing as transparent white. The milky whiteness of moonlight streaming into the room at night, accentuated by the presence of porcelain jugs, marble surfaces and cream colored basins, creates for the child a discoloration of the world. Whereas the mood of color is one of immersion, discoloration creates detachment from the world. "When [the moon] was there in the room and I awoke, I was effectively un-housed, for my room seemed willing to accommodate no one besides the moon" (SWIII: 382). One might say, echoing Wittgenstein, that in such a state the world is no longer my world: as if I am contemplating an alternate earth in which the place I recognize as "me" is already taken: This uncanny doubling is reinforced by the stillness in which even sounds deceive: "The gurgling of the water, the noise with which I put down first the carafe and then the glass – it all struck my ear as repetition. For every spot on this alternate earth to which I was transported appeared wholly occupied by what once has been. I had no choice but to give myself up to it. When I returned to my bed a moment later, it was invariably with the fear of finding myself already stretched out upon it" (SWIII: 382). The child's exhausted anxiety occasions his first engagement with metaphysics: "nothing more remained of the world than a single, stubborn question. It was: Why is there anything at all in the world, why the world?" In discoloration there occurs a falling out of attunement with the world, as though by losing the texture that makes a being belong to its world "With amazement," Benjamin writes "I realized that nothing in [the world] could compel me to think the world" (SWIII: 383). The alignment of discoloration with the question of being makes it all the more necessary to ask about the understanding that belongs to color. Indeed it would seem that colors can hardly give rise to such a fundamental question if only because there are many of them and since they are so much what they appear to be.[4]

What is the instruction the child derives from the experience of color? We think of "learning from experience" for the most part to mean learning the hard way, by encountering obstacles and pain, or, alternatively, by the numbing acquisition of habits based on regularities in experience. But, my description of the dissolution of boundaries in color might allow for neither and make experience into a Mickey Mouse world in which as Benjamin writes "it is not worthwhile to have experiences" (SWII: 544). Since everything is malleable, nothing would be worth retaining in memory. Nor would the associative function of the imagination find any occasion to bring to mind, say, heavy cinnabar when representing red. Would color then be an occasion to develop the child's imagination and foster creativity? Benjamin does write that "the imagination can be developed only by contemplating colors" and that "only in this way can it be both satisfied and kept within bounds" (SWI: 51). But he does not mean by that to refer to the imagination as a creative function that puts together out of the given material of perception new forms. Rather he distinguishes such a formative imagination (*Einbildungskraft*, as in Kant's use of the term in his aesthetics) from fantasy (*Phantasie*) that is manifest in the child's relation to color.[5]

Fantasy is not a forming faculty but rather a medium of deformation. To take color to be one of its clearest manifestations would allow to conceive of fantasy not by way of bizarre, grotesque or ironic deformation. It would be the sense color provides of "the interrelated totality of the world of the imagination" that would constitute its deformation. Fantasy would perceive the world not in its self identity, through objects individuated in space and time, and separated from one another, but rather strange as it might sound, as similar to itself. The deformation of fantasy would not be an external change such as substances undergo but would occur in the intensification of the inner relatedness of experience by way of color.

Relationships that make experience whole would not depend on the lawfulness of experience. Color involves the highest receptivity to experience, but its order does not parallel or merely reflect the *facts* of experience. It inheres in experience but at the same time is dissociated from causal, temporal, spatial, conceptual and even metaphorical determinants. And precisely that self sufficiency of color, as it allows discrimination in an order whose internal relatedness is both endless and immediate is the instruction it offers.

"When you look at colors, the intuition of fantasy, in contrast to the creative imagination, manifest themselves as a primal phenomenon" (SWI: 442). The reference

[4]In this context consider an interesting remark of Wittgenstein: "Colors spur us to philosophize… Colors seem to present us with a riddle" he writes, but he adds "a riddle that stimulates (anregt) us – not one that disturbs (aufregt) us." (Wittgenstein 1984: 66).

[5]See the fragment entitled "Imagination" in Benjamin (1996: 280–282).

to "the intuitions of fantasy" (and similarly, to "imaginative contemplation") is striking. It points to the possibility of conceiving of fantasy in terms of receptivity rather than activity. The reference to intuition further distinguishes such receptivity from perception, from the causal affection of the senses by the external world. As the manifestation of a primal phenomenon such pure passivity is rather the highest mode of openness to what Goethe, and following him Benjamin, think of as an archetype that inheres in nature.

Painting too creates under such a muse, but precisely because it imitates that model it must introduce form that is foreign to the intuitions of fantasy. The art of painting has its source in what fantasy intuits, but it cannot recreate that order in its purity. The form it depends on allows intimacy at a distance (creates what Benjamin calls an aura). It opens the space for an activity of criticism in which the work comes alive, as something promised or to be endlessly approached as an idea. This movement of approach that the work makes possible is described by Benjamin in terms of a dissolution of limits as well (for instance in his discussion of the moment of irony in Romantic Criticism). But the purely receptive, uncreative actuality of a paradisiacal order, of painless change and dissolution, of discrimination before judgment and concept, free of yearning and desire, is the prerogative of children.

It is this relation formed between the archetype, the platonic idea, and the intuitions of fantasy that motivates what is probably the most difficult and surprising claim of Benjamin's understanding of the color world of children: "if anything similar to Platonic anamnesis actually exists, it would take place in the lives of children, for whom picture books are paradise. By remembering they learn ... Children learn in the memory of their first intuition. And they learn from bright colors, because the fantastic play of color is the home of memory without yearning, and it can be free of yearning because it is unalloyed" (SWI: 264).

Our excursion into the childhood world of color lead us back to memory, moreover to the idea of learning through recollection, and with it to the opening of the *Berlin Childhood.* Though the anamnesis of color, the memory without yearning, is the prerogative of the child's world, we might want to raise the question whether and how the space of memory of adulthood can take on its characteristics. By this I do not mean the adult recovery of the experience of color in childhood, but rather making it a model for the transformation that the *meaning* of the past undergoes in memory. The new questions and problems this raises, I can only approach here suggestively and leave their systematic elaboration for another context.

In the passage entitled "Boys Books" Benjamin tells of revisiting the colors of fantasy in a dream he had about old lost books: "In these books there were stormy goings-on. To open one would have landed me in the lap of the storm, in the very womb, where a brooding and changeable text – a text pregnant with colors – formed a cloud. The colors were seething and evanescent, but they always shaded into a violet that seemed to come from the entrails of a slaughtered animal." I note several things about this dream[6]: First, I take it that it is an adult dream about the books of

[6] I am indebted to Werner Hamacher's insightful reading of this part of the *Berlin Childhood* in "The Word Wolke – if it is one – (Walter Benjamin's theory of the Mimetical)," in Hamacher (1988).

childhood, that is, about the form meaning absorbed in childhood can take. Second, such meaning as is read or articulated, so to speak in black and white, takes on the continuous fluidity of color. Third, that mutability of color is not only the paradisiacal mood but shades into an intensity which co-exists with cloudiness, even violence. Fourth, the shading into violet occurs as reading becomes of something inner, organic. Fifth, such reading of the real, by way of texts is figured as reading in entrails that is as prophetic, to be realized in the future of afterlife of meaning. Lastly, the closer one gets to those Ur – books in the dream, the cloudier it is and the less one is able to tell what their titles are. One awakens without realizing their names. Or rather one should say that the realization of meaning will not take place for the adult in dream but in awakening.

Clouds and colors, then, or if you prefer otters and butterflies: Our earlier discussion suggested that the passivity of waiting and its attendant boredom are the essential element in which experience would accumulate and precipitate into images. The other side of that grayness of waiting, is the colorful image that gathers its surroundings in meaning. The meaning opened up by that image is not unified in a narrative pattern, through succession and causality. The biographical conjuncture of being-in-a-place and at-a-time is, to use a pun Benjamin coins in the *Arcades* not only a *Zeit-Raum*, a space-time but a Zeit-Traum, a *Dream-Space-Time* (A: 389). Benjamin provides a figure for these two sides of the texture of experience in memory: "Boredom is a grey fabric lined on the inside with the most lustrous and colorful silks. In this fabric we wrap ourselves when we dream. We are at home then in the arabesques of its lining. But the sleeper looks bored and grey within its sheath. And when he later wakes and wants to tell of what he dreamed he communicates by and large only this boredom. For who would be able at one stroke to turn the lining of time to the outside" (A: 106).

This turning inside out of the garment of time, the task of memory to make the two sides into one surface involves a peculiar topology: Not that of the pair of gloves which Kant has introduced into philosophy through his reflection on space. Nor of the pair of shoes that Heidegger introduced into the understanding of the temporality of art as origin. Rather I return for a last time to the *Berlin Childhood* to tell of a pair of socks. In the passage entitled "The Sock" we are told how the child enters a wardrobe and works his way through the materials to its back: "There I would come upon my socks, which lay piled in traditional fashion – that is to say, rolled up and turned inside out. Every pair had the appearance of a little pocket. For me, nothing surpassed the pleasure of thrusting my hand as deeply as possible into its interior. I did not do this for the sake of the pocket's warmth. It was "the little present" rolled up inside that I always held in my hand and that drew me into the depths. When I had closed my fist around it and, so far as I was able, made certain that I possessed the stretchable woolen mass, there began the second phase of the game, which brought with it the unveiling. For now I proceeded to unwrap "the present", to tease it out of its woolen pocket. I drew it ever nearer to me, until something rather disconcerting would happen: I had brought out "the present," but "the pocket" in which it had lain was no longer there. I could not repeat the experiment on this phenomenon often enough" (SWIII: 374).

In the description of this childhood experiment, or 'magic trick' as one could also call it, there is a very pronounced element of desire, almost an erotic component. But what most grabs the child's attention and provokes astonishment, is not getting hold of the attractive object, but rather its disappearance, neither by having desire satisfied, nor by having it frustrated. It is dissolved by the disappearance of what allows the structure of desire at all: the economy of distance and closeness that made for the attraction. Desire that seeks to possess the attractive 'present' is itself worked through, dissolved one might say, on the way to its realization.

In terms of our earlier discussion, think of the pocket as the meaning surroundings in which the images of the past are sheltered. The images, that is the woolen mass or little present, appear to us significant far beyond any factual basis they would have, and provoke longing precisely because they are veiled by that aura of meaning. Any attempt to merely tell straight on why they create such homesickness would only result in recounting the ordinary and uneventful boredom which is their soil. Understanding is not achieved by placing the images in an objective, independently arrived at context. It is precisely the gathering power of the images that allow the surroundings to come together in meaning as a world. For the child color is the medium of such relationships. Benjamin takes the experience of correspondences to be a dissociation from the object space that demands the recognition of non-sensuous similarities, non-sensuous insofar as they are relationships between the spaces of different senses. Synaesthesia is for him a matter not of empirical psychology but a possibility of the medium of memory. More generally, the work of memory that those images allow would consist in revealing all the threads that open up their surroundings of meaning. The net of similarities within the space of memory weaved by way of the image at their center would not only allow to overcome the fixations of memory, but, also, if we follow the unfolding of the socks, result in the formation of a single plane of meaning in which the attractive or distinctive image is dissolved. (As Benjamin points out, Proust would take some 80 pages, not for the utterly ordinary dissolution of the Madeleine in a spoon of tea to take place, but for the dissolution of that impression in the surroundings of meaning it made appear.) In tightening the many fine threads that linked the image to its life, in making the surroundings that emerge out of it into one texture, through a work that would be just as much a forgetting as a remembering, the image would become unremarkable, part of a uniform weave of meaning. The dissolution of that image, the transformation of the yearning it provoked into a sense of the ephemeral in experience, can be called a mood of happiness.

References

Benjamin, Walter. 1977. *The Origin of German Tragic Drama*. Trans. J. Osborne. London: NLB.

Benjamin, Walter. 1994. *Complete Correspondence*. Chicago: Chicago University Press.

Benjamin, Walter. 1996. *Selected Writings*. vol. 1. Cambridge: Harvard University Press. "Aphorisms on Imagination and Color," 48–49; "A Child's View of Color," 50–52; "Old Forgotten Children's Books," 406–413; "The World of Children's Books," 435–443.

Benjamin, Walter. 1999a. "On the Mimetic Faculty." In *Selected Writings*, vol. 2, 720–722. Cambridge: Harvard University Press.

Benjamin, Walter. 1999b. *The Arcades Project*. Trans. H. Eiland and K. McLaughlin. Cambridge: Harvard University Press.

Benjamin, Walter. 2002. "Berlin Childhood Around 1900." In *Selected Writings*, vol. 3, 344–413. Cambridge: Harvard University Press.

Hamacher, Werner. 1988. "The Word Wolke – if it is one – (Walter Benjamin's theory of the Mimetical)." In *Benjamin's Ground*, ed. Rainer Nägele and Trans. Peter Fenves, 171–201. Detroit: Wayne State University Press.

Kant, Immanuel. 2001. *Critique of the Power of Judgment*. Trans. P. Guyer and E. Matthews. Cambridge: Cambridge University Press.

Wittgenstein, Ludwig. 1984. *Culture and Value*. Trans. Peter Winch. Chicago: Chicago University Press.

Part III
Melancholy

Leibniz's Monad: A Study in Melancholy and Harmony

Ilit Ferber

In describing his attempts to delineate the diverse faces of melancholy, Robert Burton famously compares this task to that of "capturing a many-headed beast" (Radden 2000: 8). Melancholy indeed has an extremely variegated history; however, among the extraordinary persistence of its described traits, such as an inhibition from activity, paralysis and deep sadness without cause,[1] two polar attributes dominate: *detachment* and *self-absorption*. Moreover, its dialectical nature, which has kept interest in melancholy alive for so many centuries, has veered its examination less toward its pathologies than toward those features that endowed the afflicted, usually considered to be great men with exceptional genius, with special access to truth, manifested in bursts of creativity, abstract and philosophical thought, to mention only a few.

It seems therefore that one of the consistencies running through melancholy's history has been its association with philosophy. That connection has not, however, been stable in its characteristics, going from the Aristotelian link between great men (philosophers among them) and melancholy; the Renaissance association of melancholic genius with medical imbalance attributed to the intense presence of black bile, assumed to generate detachment from the active life; the Baroque understanding of

[1] In general, the melancholic mood is defined through its detachment from causality. In all accounts throughout its history, no actual event has caused a loss, and nothing is necessarily "discovered" in the world to have caused melancholy. On the contrary, the fact is that nothing has been identified that produces melancholy. In this context, it is interesting to look into two pairs of concepts, Heidegger's fear and anxiety, together with Freud's mourning and melancholia. Both pairs maintain a similar structure of intentionality/causality as opposed to lack of intention and cause. Also in both cases, the pathological (in Freud) or authenticity (in Heidegger) lack an object and thus proximate the definition of mood.

I. Ferber (✉)
Department of Philosophy, Tel-Aviv University,
P.O. Box 39040, Ramat Aviv, Tel-Aviv 69978, Israel
e-mail: iferber@post.tau.ac.il

H. Kenaan and I. Ferber (eds.), *Philosophy's Moods: The Affective Grounds of Thinking*, Contributions To Phenomenology 63, DOI 10.1007/978-94-007-1503-5_5,

philosophical rigor as melancholic detachment from the allusive visual world; and finally Freud's curious comment, in which he admits, without further explanation, that the melancholic patient is withdrawn from any object-relations or active life although he does have what Freud calls "a keener eye for the truth."

The spectrum of these accounts of the relationship between melancholy and philosophy not only testifies to the stability of the connection, it reveals that melancholy is not conceived merely as an obstacle to creativity and productivity, it is, first and foremost, depicted as a mood or state of mind that is positively associated with the impetus to think. This bond, however, poses one fundamental and dogged problem: How is it possible that a mood so persistently characterized by closure and detachment can be the same mood that gains us access to truth, which requires openness and involvement? If truth is not internal or subjective but the subject matter of philosophical activity itself, how do we reconcile philosophy with melancholic closure and self-absorption? Furthermore, how can melancholic avoidance of action and the external world be associated with philosophical expression of that same world?

In what follows I attempt to unpack this paradox and offer a possible solution in the form of a productive co-existence between these allegedly contradictory approaches. The implications of exploring such co-existence reach beyond the understanding of melancholy's special relationship to philosophy: They divulge the essential bond between philosophy and mood (or attunement) in general. I begin with an outline of Heidegger's celebrated account of moods while focusing on the way in which they condition and determine Dasein's being-in-the-world. I then suggest looking at this problem through Leibniz's work, particularly the monad's structure.

My aim here is not to propose a new interpretation of Leibniz but, rather, to use his metaphysical model in tackling what I take to be the essence of the relationship between philosophy and attunement. Rather than portraying the monad as inherently melancholic, I explore the monadological system as capturing a relationship with the world, that is, I view this entity as self-absorbed yet open to the world; in other words, the monad is not melancholic but melancholically structured. This approach allows me to elaborate the special affinity holding between philosophy and melancholy while demonstrating the possibility of a productive link between the two.

I. Heidegger: Being-in-the-world

One of the elemental characteristics of Dasein, according to Heidegger, is the special structure of its being as Being-in-the-world. Heidegger frequently reiterates this premise from different perspectives and in different contexts. The importance of Being-in-the-world lies in its harboring many of the characteristics that Heidegger attributes to being and its configuration: Its encounter with the world as totality rather than intentionality, abandonment of the classical subject-object opposition, avoidance of a causal structure in its encounters with the world, and so forth.[2]

Description of the internal structure of Being-in-the-world requires a special type of analysis, one that would retain that structure's inherent unity yet simultaneously elucidate its discrete elements. As Heidegger explains: "The compound expression 'Being-in-the-world' indicates in the very way we have coined it, that it stands for a unitary phenomenon. This primary datum must be seen as a whole. But while Being-in-the-world cannot be broken up into contents which may be pieced together, this does not prevent it from having several constitutive items in its structure" (Heidegger 1962: 78 [53]).[3] This unity, inherent to "Being-in", is not, as implied, similar to that of water 'being in' a glass, or to a garment 'being in' the cupboard (Heidegger 1962: 79 [54]). Being-in implies a much more complex structure and determines Dasein's own necessity by representing an existential state. This determines an encounter with another of Dasein's hallmarks: It always has a state of mind (Heidegger 1962: 173 [134]; Heidegger 1962: 183 [144]) or, as Heidegger puts it elsewhere, "We are never free of moods" (Heidegger 1962: 175 [136]).[4]

My aim here is to think about the convergence between the previously mentioned two components while developing the form of that encounter in order to illuminate the structure of Being-in-the-world and the role moods play in it. My question is, therefore, how is the intrinsic state of being-in-a-mood threaded into the structure of Being-in-the-world? Does it induce contradiction or collaboration?

A term useful for understanding the complexity and richness of this structure is *Befindlichkeit* (state-of-mind),[5] which Heidegger conceived as the receptivity of Being manifested in Dasein and the way it finds itself situated within the world; And moreover, the way that Dasein finds the world within itself (the two should be understood as inseparable). *Befindlichkeit* therefore relates to both aforementioned characteristics of Dasein: It describes the special way of being within-a-world and, at the same time, describes this being as determined by how Dasein and the world find one another. Heidegger deliberates on the use of terms such as care, concern and mattering, all of which stress that 'finding oneself' has no spatial referents but is related exclusively to the *manner* in which the world enters Dasein's circle of concerns and comes to matter to it.

The implications of understanding Being-in-the-world also refer to how the world becomes open to Dasein from within its own circle of concerns and the

---

[2]For further explanation of the nature of mood in Heidegger's thought, see the Introduction, pp. 4–5.

[3]Heidegger (1962). Hereafter for each citation, I also provide the German pagination in brackets.

[4]The relationship between "mood" [*Stimmung*] and "state-of-mind" [*Befindlichkeit*] in Heidegger's use, unfolds later in this article.

[5]"State of mind", as used here, is Macquarrie and Robinson's translation (see their footnote on the term's translation in Heidegger 1962: 172, n. 2). Dreyfus's note on this translation and his suggestion to understand *Befindlichkeit* as "affectedness" is interesting (Dreyfus 1991: 168 ff).

special way it is constituted as something mattering. The association between Dasein's Being-in-the-world and its constant being within a mood, indicates the specific way in which the world discloses itself. Mattering is, then, in affinity with disclosure: "Dasein's openness to the world is constituted existentially by the attunement of a state-of-mind" (Heidegger 1962: 176 [137]). Only in this way can Dasein be "touched" by anything or have a sense of the world as meaningful.

"*Dasein is its disclosedness*" (Heidegger 1962: 171 [133], stressed in the original), writes Heidegger. Disclosedness is, however, quite different from any form of representation of the world or specific knowledge about it. Its distinctiveness stems from Heidegger's rejection of the classic separation between subject and object lying at the heart of Husserl's theory of intentionality (which Heidegger contests). The structure of Dasein as always Being-in-the-world, which constitutes the most radical demonstration of Heidegger's critique of intentionality, is sharply marked by his statement that "subject and object do not coincide with Dasein and the world" (Heidegger 1962: 87 [60]). Dasein is therefore never discussed from the perspective of its psychological or even subjective nature but always from within its fundamental unity with the world. According to Heidegger, it would be misleading to think of Dasein as standing "in between" subject and object because once these phenomena are separated, it will be difficult to reunify them (Heidegger 1962: 170 [132]). What is decisive, then, is to "prevent the splitting of the phenomenon… to hold its positive phenomenal content secure" (Heidegger 1962). And so, despite Heidegger's initial insistence on disposing of this separation, doubts remains as to whether any complete separation can be accomplished at all (this ambiguity is evidenced in Heidegger's repetitive use of the separate terms).

At this point I would like to shift my focus to Leibniz's basic metaphysical entity, the monad. This move entails a departure from our discussion of Dasein as a human entity to another plane, more abstract or structural, as we explore the identity between Dasein and the monad. This shift is not unproblematic. I by no means wish to claim that Dasein and the monad are similar or even parallel entities, and it is not my intention to compare them here. The purpose of this exploration is to join two extremely different discussions and show how one can illuminate the other as I attempt to offer a solution to the puzzling relationship between philosophy and melancholy as necessary for understanding the correspondence between philosophy and mood.

As a preliminary, I find it necessary to note the interesting echoes of the special connection of Leibniz's monad with the world, in Heidegger's attempt to offer *Befindlichkeit* (state-of-mind) and *Stimmung* (mood) as alternatives to the customary subject-object relationship. I first point to what I take to be the monad's prototypical melancholic structure (which I consider to be a specific case of mood), found in the relationship it maintains with the world it expresses. Consequently, I link this structure to Heidegger's account of mood and its role in Dasein's encounter with the world on the one hand, and to the two focal attributes of the melancholic stance, detachment and abiding self-absorption, on the other hand. In doing so I show that the monad is an entity whose closure does not hinder it from expressing the world of which it is a part.

The case of the monad lucidly presents a state in which complete closure and detachment accompany an endless expression of the world together with the perfection of that expression. Moreover, the monad provides an interesting interpretation to Being-in-the-world, or the world as being in the monad, when viewed as a relationship avoiding representation and intentionality. I claim that Leibniz's system of monads represents a paradigmatic concretization of the encounter between philosophy and the world, with the question of mood situated in at its nucleus. My reading explores the special structure of the monad's encounter (or lack of encounter) with the world together with the imperative role mood plays in that encounter. I therefore perceive Leibniz's system of monads as proffering a metaphysics of mood.

II. Leibniz: Expression

When thinking of the constitutive relationship holding between philosophy and mood (or attunement), it may be enlightening to turn to philosophical arguments in which this connection is implicit or latent rather than explicit. Such cases have special force in that they invite us to delve into the conundrums marking this connection.

If mood, or attunement, is defined, following Heidegger's account, as an openness to the world, an attitude incorporating the world within one's sense of self, time and place, then the monad and its functioning, as continual expression of the world, exemplify attunement. Leibniz describes the monad as being in a continuous and unremitting correspondence with the world, a stance not rooted in an encounter with a specific object but in a perpetual accord, sustained with the world as a whole. This accord, following Heidegger, can be understood as an attunement in which the world as totality is engulfed by and expressed by the monad.

Leibniz describes attunement in various places and contexts, a sample of which follows, when accounting for the congruity of monads vis-à-vis the world: "every simple substance … [has] relations which express all the others and consequently… [is] a perpetual mirror of the universe" (MO: 648)[6]; "Each created monad represents the whole universe…" (MO: 649); "In the smallest portion of matter the whole world resides…" (MO: 66); "…expression takes place everywhere because

[6]Most citations of Leibniz's texts are taken from the second edition of Loemker (Leibniz 1969). For each citation, I provide abbreviations, based on the initials of the text's title, and the page number in the Loemker edition. The main abbreviations are: "The Monadology": MO; "Correspondence with Arnauld": CA; "What is an Idea?": WI; "Principles of Nature and Grace": PNG; "New System of the Nature of Substances and Their Communication, and of the Union which Exists Between the Soul and Body": NS; "Second Explanation of the New System (postscript of a letter to Basnage de Beauval, January March 13, 1696)": NS2; "First Truths": FT; "Reply to the Thoughts on the System of Pre-established Harmony Contained in the Second Edition of Mr. Bayle's Critical Dictionary": RPH; "Letter to Magnus Wedderkopf, May, 1671": MW.

every substance sympathizes with all the others and receives a proportional change corresponding to the slightest change which occurs in the whole world…" (CA, 9.10.1687: 339).

However, the accord described has a unique character. It is not a simple external encounter between two independent entities, the monad and the world. Leibniz claims that a monad, having no apertures ("windows"), is discrete and consequently isolated from the world with which it is in accord. The monad's openness to the world is, in fact, rooted in a basic impediment within its own structure: Outside its confines, the world is inaccessible to the monad[7]; rather, the world resides within it, in a peculiar relationship termed *expression*.[8] In Sect. 7 of the *Monadology*, Leibniz elaborates on this relationship:

> There is… no way of explaining how a Monad can be altered or changed internally by any other creature, since nothing can be transposed in it, and we cannot conceive in it… that any internal motion can be excited, directed, increased or diminished from without. Monads have no windows through which anything could enter or depart. (MO, 643)

Hence, despite their concurrent seclusion, the world is never independent of the monads constituting it; in consequence, every expression of the world is necessarily an expression of all monads. This raises the question of self-expression. Does the monad express itself directly or indirectly, as mirrored by other monads? Is its power of expression stunted when it comes to expressing itself? These questions reveal that a special form of communication is integral to the act of expression. Leibniz calls it *sympathy*: "This [form of] expression takes place everywhere because every substance sympathizes with all the others and receives a proportional change corresponding to the slightest change which occurs in the whole world…" (CA, 9.10.1687: 339).

This account frames the inherently *non-causal* character of expression associated with the monad: Nothing external can directly initiate any act of expression within the monad's confines. As a result of its closure, the world as an object does not reside within the monad; rather, it exists as an expression free of any causal

[7] According to Leibniz, it is only God who possesses this eternal point of view. He is the only one 'outside' of any individual perspective or, rather, the only one with an all-encompassing perspective, which includes all others. The universe, however, is not equivalent with God.

[8] Leibniz defines the relationship of expression, the monad's principal activity, in several ways; in none of them is the relationship external. With this almost counter-intuitive structure of expression, Leibniz detaches the monad's perception from what we usually understand by this term, and renders it completely internal. Leibniz illustrates his conceptualization with five examples: miniaturization or abbreviation (See also, "…the monads produce something that resembles the works of God but in a miniature" (PNG: 640)); projective delineation; speech as expressing thought; character as expressing a number; and the algebraic equation. This five examples share one trait: with their help, "…we can pass from a consideration of the relations in the expression to knowledge of the corresponding properties of the thing expressed. Hence it is clearly not necessary for that which expresses to be similar to the thing expressed, if only a certain analogy is maintained between the relations" (WI: 207–208) or, as Leibniz formulates this idea in a letter to Arnauld: "One thing expresses another, in my usage, when there is a constant and regular relation between what can be said about one and about the other" (CA: 9.10.1687: 339).

derivation stimulated by actual encounters with the exterior. 'Expression' thus has nothing to do with any direct or causal relation with the expressed object. It is, as Leibniz defines it in "What is an Idea?", a state in which

> we can pass from a consideration of the relations in the expression to a knowledge of the corresponding properties of the thing expressed. Hence, it is clearly not necessary for that which expresses to be similar to the thing expressed, if only a certain analogy is maintained between the relations (WI: 208).

By turning to analogical affinity, or to proportion or to ratio, as he does elsewhere, Leibniz establishes the pristine closure he attributes to the monad. Lacking an opening, a window, the monad is secluded, together with its own history and future, in a mirror-image of the world it expresses. Importantly, because the monad lacks causal relationships with anything outside it, it is not only detached from its exterior, it is completely self-absorbed in total self-retention.

Why is the monad's status that of inherent confinement? Leibniz presents a system based on detachment and seclusion, a system in which no communication between the monads is possible. Yet, Leibniz also maintains that all monads express the same universe. What we have here is utter confinement merged with all-encompassing unity.

This seemingly paradoxical formulation, according to which the same universe is expressed by substances that are not only completely detached from one another but also from the universe itself, is what underlies Leibniz's special conception of individuality. Each monad, as a complete entity, expresses the same world from its own point of view (CA 14.7.1686: 337; PNG: 637), a point of view that individuates the monad. According to Leibniz's principle of 'the identity of indiscernibles', no monad can be completely similar to another, otherwise there would be but one single object (as in Spinoza). The infinite individuation of monads is shaped and determined by their different perspectives on the same world. Yet, these substances' encapsulation and detachment are insufficient to maintain their *individuality*. Individuality is therefore established by the different ways in which the monads find themselves in relationship to something else. In that sense, monads seem to express a Heideggerian principle: Their being is defined and determined by their being-in-their-world or, more precisely, the world being-in-them, and the specific ways they relate to this world.

Leibniz's famous illustration of a city around which groups of substances are organized exemplifies how the same object can be observed from what Leibniz describes as infinite points of view. These perspectives not only define the monad's individuality, they also amplify as they refine the representation of the world (in this case, the city) by enforcing variety in its expression: "That every substance expresses the whole of the universe, but some more distinctly than others, each one more particularly with regard to certain things, and according to its own point of view" (CA, 23.3.1690: 360). Hence, although the world in its totality exists in each individual monad, it is the monad's distinctive point of view that defines which *portion* of this world is expressed clearly and which is not. What Leibniz conceives of as a 'clear portion' is that level of perfection in expression, each monad is capable of achieving.

Similarly, while the city in its entirety is expressed, what Leibniz considers the chimerical, unconscious "image" of the city remains only that narrow portion captured within the boundaries of the individual monad's point of view that can be clearly and consciously expressed. It is as if the ray of its individuality defines the monad's unique perspective.

The role each monad plays in the system, like its relationship to other monads, is thus determined by the specific and unique way in which the monad expresses the world. The system's complexity thus emerges from the various levels of clarity marking the expression that each monad manifests. The specific way in which the world comes to "matter" to the monad, to use Heidegger's term, is determined by each monad's own, individual point of view. This structure (or relationship characterized by "mattering") is interestingly confronted in Heidegger's discussion of anxiety (what he takes to be a fundamental mood)[9]; when he writes that "anxiety individualizes Dasein and thus discloses it '*solus ipse*'" (Heidegger 1962: 233 [188]). Although Dasein's possibilities are determined, its individual formation of mood (in this case, anxiety) is *solus ipse*, in the same way that the monad's distinctive point of view provides the basis for its individuality. For Heidegger, these possibilities imply Dasein's ability to "project",[10] to "sketch" or delineate its potential for action in the world; in Leibniz, possibility means the specific (and individual) way in which each monad has access to and expresses the world.

What determines the distinctive portion in which the world is expressed – the portion in which the world appears in perfect accord – is, interestingly enough, the monad's *feeling* of its own *body*, and everything directly related to that substance. In order to clearly express that part of the world closest to it, the monad needs to feel itself, its own body, very precisely; that is, it needs to feel a distinct change in its substance.[11] However, it is not simply the body and what affects it that the monad distinctly feels; in deepening his definition, Leibniz writes that it is *the body in pain* that we feel most clearly and thus express most distinctly:

> The soul expresses the world according to the relationship which other bodies have to it. It expresses the parts of its own body more immediately. This soul must, by virtue of the laws of relationship which are essential to it, particularly express certain unusual motions of the parts of its body. This happens when it feels *pain* (CA, 9.10.1687: 339; emphasis added).

Leibniz posits that we have a confused and indistinct sense of our own body because we are so accustomed to it that we cease to feel its presence. It is only

---

[9]For Heidegger's Discussion of Anxiety see, Heidegger 1962: 228–235 [184–191].

[10]By "projection," Heidegger means the existential structure in which Dasein marks its own limits by sketching its possibilities. Dasein can only understand itself through fathoming the possibilities through which it projects itself unto the world by planning and relating to its future (an existential capability not shared by animals). On Projection see for instance, Heidegger (1962: 184-185ff [144–145ff]).

[11]Another well-known illustration Leibniz gives to explain the concept of confused perceptions is the roar of the sea, which is composed of noises made by separate waves (CA 9.10.1687: 339).

instates of illness or pain that our body "reappears" before us in all its clarity, a state that motivates reflection:

> So we also sense some confused result of all the motions taking place within us, but, being accustomed to this internal motion, we do not perceive it clearly and with reflection except when there is an important change as in the *beginning of illness* (CA, 9.10.1687: 339–340; emphasis added).

It is as if being in pain allows us to feel our bodies anew, and in many ways even redefine them. In extreme instances of pain, we suddenly seem to rediscover organs and redefine our body's boundaries; put differently, pain is a state in which the attunement and accord we have with our own body changes and the lucidity with which we sense our body is renewed and deepened. Hence, the soul expresses most articulately what pertains to its own body when it is in pain. We can thereafter reorient ourselves to our bodies. The immediacy of our access to pain, whether physical or mental, can account for the clarity of our expression. What Leibniz hypothesizes here is a kinship between adversity and the clear, precise expression of the world. This means that the acknowledgement of pain and the special feeling of individuation it induces has the potential to bring us closer to clear and perfect expression.

Returning to the aforementioned account of melancholy, we can claim that just as in Leibniz's allusion to the pain that intensifies feelings of the body, intensification of the melancholic stance allows truth and lucidity to emerge. Stated differently, what we tend to understand as a pathological psychological state, conducive to symptoms of dejection in its sufferers, can also be shown to generate another, vital condition. The history of melancholy is indeed a history of psychological and physical symptoms, but it also reveals dominant traits that render it productive and generative. It is a mood that allows one privileged access to truth and meaning.

III. A Melancholic Harmony

The positive and productive relationship between melancholy and philosophy rests on a certain type of philosophical activity; clearly, construction of an affinity between melancholy and philosophy as such is unjustified. The assumption underlying my reading of Leibniz, an assumption responding to and reflecting the historical connection between melancholy and philosophy, demands that philosophical work be understood as the constant practice of expression and the unremitting attempt to perfect expression. I take this conception from Walter Benjamin's work, which I have justified elsewhere in detail. And indeed, my approach to Leibniz originated in my work on Benjamin, whose texts reverberate with the pair 'monad' and 'melancholy'. This current exploration grew out of an attempt to fathom Benjamin's persistent interest in Leibniz's monad (mainly in his book on *Trauerspiel,* dealing with the baroque theater active in Leibniz's lifetime). The link I found between the monad and melancholia can be defined as the paradigmatic state of mind dominating Benjamin's work.[12]

In unfolding the problematics of the relationship between melancholy and philosophy as they emerge from the aforementioned characterization of philosophical work as the practice of expression, I return to Leibniz. My claim is that the monad conspicuously contains the solution to the conundrum of the connection between the paralysis of solipsistic self-retention and the productivity of philosophical expression. The structure of the monad entails detachment and utter closure from the world on the one hand, together with an intensely vital expressiveness regarding that world on the other. My claim here is *not* that the monad is itself melancholic. Instead, I argue that the monad's relationship with the world is *constituted* by melancholic attunement.[13] In effect, the same problem is confronted in the melancholic mood and in the monad: Both are imbued with detachment and both are fundamentally inhibited from relating to the world.

Leibniz does not allude to melancholy directly, and is in fact known for his persistent optimism. Yet, the structural elements of melancholy as I present them here are present in his writings on monads:

> …in metaphysical strictness we are in a state of *perfect independence as concerns* the influence of all other created beings. This throws a wonderful light on the immortality of our soul and on the always unbroken conservation of our individuality, which is perfectly regulated by its own nature and fully *sheltered from all external accidents… every mind is as a world apart* and sufficient unto itself, *independent* of every other created being, enveloping the infinite and expressing the universe, it is as lasting, as continuous, as absolute as the universe of creatures itself (NS: 458, emphasis added, translation revised by the author).

The radical independence of the monad, grounded in its detachment from external reality, diverts its gaze inwards, to its state of perpetual self-absorption. Yet, Leibniz continues, while activity is metaphysically necessary (Russell 1937: 44)·, this activity is always spontaneous since no external reality can provoke it: "Anything which occurs in what is strictly a substance must be a case of action in the metaphysically rigorous sense of something… spontaneously arising out of its own *depths*" (Leibniz 1896: 218), and elsewhere: "Except for its dependence upon God, all its actions come from its own *depths*" (CA 23.3.1690: 360, emphasis in original).[14]

Leibniz's emphasis on 'depth' in describing the monad's spontaneity is meant to accentuate its basic self-absorption, the sole stance from which the monad can structure its attunement with the world. Since all the monad's predicates have always

[12] See Ilit Ferber, *Melancholy and Philosophy: Walter Benjamin's Early Writings*, Manuscript in preparation.

[13] It is interesting to note in this context that Leibniz gives happiness a prominent place in his philosophy. For Leibniz, what I call a "melancholic system" is in fact very optimistic. That is, each monad maximizes its happiness by refining its expression of the world.

[14] See also "a nature or an internal force that can produce in it, in an orderly way, all the appearances or expressions it will have, without the help of any created being" (NS, GP iv 486/AG 144). Another version of this claim can be found in MO, §15.

belonged to it, and since these predicates include the monad's complete history, it follows that the monad's activity and development in time are mere consequences of its own notions, spontaneously derived from its own depths, never from other substances.[15] The monad thus encapsulates everything in a gesture curiously similar to what Freud describes as the "narcissistic" facet of melancholy. This lack of worldliness – or basic detachment from anything that might be considered as exteriority – is associated with radical inwardness and self-absorption, what Leibniz designates as being in one's own 'depths,' a withdrawal not motivated by loss but by its own basic spontaneity or existential enterprise.[16]

Leibniz offers here a special type of melancholic solipsism. It is not that the monad detaches itself from the world and is fully absorbed in its solipsistic subjectivity (as in Leibniz's contemporary, Descartes). On the contrary, Leibniz creates a solipsism in which the world is *incorporated* in each monad, rather than left out and secluded: "It is clear from this that there is a world of creatures, living beings, animals, entelechies, souls, *in the smallest particle* of matter" (MO: 650).[17] The monads are secure from absorption into the external world; yet, that very world completely exists within them and is present in their distinctive expression of it.

This melancholic stroke also encompasses another quality essential to the monad: melancholy arises when the impossibility of complete and perfect accord with the world and its expression is finally recognized. It is in this sense that the Baroque scholarly state-of-mind reputedly sank into dejection upon discovering the discord between the perceived world and its abstract mathematical and scientific formulations (such discord can be taken as the basis for Descartes' categorical doubt). Within the monad's configuration, this facet, more closely anthropological than the others, can be identified in the substance's elemental *incapacity* to express the world in complete, perfect clarity. There is always some obscurity in its expression, as well as a persistent melancholic attempt to overcome that obscurity. Melancholy is therefore inherent in the 'limits of expression' so to speak, and in the endless task of perfecting expression.[18]

This picture of an infinite number of substances, all self-absorbed and completely detached from one another, not only grounds the presence of melancholy in Leibniz, it establishes the centrality of mood in general. *Stimmung*, if we take Leibniz's own

---

[15]This formulation is adapted to some extent from Russell's account of substance. (See Russell 1937: 43).

[16]One aspect of loss is Leibniz's "best of all possible worlds" – the choice of the best world inherently entails the loss of other worlds. Another commonality between Leibniz and Freud regarding the description of melancholy is the constant working-though of the internalized object. In Freud, melancholy is destructive; in Leibniz, it represents a continual attempt to perfect the expression of the world or its image.

[17]See also, FT: 270.

[18]This can be thought of the philosopher himself when constrained by monadic concepts. It is specifically the philosopher who is rendered melancholic from his futile attempts to clearly express the universe.

use of the term, is to be understood as accord, attunement, or harmony. Leibniz describes his system in various places as operating under the principle of "*Zusammenstimmung*" and "*Übereinstimmung*". I argue here that the special type of accord and attunement that Leibniz offers, this "pre-established harmony", should be considered the outcome of the melancholic structure found in the monad.[19] This unique type of accord is based on the fact that no external relations whatsoever exist, not between the monad and the world, and not between the monad and other substances. This fundamental detachment reinforces Leibniz's need for the pre-established harmony within his theory. No means are available for monads to operate as a system other than submission to a principle of internal accord and attunement. Pre-established harmony can thus be conceived as *melancholic harmony*. This harmony is dual, established first by virtue of each expressive substance and that substance's own spontaneity, and second by virtue of the common element that introduces harmony between all "expressive spontaneities" (Deleuze 1993: 134).

Yet, what does it mean to be in harmony with another substance without being in communication with it? How are we to understand the workings of a metaphysical system entirely based on detachment and inclusion? Leibniz writes that although there is no external causal connection, monads are not completely unconnected; they are, in effect, united in non-causal concomitance, agreement and harmony (CA 23.3.1690: 360). In a letter to Wedderkopf, Leibniz asserts that no reason is necessary for pre-established harmony since it embodies the "essence" of the monad. He writes:

> What then is the reason for the divine intellect? The harmony of things. What is the reason for the harmony of things? Nothing. For example, no reason can be given for the ratio of 2 to 4 being the same as that of 4 to 8, not even in the divine will. This depends on the essence itself or the idea of things....[20]

When Leibniz defines the nature of expression in the monad, he uses terms such as proportion, ratio and abbreviation – all of which stress the fact that expression, as a relationship, is not based on either complete similarity or direct causality (WI: 207–208). Pre-established harmony is, therefore, an internal state, expressed and reflected in the interior of every monad.[21] On one level, an accord is found between each monad and the world it expresses; on another level, it is found between the various expressions of the monads and the accord existing among them (i.e., the fact that the very same universe is expressed from different viewpoints). The pre-established harmony is conditioned by the melancholic nature of the

---

[19] Although Leibniz attributes his pre-established harmony to the entire system of monads, he uses this concept mainly in his discussion of the body-soul problem. I nevertheless use it here in its broader context.

[20] "...it is impossible for... [God] not to be affected by the most perfect harmony, and thus to be necessitated to do the best by the very ideality of things" (MW, 5.1671: 146). The necessity of harmony is therefore so great that even God is subject to it. This is the basis for Leibniz's famous declaration: that the created world is the "best of possible worlds".

[21] There are no causal relations because every monad incorporates its entire history and future; as Russell explains, any external relation is therefore superfluous (Russell 1937: 134).

monads and expressed in their different individual perspectives. Leibniz's 'solution' to what I refer to as the monad's melancholic structure is, therefore, the part it plays in the configuration of the system's harmony.

Leibniz's special type of melancholy-based harmony is related to *Stimmung* as music on the one hand and mood on the other. As Wellbery points out, the German word *Stimmung* encompasses both these denotations, capturing both inner feeling and attunement or accord with the world. In *Stimmung*, all distinctions between the internal and the external, the subject and the world, collapse. Heidegger clarifies this beautifully in his *Fundamental Concepts of Metaphysics*:

> We speak of a 'laughing meadow' and do not mean that the meadow itself is laughing, we speak of a 'cheerful room', of a 'melancholy landscape'. The landscape is not itself melancholy [*schwermütig*], but merely attunes us in such a way, causes this attunement in us. (Heidegger 1985: 85).

The English word 'mood' also describes something that is not entirely objective (the landscape) nor entirely subjective (my own melancholic mood); however, it lacks the significant musical associations carried by *Stimmung*. The German *Stimmung* originates from the Latin *concentus* and the Greek *armonia*, both having strong musical connotations that the English "attunement" can only approximate, albeit with a technical accent.[22]

The different facets of *Stimmung* articulate the richness of Leibniz's melancholic harmony. The central role of melancholy is found in enforcing the complete closure from which the monad approaches the world, a condition that reveals something substantial about the way in which the monad configures its 'openness' to the world, precisely from within this radical closure. If philosophy is to be reckoned as monadic in nature, Leibniz's articulation of *Stimmung* provokes us to ask how, then, should philosophy itself constitute its openness to the world it seeks to express? In what way is an encounter from within closure so crucial to its operation?

I maintain that harmony is not to be understood merely as synonymous with perfection and order, or as unity in variety. Moreover, I claim that harmony should be considered more broadly, as going beyond the body-soul problem, the context in which it frequently appears in Leibniz. Rather, I will show that harmony's musical connotations are crucial to unfolding the problematization of the monad's special encounter with the world together with its philosophical implications. I therefore understand harmony as the state of being in accord with or attuned to the world, as setting oneself in a position of agreement with it. Bearing this in mind, I return to Leibniz who himself employs musical metaphors to describe his pre-established harmony.

> To employ a comparison, I will say in regard to this concomitance, which I hold to be true, that it is like several bands of musicians or choirs separately taking up their parts and placed in such a way that they neither see nor hear one another, though they nevertheless, agree perfectly in following their notes, each one his own, in such a way that he who hears the

[22] Wellbery (2003: 703) and Agamben (1991: 55). In this text, Agamben links *Stimmung* and *Stimme* and claims that *Stimme* is more primary than is *Stimmung* by pointing to the voice's structure as the most original and negative of metaphysical foundations (59).

whole finds in it a wonderful harmony much more surprising than if there were a connection between the two performers. It is quite possible also that a person who is close by one of two such choirs could judge from the one what the other was doing, and would form such a habit (particularly if we supposed that he was able to hear his own choir without seeing it and to see the other without hearing it), that his imagination would come to his aid and he would no longer think of the choir where he was, but of the other, and he would take his own for an echo of the other, attributing to his own only certain interludes, in which certain rules of symphony by which he understood the other did not appear, or else attributing to his own certain movements which he caused to be made from his side, according to certain plans that he thought were imitated by the other because of the inter-relationship which he found in the kind of melody, not knowing at all that those who were in the other choir were doing also something which corresponded according to their own plans (CA, 30.4.1687).[23]

And elsewhere:

It is therefore the[se] present perceptions, along with their regulated tendency to change in conformity to what is outside, which form the musical score which the soul reads. "But", says Mr. Bayle, "must not the soul recognize the sequence of the notes (distinctly), and so actually think of them?" I answer '**No**'; it suffices that the soul has included them in its confused thoughts in the same way that it has a thousand things in its memory without thinking of them distinctly. (RPH: 580)[24]

The two choirs demonstrate a structure of agreement devoid of any external relations or any communication between them. Yet, despite the lack of overt connection, a system does exist, constructed upon the principle of agreement and attunement. Each choir is in accord with the other, without each actually hearing or seeing the other. Each occupies a place in the overall harmony by simply singing its song; harmony is constructed out of this accord. Considered from this perspective, Leibniz's use of the word "echo" elsewhere in the text is compelling since it alludes to a state in which the monad hears only itself, its inner voice projecting and echoing back to itself.[25]

The congruence between the two choirs, writes Leibniz, should be understood as a set of musical notes read by the monad. It is not, as Bayle implies, an external rule to which the monad consciously conforms. Rather, congruence is "included" among the monad's internal and minute but indistinct perceptions and memories. This accord can only be intuitively felt, springing as it does from the depth of indistinct perceptions, in the same way that music is enjoyed precisely from the unconscious perception of its harmonic structures.[26] The monad is in tune with the world, as Leibniz writes elsewhere, "like two strings tuned to each other" (NS2: 459).

---

[23]Leibniz 1973: 188 (This citation is not included in the Loemker edition).

[24]Another interesting citation that employs the concept of the echo is: "Harmony is diversity compensated by identity; or the harmonious is the uniformly deformed. Praise is a kind of echo and duplication of harmony. If God had no rational creatures in the world, he would still have the same harmony, but alone and devoid of echo; he would still have the same beauty, but devoid of reflection and refraction and multiplication" (Leibniz, *Opera Omnia*, Academy ed., VI, i, 484, 438 [1671], cited in Loemker 1972: 177).

[25]Novalis defines *Stimmung* as "the acoustics of the soul" (cited in Agamben 1991: 56).

[26]See Loemker (1972: 182).

Music's connotations enrich our understanding of the special character of the accord the monad maintains with the world. Its pre-established harmony is a form of listening to the world, of being attuned to it, of perfecting and fine-tuning its expression of that world. There is also the unique structure of musical harmony, to which Leibniz has an affinity due to its close connection to mathematical proportion and the wider category of order. Music's richness and abundance, based on simple harmonic relations, also conforms to Leibniz's principle of perfection: the greatest possible variety together with the greatest possible order (MO: 648). Musical harmony, as a fundamental metaphor of pre-established harmony, is the productive and positive solution that Leibniz offers to the problematics of melancholy. Within the boundaries of musical harmony, detachment and self-absorption serve as foundations for the philosophical productivity articulated in expression. It is harmony that ensures that Leibniz will retain his famous optimism, which initially appears incongruous with the aforementioned melancholic relationship. It is through harmony that we can trace the affinity between melancholy and philosophy, and between mood and philosophy as promulgated by Leibniz.

IV. Conclusion

The monad can be thought of as the condensed embodiment of the philosophical encounter with the world, rooted in expression. Through its study, we can examine questions of mood in general and of melancholy in particular. The monad displays mood, or attunement, through which it approaches the world and takes it in; moreover, this attunement is the medium that determines the nature of this encounter. Furthermore, exploration of the monad is an exemplary setting for the presentation of the philosophical encounter with mood because it is neither a subject nor subjectively constructed. Being a purely metaphysical entity, the monad does not provoke the risk of a merely psychological understanding of *Stimmung*, and is revealed stripped of all possible psychological and subjective connotations.

Hence, the monad embodies the *non-subjective version of mood*, in this case – of melancholy. This non-subjective character explains why in Leibniz, the melancholic *Stimmung* encounters the totality of the world, free of any intentional encounter with a specific object. Within this context, melancholy thus radically raises questions regarding configuration of a non-causal and non-object-related accord with the world.

Heidegger's use of *Stimmung* is particularly appropriate for this interpretation because *Stimmung* (in *Being and Time*) is what enables the primary, most preliminary discovery of the world; through it the world is more fundamentally disclosed, beyond what any knowledge or perception can ensure. In overcoming the dichotomy between subject and object, Heidegger not only fully detaches *Stimmung* from its psychological significance, he also grasps it from without, in isolation of any intentional structure. If we follow the lines of this argument, the monad, as I have shown, also blurs or, perhaps as in Heidegger, surmounts the internal and the external.

The monad captures a radical interiority intimately bound up in and interlaced with complete exteriority – with the world itself.

The importance of the figure of the monad lies precisely in the structure that I have termed the "melancholic": An encounter with the world that originates from complete closure, detachment and self-absorption, a state in which the monad is attuned to the world (attunement understood here as internally constituted) while continuously expressing it. Melancholy, as presented here, is discovered to be of a status different from its usual conceptions: It is no longer a state of passivity and paralysis, deterred from any activity and inhibiting an engagement with the world. Quite the opposite: In the monad, melancholy proves to be the basis for a productive and positive state, a state in which the world is not concealed but disclosed. The monad's melancholic structure therefore radicalizes how we think of mood and offers a model of melancholy metaphysics.

References

Agamben, Giorgio. 1991. *Language and Death*. Minneapolis: University of Minnesota Press.

Deleuze, Gilles. 1993. *The Fold: Leibniz and the Baroque*. Minneapolis: University of Minnesota Press.

Dreyfus, Hubert L. 1991. *Being-in-the-World: A Commentary on Heidegger's Being and Time, Division I*. Cambridge: MIT Press.

Ferber, Ilit. 2011. *Melancholy and Philosophy: Walter Benjamin's Early Writings*. Manuscript in preparation.

Heidegger, Martin. 1962. *Being and Time*. Trans. John Macquarrie and Edward Robinson. New York: Harper & Row.

Heidegger, Martin. 1985. *The Fundamental Concepts of Metaphysics: World, Finitude, Solitude*. Bloomington: Indiana University Press.

Leibniz, G.W. 1896. *New Essay Concerning Human Understanding*. Trans. A.G. Langley. Montana: Kissinger Publishing.

Leibniz, G.W. 1969. *Philosophical Papers and Letters*. Trans. and ed. Leroy E. Loemker. Dordrecht: Kluwer Academic Publishers.

Leibniz, G.W. 1973. *Discourse on Metaphysics, Correspondence with Arnauld, Monadology*. Trans. George R. Montgomery. Chicago: The Open Court Publishing Company.

Loemker, Leroy E. 1972. *Struggle for Synthesis*. Cambridge: Harvard University Press.

Radden, Jennifer. 2000. *The Nature of Melancholy*. Oxford: Oxford University Press.

Russell, Bertrand. 1937. *A Critical Exposition to the Philosophy of Leibniz*. London: G. Alen and Unwin.

Wellbery, David E. 2003. "Stimmung." In *Ästhetische Grundbegriffe: Historische Wörterbuch in Sieben Bänden*. Band 5, ed. Karlheinz Barck. Stuttgart/Weimar: J.B. Metzler.

"Perhaps Truth Is a Woman": On Shame and Philosophy

Daniel Strassberg

Since I earn my living as a psychoanalyst, it should come as no surprise that my reflections have their starting-point in clinical situations in which people have specific difficulties dealing with shame.

Let's say a person suffering from guilt feelings seeks psychoanalytical treatment. The patient complains about guilt feelings or a symptom which can easily be discerned as an equivalent of guilt feelings, but usually the person herself does not know the reason for her suffering, she does not know what offence she is guilty of, but he nonetheless suffers tremendously from a burden of unknown origin. If everything goes well, in the course of analysis the unconscious reason for her agonizing guilt feelings is revealed, historically it usually turned out to be her incestuous desire. But this case has become rare, this is the case for which Freud specifically developed psychoanalysis, the theory of the Oedipus complex.

However, today many more patients suffer from the unbearable feelings of shame (rather than those of guilt). If we have a close look at most anxiety disorders, social phobias, narcissistic neuroses and depressions, we may find that in the core of those disturbances lies an insupportable feeling of shame. Here, the course of treatment proceeds exactly the other way round: At the beginning, the patient seems to be convinced that she knows what she is ashamed of: a nose that is crooked, of going bald, wrinkles in her face, or having said something stupid in public. Step by step, analysis destroys these presumed certainties, the patient begins to understand that it cannot be one of those problems that she is ashamed of, and she – and the analyst as well – are left with the uncomfortable insight that she is ashamed of nothing. But the insight that there is nothing to be ashamed about does not render her shame more tolerable. On the contrary, it seems to aggravate it. The following reflections are an attempt to approach this "nothing" we are ashamed of.

D. Strassberg (✉)
Weinberg Street 145, CH-8006, Zürich, Switzerland
e-mail: dastrass@swissonline.ch

H. Kenaan and I. Ferber (eds.), *Philosophy's Moods: The Affective Grounds of Thinking*, Contributions To Phenomenology 63, DOI 10.1007/978-94-007-1503-5_6,

Psychoanalysis conceives of this 'nothing' as something missing which should be there. The term 'castration', which it coined for this absence, implies that shame is referring to a primordial experience of corporeal insufficiency which is a result of a penalty for our incestuous desires. Thus the concept of castration links the realm of guilt to the realm of shame and turns shame into a kind of guilt; because, as Jacques Goldberg puts it, guilt is the main axiom of psychoanalysis to which all other emotions can be traced (Goldberg 1985).

In *Being and Time* Martin Heidegger attempts to approach the 'nothing' in a different manner, not as an absence or a deficiency, but as a lack of meaning, which manifests itself as anxiety. One has to be precise: anxiety is not *caused* by one's insignificance, but *is* in itself an absence of meaning. There is not primarily a cognition of meaninglessness which leads to anxiety, but real (*eigentliche*) anxiety is the manifestation of insignificance itself.

> The obstinacy of the 'nothing and nowhere within-the-world' means a phenomenon that the world as such is that in the face of which one has anxiety. The utter insignificance which makes itself known in the 'nothing and nowhere, does not signify that the world is absent, but tells us that entities within-the-world, the world in its worldhood is all that still obtrudes itself. [...] But this 'nothing ready-to-hand' (Zuhandenheit), which only our everyday circumspective discourse understands, is not totally nothing. The 'nothing' of readiness-to-hand is grounded in the most primordial 'something' – in the *world*. Ontologically, however, the world belongs essentially to Dasein's Being as Being-in-the-world. So if the 'nothing' – that is, the world as such – exhibits itself as that in the face of which one has anxiety, this means that *Being-in-the-world itself is that in the face of anxiety is anxious*. (Heidegger 1962: 231–232)

When one speaks in everyday language of anxiety as having no object or no reason ("I am afraid of nothing") she doesn't mean to say that there are no objects in the world, but only that those objects have lost any significance for us. In anxiety things are simply what they are, they have no meaning for us anymore, they are not 'ready-to-hand', they have in a sense become hostile to us, because they serve no purpose. In other words the world has lost its symbolic coherence and its order; it has become simply an accumulation of things.

This explains why, in Heidegger's view, anxiety is the privileged gateway to truth. In fact things are simply what they are, they have no meaning. Significance is merely a human attempt to give things an order and make the world coherent in order to tranquilize human beings. In other words, the symbolic order is nothing but a conventional veil to prevent human beings from getting lost. In anxiety, however, this veil is torn apart and we see thing as they are – meaningless.

It is in the face of the inescapable possibility of death that we become aware of the fact that our existence has no transcendental meaning. Confronted with death, we have no option other than taking responsibility for our existence. "Death is a possibility-of-Being which Dasein itself has to take over in every case. With death, Dasein stands before itself in his ownmost potentiality-for-Being" (Heidegger 1962: 294). Heidegger calls the possibility of death non-relational ("unbezüglich"), because death is a mere fact without meaning. Therefore our existence is a mere fact into which we are thrown. Anxiety is the emotion which confronts us with this.

> [I]f Dasein exists, it is already been thrown into this possibility. Dasein does not, proximally, and for the most part, have any explicit or even theoretical knowledge of the fact that it has been delivered over to this. Death reveals itself to the Dasein in a more primordial and impressive manner in that state-of-mind which we have called 'anxiety'. (Heidegger 1962: 295)

Heidegger is mainly interested in our relation to the world, in our 'Being-in-the-world' (*in-der-Welt-Sein*). Within this relation anxiety plays a key role as a gateway to truth. But when it comes to the relation to oneself it is not anxiety, but shame which shows us truth. While in anxiety we see the world at it is, namely essentially meaningless, in shame we see ourselves as we are: we perceive ourselves as nothing.

In 1951, the philologist Eric R. Dodds identified Greek culture as a culture of shame, opposing it to our own culture of guilt (Dodds 1951). Despite the fact that contemporary anthropology disregards this distinction, Dodds was certainly right to identify shame – and its counterparts, glory and honour -, as the decisive moral sentiments of early Greek culture, the sentiments which regulated most social interactions.

Aidōs – which is one of the Greek terms for shame, – can be understood as the desire of the Greek knights to be acknowledged by their fellow knights. It played a prominent role in three areas of Greek culture. In times of war, it guaranteed the bravery of the knights, because displaying cowardice in face of the enemy meant losing one's honor, which was much worse than losing one's life. In a religious context *aidōs* meant reverence regarding the holy, – which included gods, as well as parents and nobility -, and, in sexuality, *aidōs* meant feeling bashful about exposing one's body to the other sex.

On the one hand *aidōs* is a system of moral values, on the other hand, it is a specific emotion which occurs when a member of the community violates one of its rules. But other than in guilt, *aidōs* is not about what one is forbidden or allowed to do, but about what has to be concealed and what can be shown. But what is it exactly that must be concealed so desperately? What links these three areas – bravery, holiness and sexuality – which seem to be so far apart one from each other at first glance?

What has to be hidden is nature itself: At war, *aidōs* hides the natural feeling of fear, in sexuality it hides the naked body – in the form that nature created – and in religion it hides the finiteness of human existence in the face of transcendence. So shame seems to sever nature – natural feelings, natural bodies and natural finiteness – from human experience; or, in other words, shame suppresses natural motivation in human action. Naturally – we would feel terrified in a battle and run away, naturally – we would behave like sexual maniacs, and, naturally – we would act as if the gods didn't matter. Only because of shame are we capable to counteract those natural inclinations.

So, *aidōs* – as a system of social values – draws a line between nature and culture, between natural and civilized behaviour. But at the same time, shame – as an actual feeling arising when breaking the rules of *aidōs* – breaches this line, because in the actual feeling of shame we become aware of our natural, uncivilized inclinations, we become aware that we still haven't – and probably never will – overcome our own nature. In other words, in shame we perceive ourselves just *as we are*, we realize, who we are, similarly in anxiety we see things just as they are. Therefore, shame simultaneously conceals and also discloses man's origin in nature.

The thing which grants shame the power to separate natural from civilized behavior, is nature itself. Shame can only be expected to have the force necessary to keep natural drives and dispositions of human beings at bay, *because shame in itself is based in nature.* For early Greek culture, it was beyond any doubt that *aidōs* was more than just a mere conventional agreement among human beings, it was also deeply anchored in human nature. Therefore, shame became a hinge between culture and nature, it is the natural force that turns against nature in order to stop its disruptive forces. Man can only overcome his nature on account of a natural disposition called shame. Only in this way do we come to understand the obscure saying of the Ephesian Heraclitus: *physis kryptestai phileī:* nature likes to conceal itself (Heraclitus 1987: 123). Nature conceals itself by producing culture; that is by producing its own veil. Through shame, nature orchestrates its own veiling. Thereby, civilization is construed as a "fold" in nature, using natural forces to tame nature: Shame is nature-against-nature.

In the classical period of Greek philosophy this very intimate interweaving of nature and culture was disrupted, and nature and culture entered a dialectical relationship.

Nature is no longer the visible appearance of Gods creation, but its eternal and unchangeable substance; it now gradually became identified with essence, and therefore with truth and culture with appearance, and therefore with lie. For Plato culture is based on conventions only and therefore considered as the realm of *doxa,* of mere opinion. Culture is as far away from truth as it could possibly be.

In the second book of the Physics, Aristotle explains this juxtaposition of nature and truth. Nature is the being, which has its principles of modification in itself. He provides us with an intriguing example. If you were to bury a wooden bed, a bed would not grow from the soil but, instead, a tree (Aristotle 1964: 193a13). The principle of modification lies in the wood itself. Aristotle writes: while the bed has its principle of modification in human handicraft, in *technè*, so nature is the being which is neither disfigured nor veiled by any human intervention, it is the Being as it is: it always becomes what it is. Nature is true, because it remains unmodified by human action; nature is true because it is not under human control. Although *technè* uses nature and at times even improves nature, it also disfigures it. Heidegger has taken up the Aristotelian idea of truth as nature unveiled in his etymological definition of truth as *aletheia*, and so equates culture, the 'Man', with untruthfulness (Heidegger 2002: 6).

This juxtaposition of nature and truth in classical Greece altered the attitude towards shame profoundly. Since the noblest task of philosophers is to unveil truth, shame was no longer seen as a positive power bringing forth socially desirable behaviour, instead, it became a major obstacle on the path to truth.

Since nature is veiled by shame, it can only be unveiled by shamelessness. Usually, wonder is considered to be the incentive for engaging in philosophy, as exemplified in the primordial myth of philosophy, the story of Thales and the Thracian maid. In the Theaetetus-dialogue Plato tells us about Thales who, looking at the sky full of wonder, falls into a well and is therefore laughed at by the Thracian maid. But this is as much a story about shame as one about wonder. Thales made a fool of himself, but being a true philosopher, he had to be *ready* to make a fool of himself, because true philosophy is ridiculous ("Theaetetus," Plato 1961: 174a–b). Where truth is at stake, one couldn't care less about appearance or good behaviour. In fact, the Platonic dialogues demonstrate again and again that the *capacity* to be ridiculed and to bear shame is a prerogative for the search for truth.

In his defence before the court, Socrates accuses his prosecutors of being brazen, i.e. shameless, because they "have said little or nothing that is true" ("Apology," Plato 1961: 17b). Although they spoke "in flowery language, decked out with fine words and phrases" they only managed to string together a continuous series of lies. However, Socrates, despite being a poor orator himself, speaks the whole truth and nothing but the truth. The judges themselves do not feel ashamed, because they have a good command of the rhetorical codex. But they don't actually care about what they say as long as they say it in an appropriate manner. The court asks Socrates, "Do you feel no compunction (i.e. shame, DS) at having followed the line of action which puts you in danger of the death penalty?" ("Apology," Plato 1961: 28b). Socrates replies firmly: "Where a man has once taken up his stand, either because it seems best to him or in obedience to his orders, there I believe he is bound to remain and face the danger, taking no account of death or anything else before dishonour" ("Apology," Plato 1961: 28d).

Socrates and his judges have entirely different concepts of shame and dishonour. While the honourable gentlemen of Athens think of shame as a mark of disruption with society, for Socrates the betrayal of his own inner voice would be the utmost dishonour. To fulfil the orders of his inner voice he has to be ready to break with society, up to the point where he can be expelled from society by being banned from the city or even by suffering the death penalty.

It is by no means insignificant that Socrates sees himself as a bad speaker. It seems clear to him that sticking to conventional rules – for example to the rules for a good speech as they are laid down in the art of rhetoric – would prevent him from speaking the truth. Transgressing culture is a condition *sine qua non* to listen to one's inner voice: "Gentlemen, I am your very grateful and devoted servant, but I owe a greater obedience to God than to you, and so long as I draw breath and have my faculties, I shall never stop practicing philosophy and exhorting you and elucidating the truth for everyone that I meet" ("Apology," Plato 1961: 29d).

In his search for truth, Socrates calls himself a ridiculous figure time and again, and he is also not afraid of mocking his pupils with the aim of bringing them closer to truth. We might surmise that, because of his ugliness, Socrates had become accustomed to ridicule and shame from childhood onward, and that fact might have facilitated his path to philosophy. To love wisdom and thus to be a philosopher means to be capable of bearing shame; it means to disregard opinion and acknowledgment. Thus, ridicule was considered to be a crucial threshold that had to be crossed on the way to truth. Crossing this threshold meant leaving the pretence of mere conventionality, of mere *doxa* behind. To a certain degree, bearing shame marks the transition from the world of appearance to the world of being, because it unmasks social conventions as being mere opinion. Leaving the city was not an option for Socrates, because the true philosopher – i.e. the philosopher committed to truth – has to transgress the public order *within* society itself in order to propagate truth and spread it among the people.

However, in Platonic philosophy shame is also the philosopher's crucial emotion and an indispensable faculty in his search for truth. This intimate connection which links shame with truth is not idiosyncratic at all, but arises from Plato's concept of truth itself. Socrates' defence exposes a peculiar contradiction. On the one hand he claims to be the only one speaking the truth; on the other hand he confesses to not knowing anything at all. The only difference between him and a citizen of the Polis is that he is aware of the fact that he is ignorant, while the citizen believes that he knows something: "Well, I am certainly wiser than this man. It is only likely that neither of us has any knowledge to boast of, but he thinks that he knows something which he does not know, whereas I am quite conscious of my ignorance. At any rate it seems that I am wiser than he is to this small extent, that I do not think that I know what I do not know" ("Apology," Plato 1961: 21d).

How can he pronounce truth and teach it to his fellow citizens, when he himself is ignorant of it? Obviously it is the very truth of his ignorance which he seeks to proclaim. This is certainly a pretension for didactical reasons. Pretending not to know anything allows for the maieutic principle of extracting the truth hidden in everyone of us. But it is more than that. Ignorance also designates the essence of truth, which brings us back to Heidegger's notion of nothing.

In Plato's doctrine, truth appears on three different levels. On the first level, the level of opinion (*doxa*), truth is conventional and is thus a mere *simulacrum* of truth. It is the way in which culture allows for dealing with mere appearance. On the second level truth is relational and reigned by logic. The *logon didonai* provides an insight into differences, and also into identities, and therefore establishes a relational and meaningful reality in which things are presented in their proper order. Since understanding means recognizing the relations of things, it is only on this level where we can actually speak of knowledge.

But this level is also only an image of truth, because it depends on an insight into the essence of things, the ideas. You can only establish meaning (i.e. the relation of things) when you are aware of the things themselves; this is the core of Socrates' teaching. The ideas are the initial premises of the *logos* and, as such can not be deduced by logical means. One can not know or understand ideas, although one needs them to establish knowledge and understanding. In other words, meaning is based on meaningless entities.

So, when Socrates declares his ignorance time and again, he doesn't do it for didactical purposes only, but also to indicate that the awareness of ideas is *sensu stricto* not knowledge because it is not relational. Thus, if the ultimate truth is non-relational *(unbezüglich)* it is, in a Heideggerian sense, *nothing* – or, as Plato puts it, worthless.

In Plato's *Parmenides*, where the problem of nothing is extensively discussed, the young Socrates is confronted with the scandal of the ideas:

> And also in cases like these, asked Parmenides, is there, for example, a Form of rightness or of beauty or of goodness, and such things?
>
> Yes.
>
> And again, a Form of man, apart from ourselves and all other men like us — a Form of man as something by itself? Or a Form of fire or of water?
>
> I have often been puzzled about those things, Parmenides, whether one should say that the same thing is true in their cases or not
>
> Are you also puzzled, Socrates, about cases that might be thought absurd, such as hair or mud or dirt or any other trivial and undignified objects? Are you doubtful whether or not to assert that each of these has a separate form distinct from things like those we handle?
>
> Not at all, said Socrates. In these cases, the things are just the things we see; it would surely be too absurd to suppose that they have a Form. All the same, I have sometimes been troubled by a doubt whether what is true in one case may not be true in all. Then, when I have reached that point, I am driven to retreat, for fear of tumbling into a bottomless pit of nonsense. Anyhow, I get back to the things which we were just now speaking of as having Forms, and occupy my time with thinking about them ("Parmenides," Plato 1961: 130b–d).

Supposing for the time being that *Form* is used synonymously with *Idea*, there can be no doubt that rightness, goodness and beauty have ideas. At the same time, it seems perfectly clear that things like hair, mud and dirt *cannot* have ideas. For this conviction Socrates gives a rather peculiar reason: Things that are too trivial and undignified to have ideas, are just what they are. But is that not precisely the definition of a Platonic idea, depicting things as what they are and not in relation to other things? Socrates gives it a second thought and he is troubled: How can something be true in one case and false in another one?

Consequently undignified things as mud, dirt and hair *must* have their ideas as well.

This decay confronts Socrates with the very essence of ideas, namely that they are what they are, meaningless nonsense. Is it not the very reason that one can only *view* ideas and not *deduce* them logically that an idea of something is just what this thing is? Socrates is too young to cope with this insight. Shivering, he turns away from this impasse and he flies back to the higher sphere of goodness and beauty, where he feels much more comfortable. What befalls Socrates precisely meets the definition of anxiety which Heidegger has given us: Anxiety is the mood which *Dasein* experience when confronted with the things of the word as they are, stripped of all meaning, i.e. void of all relations. In other words: The impasse which Socrates encounters is that the essence of being is the nothing: nothing understood as the breaking down of order.

When Socrates grows older he no longer turns away from this insight, but starts to reflect on the conditions in which human beings can gain access to the realm of ideas, i.e. the realm of things as they are. Technically, the gateway to ideas is to view them directly and not to deduce them logically. But to be able to view ideas one has to bring herself in a state corresponding to ideas: When to view the idea of something means to see that something as what it is, and not view it in relation to other things, so the corresponding mood of the subject must be also what it is, stripped of all relations, and this mood is shame. Just as anxiety is the mood in which we perceive the outside world as it is, meaningless and non-relational; in shame we are just what we are, excluded from the social and symbolic order. In other words, in shame we become an exemption from the social order and, so, relative to the social order, we become nothing.

Recently, a patient told me about a course which she had attended to improve her skills in a hobby that she has pursued for many years. "I felt terribly ashamed, not because I was not as good as the others, but because I was just myself and nothing other than myself, I literally felt that I was nothing. I felt naked and I would rather have died."

It is not a stain, which leaves us alone with shame, but the mere fact of being who we are … and nothing else. For Plato this is the only gateway to truth.

So it seems that human beings can only conceive truth after dropping out of the social order. Although in Platonic philosophy being exposed to shame and overcoming it is one essential step on the way out of the cave, it is by no means the final one; it is a necessary but not sufficient condition for truth. But the Cynics, who considered themselves the only true heirs of Socrates, inflated this Platonic feature out of proportion by considering shamelessness the one and only prerogative of truth, proceeding from the idea that truth can only be perceived by unmasking and destroying all social conventions and thereby giving way to an undisguised view of pure nature. We don't actually know of any writings by the Cynics, but some famous anecdotes about their most prominent representative, Diogenes of Sinope have been passed on: Diogenes, who told Alexander to get out of the sun, Diogenes who masturbated, fornicated, and urinated in public; Diogenes, who went to market in broad daylight with a lantern, because he was seeking the truth, Diogenes who lay in the dirt face-down because very soon everything would turn upside-down. Here, shamelessness became the one and only philosophical principle.

The Cynics equated nature with the world of ideas, conceiving of it as the realm beyond the symbolic order of culture, beyond the veil of conventions. Therefore it suffices to transgress social rules, and return to the state of nature in order to view ideas and gain truth. So, for the Cynics, shame and shamelessness are no longer preconditions for viewing truth, but merely philosophical gestures.

But the Cynics – and their followers throughout the centuries – are all blind to the fact that this concept of nature is also nothing but a symbolic concept itself; it is the cultural code for the realm which is not codified. In this way the cynical approach still depends on the very conventions it is eager to destroy. Diogenes of Sinope was in no way the hermit he is often described to have been. Rather he was a kind of performing philosopher, who made his living by frightening his civilized fellow citizens, and expressed his scorn of civilization by making the public scorn him. His public performances were by no means pure uncontrolled natural behaviour; on the contrary, they were calculated political actions. In other words: exposing one's nature is not at all natural, but an enactment of the most advanced cultural attitude of the time: the attitude that critique. Shame could be conceived of as critical emotion.

The great renaissance of *cynisme* occurred in the eighteenth century. It is not by coincidence that in the age of enlightenment shame, and not guilt, is considered to be the main moral sentiment, since nature has by this time become the vantage point of ontology. While guilt refers to a cultural code of what is considered right or wrong, shame refers to what is considered natural or unnatural, equating natural to good, true and free, and culture to repression and prejudice.

In eighteenth century France, *cynisme* meant sexual freedom as well as relentlessly candid language. And the pornographic novels of that time explicitly pursued the program of cynicism in order to attain truth by overcoming shame. Justine and Juliet of the Divine Marquis begins as follows:

> Doubtless it is cruel to have to describe, on the one hand, a host of ills overwhelming a sweet-tempered and sensitive woman who, as best she is able, respects virtue, and, on the other, the affluence of prosperity of those who crush and mortify this same woman. But the writer, enough of a philosopher to explore truth, overcomes such inconvenience; and, forced to be cruel, with his one hand he pulls down the superstitious squiggles with which unreason embellishes virtue without mercy, while with his other hand he shamelessly discloses to the deceived and naive man the very vices amidst lust and joy by which he is haunted and overwhelmed continually (de Sade, DAF. 1965: 458. Translation modified by the author).

The philosopher who is entitled to explore truth has to overcome his own feelings of shame as much as those of his readers.

Without any doubt, Jean-Jacques Rousseau is the most important cynic of his time. He does not only want to destroy social conventions and prejudices by speaking openheartedly, that is, by speaking without shame, he aims higher. His "confessions" pursue the idea that it is possible to uncover man's nature, his very truth, by being relentlessly candid and overcoming one's own shame. He writes: "I wish to show my fellows a man in all the truth of nature; and this man will be myself. Myself alone. I feel my heart and I know men" (Rousseau 1998: 5).

Here it is sufficient to hear the voice of one's own heart to be able to know every man's truth, and this can only be achieved by ignoring all conventions and not bothering about people's opinion. Therefore, his *Confessions* are much more than the autobiography of some person or other; they are an experiment with one's self which aims to epitomize as well as to bring forth the exemplary natural human being by transgressing all boundaries of shame.

His project of relentless *unmasking of the self* implies that one must use shame itself as a point of departure to be able to overcome it, for only the feeling of shame indicates to him where to pass beyond conventions. So, for Rousseau shame is more than a just mood he adopts willy-nilly in his search for truth. He has to go further and to seek shame actively, as it is both a mark for him and a sign to others which makes the boundaries between the realm of nature and the realm of the social order visible. In other words, seeking shame is a philosophical gesture which makes truth perceivable.

The famous episode with his beloved Marion, which is reported at the end of the second book of his confessions, shows the crucial importance of shame for his endeavour. After the death of his employer, Mme de Vercellis, Rousseau stole a little pink and silver coloured ribbon to give to Marion, whom he had loved secretly for quite a long time. After being caught with the ribbon, he accused Marion of having given the ribbon to him. (Rousseau 1998: 70–73)

Rousseau himself considers this episode with Marion as the most pivotal moment of his life. It was his main incentive for writing the *Confessions* and even in his last book, the *Reveries of a Solitary Promenader* he returns to it. (Rousseau 2000: 28). The interesting point of this little story is that Rousseau failed because of shame. He didn't deny his petty theft because he feared punishment, but because he feared disclosing his desire for Marion. His utmost failure was not the betrayal of Marion, but the betrayal of his inner voice. The voice in his heart told him clearly and unmistakably that it was wrong to blame Marion, but he felt unable to follow the order of nature because he feared being rejected by her and appearing ridiculous in the eyes of others.

As a consequence, and contrary to his contemporaries, Rousseau considers guilt as a natural moral sentiment because it is the Voice of Nature which directly conveys to the heart what is right and what is wrong: "[M]y heart replied better than my reason." (Rousseau 2000: 21)

Shame, on the other hand, is not only conventional, but it is the very basis of all conventions. As Rousseau states in the Second Discourse, culture grows out of shame. Once human kind had managed to satisfy their basic needs, they began to leer at their neighbours possessions. They envied others' achievements and began to compare them to their own. In conceding their own shortcomings, they then attempted to keep up with their fellows or even to surpass them. Moreover, they tried to hide their failures from the public and began to pretend to be more than they actually were. All cultural achievements of human kind are the result of a competition and a fear of loss of reputation, for better, or for worse. (Rousseau 2004)

Looked at this way, culture arises from comparison, and comparison is responsible for the human inclination to hide one's own truth and hence for our degeneration. It is a tragedy for human kind that over the years hiding became second nature, and people lost track of their own nature. To regain truth – or, as Rousseau puts it: to return to nature – one has to reverse this process. Writing his *Confessions* is nothing less than the endeavour of reverting to nature; i.e. removing the cultural cult of comparison.

In writing his memoirs, he puts himself on stage as an absolute exception, beyond any comparison: "I am forming an undertaking which has no precedent, and the execution of which will have no imitator whatsoever." (Rousseau 1998: 5) In human society he is an exception in the sense that he is speaking out candidly and making himself transparent to both himself and to others. He doesn't care anymore, certainly not about what the public think of him, and thereby he renounces all boundaries of social conventions. In other words, he no longer compares himself with others. To advance his project he has to seek the instance of his own utmost shame, because this would be the turning point, that which singled him out from humanity – and this instance was the episode with Marion.

This episode is at the same time the moment of his deepest fall, and, by confessing it, of his highest exaltation, because it testifies that he succeeded in reversing the cultural process.

But as much as Rousseau longs to be an exception from humanity, he also aims to be an example for all human beings; he wants his fellow citizens to emulate him, and, therefore, to compare themselves with him. A double impasse: To ascertain the status of an exception – as the only one who doesn't compare – he has to compare himself with others – and to emulate him, others have to compare themselves with him.

Hence, both for propagating his struggle against culture and for establishing himself as an absolute exception from culture, Rousseau depends desperately on culture. His dilemma manifests itself in his ambivalence towards writing: He can only struggle against writing … by writing. When he states in his *Confessions* that starting to write was the beginning of his life-long suffering, he is referring to the fact that his contempt for culture can only be expressed within the boundaries of this very same culture, that it is impossible to transgress the boundaries of culture and to reach the realm of nature he is so desperately longing for. (Rousseau 1998: 295) Nature is, in other words, nothing other than the exception from culture.

As a part of this tragedy, – which is the tragedy of all Cynics he depends upon an observant and acknowledging public for this experiment of not belonging to human kind to work; and this dependency will ultimately develop into full-blown paranoia towards the end of his life. In the Dialogues, the main testimony of this illness, Rousseau describes his existence as an absolute exception, singled out from the 'conspiracy' by his honesty and candidness. (Rousseau 1989) Thus his paranoia can be understood as a sublation (*Aufhebung*) of his shame; both its climax and its abolishment. On one hand he carries the situation of absolute exception to its extremes; on the other hand he doesn't feel shame anymore, because he doesn't ascribe his excommunication to himself anymore but, instead, to the bad faith of society.

To recapitulate Rousseau's attitude towards shame, it is first of all a sign posted on the path from culture to nature; it indicates where to burst the bonds of cultural conventions. Secondly, shame is also a proof of the fact that this journey is ultimately impossible, because if it were possible, and he was only a natural man without any alliance to culture, shame would be both unnecessary and impossible.

So, shame marks the border between the codified and the non-codified, between symbolic order and natural. However, this border is at the same time both transgressed *and* sustained by shame. Shame establishes the boundaries of cultures by producing a fictional realm beyond culture, called nature, understood as an exception from culture. But, at the same time, shame veils the fact that this realm beyond culture is literally – nothing, for it exists only as a cultural fiction,

This feature corresponds with clinical experience: When we are attacked by shame, we feel that we are being expelled from society. All links with our fellows are cut down, we lose our solid grounding, and we perceive ourselves as an absolute exception. But exceptions are extremely visible. As much as we wish to vanish from the surface of the earth, we cannot turn away from the glances of others; we are standing naked before their eyes, in the midst of society, but nevertheless without any connection to it. It is this loss of connections, which makes us feel – nothing.

It is with this grand failure of the cynical venture to find truth by overcoming shame, where Nietzsche begins. I should like to quote the pivotal passage of the preface to the *Gay science* in full:

> 'Is it true that God is everywhere?' a little girl asked her mother; 'I find that indecent" — a hint for philosophers! One should have more respect for the *bashfulness* with which nature has hidden and iridescent uncertainties. Perhaps truth is a woman who has grounds for not showing her grounds? Perhaps her name is - to speak Greek - *Baubo*? ... Oh, those Greeks! They knew how to *live*. What is needed for that is to stop bravely at the surface, the fold, the skin, to worship appearance, to believe in shapes, tones, words, in the whole Olympus of appearance! Those Greeks were superficial - *out of profundity*! And is not this precisely what we are coming back to, we daredevils of the spirit who have climbed the highest and most dangerous peak of current thought and looked around from up there looked *down* from up there? Are we not just in this respect - Greeks? Worshippers of shapes, tones, words? And therefore — artists? (Nietzsche 2001a: 8–9)

Here again Nietzsche proves to be the "re-valuer of all values". While the ancients might have wanted to bear and to overcome shame in order to attain truth, to abandon appearances in order to grasp being as it is, Nietzsche honours shame in order to worship appearance. To understand that this revaluation of shame is more than a simple provocation, it might be worthwhile to take a better look at the myth of Baubo.

In Greek mythology, Baubo is the personalized vulva. She belongs to the orphic rites and therefore to the cult of Dionysus. While Demeter is wandering around in search of her daughter, who was stolen by Hades, she encounters Baubo. Baubo pays homage to her by offering her a drink, which Demeter refuses because she is in mourning for her daughter. In order to persuade Demeter to accept her hospitability, Baubo lifts her skirt and lets her look at her crotch. At that, Demeter becomes cheerful, she starts to laugh and finally accepts the drink. The historical sources diverge concerning the question of what Demeter actually saw. According to Clemens of Alexandria she saw Iacchos – another name for Dionysus – who waved at her laughingly; according to Arnobius, 200 years later, she saw Baubo's shaved sex. (Gsell 2001)

What is important in this historical tradition is the fact that the female sex induces merriness. Well schooled in Freud's fear of castration we should have expected fear and terror in the face of the missing phallus, and, as a matter of fact, the figure of the terrifying female sex also exists in Greek mythology, but her name is Gorgo. However in this instance the contrary happens: Demeter is cheered up and the question should be asked, what exactly induces her merriness?

What Baubo offers the mourning Demeter, doesn't seem to be some kind of deficiency but, instead, the origin of life, life as it is in itself. By showing her sex she brings Demeter back to life. But if Baubo is the sign of life, we must ask ourselves, why does Nietzsche advocate the hiding of life? Wasn't the main incentive of his philosophy his desire to affirm life without any reservation?

The problem is that the Dionysiac principle – that is, honouring life as it is – never exposes itself unveiled. Nietzsche is anything but a mystic advocate of the immediate who believes that there is an immediate access to real life. Rather, the Dionysiac is always exposed in its Apolline representation. Life expresses itself only as tamed by *appearance, by shapes, tones, words*, that is: by art. So, in his

Birth of Tragedy, Nietzsche states that the Appoline is the truth of the Dionysiac. Albeit the "Apolline consciousness alone, like a veil, hid that Dionysiac world (Nietzsche 2001b: 21)", "[o!]nly trough him [i.e. Apollo] does the perpetually attained goal of primal Oneness [i.e. the Dionysiac] ... reach consummation." (Nietzsche 2001b: 26) Life needs a mask, a simulacrum to be able to express itself.

"Everything profound loves the mask." (Nietzsche 1973: 69). The true philosopher loves masks and adores appearances, because they allow for interpretation. Life – Nietzsche's term for Nature – is not a hidden space beyond the surface of appearance, but the force of appearance itself; it is the Will to Power. In other words: Life is nothing but the Will to Power itself; it is the force of interpretation. Truth is only a perspective, but a perspective powerful enough to subdue other perspectives. Therefore knowledge is not a process of unveiling the hidden, as it is in traditional philosophy, but a means by which to give a conquering interpretation.

But what is the criterion to decide whether one particular interpretation is more powerful than any other one; so that it wins over other interpretations? Certainly it is not the number of those who adhere to a certain interpretation. Nietzsche is not advocating a democratic poll for truth; on the contrary, the 'best' interpretations are only for the few. The winning interpretation is the healthiest one, i.e. it is the interpretation, which allows for the most possibilities of life; or, indeed, possibly the other way round: it is that interpretation which chokes even the smallest expressions of life in others. But as life expresses itself only in interpretation, life also depends on a continuing series of interpretations. No single interpretation should win once and for all, because if interpretation comes to an end by finding the final truth, by discovering the things as they are, life itself comes to an end as well, and so does truth. Finding truth is smothering truth. At this point shame comes into play: shame both modulates the process of interpretation as a kind of 'hermeneutic brake' and hints as to where it should move toward. In *Daybrake 527*, Nietzsche speaks of "the shame of moderation" (Nietzsche 1982: 529; translation modified by the author) Here, shame both a gesture of hiding *and* a sign for the hidden, is a necessary condition of knowledge. This is why shame is not only a philosopher's emotion or an attitude, but is also ascribed to nature itself as its regulatory principle. Nature is hiding shamefully in order to reveal herself: "In the effort to conceal herself Nature reveals the essence of her contradictions." (Nietzsche 1990: 279, IV.7). Nature is hiding herself to provoke interpretation, and by this she reveals her very essence as Will of Power.

How should we interpret all these philosophers, beginning with Socrates, who pretend to have found the ultimate truth? "A terrible moral dishonesty (or shamelessness) [*Eine ungeheure moralische Verlogenheit (oder Schamlosigkeit)*]"[1] (Nietzsche 1988a: 249). They are shameless and dishonest, because they deny their own interpretations the status of interpretations; they claim to have actually viewed the essence of things as they are. Socrates' deep hostility towards art is the same as his contempt for shame: it is due to the fact that he doesn't honour masks, surfaces

[1] The quotations of the *Nachlass* are translated by the author.

and appearances; that he is still searching for the truth beyond images. Socrates debases surfaces in favour of the depth of the *unum, bonum et verum*. In doing so he devalues life as it appears before our eyes in favour of the supposed hidden values beyond life. The Platonic gesture of overcoming shame nurtures the priest's phantasm that truth can only be found beyond life. Thereby he brings the process of interpretation to an end: the most forceful and at the same time the meanest interpretation of all. Christianity, for example, has become so powerful and so shamelessly destructive by pretending to have solved every problem: "The shameless levity, with which is spoken here (i.e. in Christianity, DS) of the most inaccessible problems, as if those were no problems at all: life, world, God, meaning of life. [*Die unverschämte Leichtfertigkeit, mit der hier von den unzugänglichsten Problemen geredet wird, wie als ob sie keine Probleme wären: Leben, Welt, Gott, Zweck des Lebens'*]" (Nietzsche 1988b: 581)

For Nietzsche shame is more of a metaphysical concept than an emotion; more of a conscious attitude than something which befalls the subject. Shame is the mark of a necessary distance from truth, a means of preserving truth through continuing interpretation. In this way, shame teaches us to keep a mysterium: "Shame exists wherever there is a 'mysterium'" (Nietzsche 1994a: 69)

"Those Greeks were superficial – *out of profundity*!" Now this enigmatic exclamation becomes more comprehensible. Truth ceases to be truth when interpretation ends: "We no longer believe that truth remains truth, when one pulls off the veils" (Nietzsche 2001a, b: 8) Because truth vanishes into nothing when exposed, it can only be preserved by using some disguise, for example myth. It is, therefore, only in a myth that Demeter is able to see the origin of life in an undisguised way, but the myth itself is an artificial and artistic creation, a simulacrum of life. Demeter's merriness seems to be the merriness of a light-hearted science, a science that knows that it is merely copying life, but that behind the copy there is .... nothing. The artist copies life, he recreates it in simulacra, but at the same time he is laughing at it, because he knows that he is merely producing a surface, a surface behind which there is nothing, and herein lies his depth.

According to Nietzsche, Socrates is not a typical Greek, for he is not deep. But his shamelessness indicates that he is sticking to depth, namely to the concept of a fictional ideal beyond life, in contrast to which life can only be perceived as defective. Thus, truth becomes the enemy of life and it is only by renouncing the cynical attitude of shamelessness that Nietzsche seems to seek the possibility of a complete affirmation of life.

However, it's not as easy as it seems. For Nietzsche "surface" is not at all identical to "truth"; his way of thinking is not a simple reversal of Socrates', as he doesn't argue that truth *does not* lie hidden *behind* appearance, but, instead, it is right *on* the surface, but this surface is itself highly artificial; it is an artist's product, consisting of masks and simulacra, consisting of artistic and artificial copies of life. It is as much a lie as the Socratic lie. But it is a lie which encourages life because it helps us to endure life. In order to affirm life, we must forget that the life which we affirm is merely a copy of life and is therefore our own product. That is why Nietzsche praises the act of forgetting again and again. "Forgetfulness is not just a *vis inertia*, as superficial people believe, but is rather an active ability to suppress, positive in the strongest sense of the word." (Nietzsche 1994b: 38)

In fact behind the surface, beyond the play of masks – there is nothing. But the "Übermensch" is strong enough to forget that there is nothing behind his projections; he adores the surface because he is profound. The concept of a surface only makes sense by opposing some kind of virtual depth – this is why he sticks to shame.

Shame then becomes a borderline affect located somewhere between forgetting and remembering, between not knowing and knowing, between nature and culture. Indeed it marks a threshold, but not – as Socrates and the Cynics wished us to believe – the threshold between truth and appearance, but the threshold which keeps us captured in the game of interpretation, which allows us to forget that there is nothing behind the masks but other masks. Shame is a screen masked as a veil; it is the screen upon which we perceive the shadows of life, the screen which makes us believe that truth and nature are located behind it. If we were to tear off the veil, we would see – nothing, certainly not any kind of metaphysical Nature or Substance.

So, shame results in acknowledging and – at the same time – denying that the life we construct for ourselves is a fiction. If Nietzsche thus advocates the honouring of shame, he also advocates our maintaining the fiction of a truth behind appearances; all the while being conscious of the fact that there is nothing. Or, in other words: He advocates keeping the abyss at a distance in favour of life.

Throughout the history of philosophy, shame and shamelessness have maintained an intimate relationship with truth. Emanating from Martin Heidegger's concept of anxiety as an emotion which equates to the experience of nothingness, i.e. the essential meaningless of Being, it was argued that shame can correspondingly be conceived as an affect of nothingness. Hereby, neither nothingness nor meaninglessness are understood as voids but, instead, as disruptions of connectivity. But while anxiety is centred on the meaninglessness of the outside world, shame is reflexive insofar it indicates the disruption of the relatedness of the subject itself.

From the time of Platonic metaphysics the lack of connectivity was identified with truth, since it made it possible to grasp things as they are, i.e. their essence or nature. While culture relates things one to another, nature is the realm of things by themselves, bare of any relation. As long as the philosopher participates in the cultural grid he is not able to grasp the essence of things.

For, it is shame which ties her to the symbolic grid, shamelessness becomes both a necessary condition and a gateway to truth because shamelessness expels her from culture.

But shame is not the only the force which keeps the subject in the bonds of conventions; at the same time it also indicates that those bonds are already loosened, because shame occurs when people have already transgressed cultural conventions. In this way, shame marks the border between culture and nature, but also produces it and breaches it as well.

And so, it becomes clear what the *nothing* we are ashamed of consists of – the question we started off with: It doesn't consist of any deficiency, called castration or narcissistic deficiency, the way in which psychoanalysis usually conceives it. Instead, it consists of the simple fact that I am never anything other than myself, but also that I can never fully identify with this self. In other words: that not only things are meaningless, i.e. unrelated, but I myself am only what I am. In the instance of shame any significant and comforting bond that ties me to my future or my past, to my ideals or my fellows is completely disrupted. I am completely myself, and nobody, at the same time.

Who is not familiar with the feeling of absolute loneliness, when one has raised his voice in public and nobody reacts to it, or even worse: when just a short and bashful laughter causes a deadly silence? Our face flushes and we wish nothing more than to disappear from the surface of the earth and to sink to the ground.

In these moments of deadly shame, all the symbolic ties and social roles we are equipped with in everyday life are disrupted. In these instants our true self is disclosed, and this alleged authentic self, stripped of our masks, turns out to be a mere nothing. We are identified as who we are and, at the same time we are also just an anybody without any marks of identification.

References

Aristotle. 1964. *Physics*. With an introduction and commentary by W. D. Ross, Oxford: Clarendon Press.

de Sade, DAF. 1965. *Justine*, ed. Richard Seaver and Austryn Wainhouse. New York: Grove Press.

Dodds, Eric R. 1951. *The Greeks and the Irrational*. Berkeley: University of California Press.

Goldberg, Jacques. 1985. *La culpabilité, axiom de la psychanalyse*. Paris: Presses universitaires de France.

Gsell, Monika. 2001. *Die Bedeutung der Baubo. Kulturgeschichtliche Studien zur Repräsentation des weiblichen Genitals*. Frankfurt am Main: Stroemfeld.

Heidegger, Martin. 1962. *Being and Time*. Trans. John Macquarrie and Edward Robinson. New York: Harpers and Brothers.

Heidegger, Martin. 2002. *The Essence of Truth*. Trans. Ted Sadler. New York/London: Continuum.

Heraclitus. 1987. *Fragments*. A Text and Translation with a Commentary by T.M. Robinson. Toronto/Buffalo/London: University of Toronto Press.

Nietzsche, Friedrich. 1973. *Beyond Good and Evil*. Trans. R.J. Hollingdale. London: Penguin.

Nietzsche, Friedrich. 1982. *Daybreak. Thoughts on the Prejudices of Morality*. Trans. R. J. Hollingdale. Cambridge: Cambridge University Press.

Nietzsche, Friedrich. 1988a. *Kritische Studienausgabe*, ed. Giorgio Colli and Mazzino Montinari, vol. 10. München: dtv.

Nietzsche, Friedrich. 1988b. *Kritische Studienausgabe*, ed. Giorgio Colli and Mazzino Montinari, vol. 12. München: dtv.

Nietzsche, Friedrich. 1990. *Unmodern Observations*, ed. William Arrowsmith. New Haven & London: Yale University Press.

Nietzsche, Friedrich. 1994a. *Human, All too Human*, ed. and trans. Marion Faber. London: Penguin.

Nietzsche, Friedrich. 1994b. *On the Genealogy of Morality*, ed. Keith Ansell-Pearson, trans. Carol Diethe. Cambridge: Cambridge University Press.

Nietzsche, Friedrich. 2001a. *The Gay Science*, ed. Bernard Williams. Cambridge: Cambridge University Press.

Nietzsche, Friedrich. 2001b. *The Birth of Tragedy*, ed. Michael Tanner, trans. Shaun Whiteside. London: Penguin.

Plato. 1961. *The Collected Dialogues of Platon*, ed. Edith Hamilton and Huntington Cairns. Princeton: Princeton University Press.

Rousseau, Jean-Jacques. 1989. *Rousseau, Juge of Jean-Jacques*. The Collected Writings of Rousseau, vol. 1, ed. Roger D. Masters and Christopher Kelly. Hanover: University Press of New England.

Rousseau, Jean-Jacques. 1998. *The Confessions*. The Collected Writings of Rousseau, vol. 5, ed. Christopher Kelly, Roger D. Masters and Peter G. Stillman, trans.Christopher Kelly. Hanover: University Press of New England.

Rousseau, Jean-Jacques. 2000. *The Reveries of the Solitary Walker.* The Collected Writings of Rousseau, vol. 8, ed. Christopher Kelly, trans. Charles E. Butterworth, Alexandra Cook and Terence E. Marshall. Hanover: University Press of New England.

Rousseau, Jean-Jacques. 2004. *Discourse on the Origin of Inequality*. Mineola: Dover.

Philosophy's Nostalgia

Jeff Malpas

"weeping, his eyes never dry, his sweet life flowing away/with the tears he wept for his foiled journey home [*nostos*]/… all his days he'd sit on the rocks and beaches/ Wrenching his heart with sobs and groans and anguish [*algos*]" – Homer, *Odyssey* 5.169-174 (Fagles 1997: 157).

What is wrong with nostalgia? How and why has it come to be the case, as it surely has, that to say of a philosophical position that it is 'nostalgic' is already to indicate its inadequacy? In the inquiry that follows, I examine nostalgia both as a mood or disposition in general, and as a mood or disposition that is characteristic of philosophical reflection. Part of that inquiry will involve a re-thinking of the mood of nostalgia and what that mood encompasses. Rather than understand the nostalgic as characterised solely by the desire to return to a halcyon past, the nostalgic will be explored through the connotations suggested by its Greek etymology as precisely a *longing* for the return home – a return that cannot be achieved – a form of homesickness, and so as *discomfiting* rather than comfortable, as bringing with it a sense of the essential *questionability* of our own being in the world.

The origins of nostalgia or, at least, of the term itself, lie in the seventeenth century and its use to refer to a form of melancholia most often found among soldiers serving away from their homelands.[1] Nostalgia combines the Greek *nostos*, meaning home or the return home, with *algos*, meaning pain, so the literal meaning of the term is a pain associated with the return home – a pain originally taken to arise as a consequence of the unfulfilled desire or longing for such return. 'Nostalgia' thus appears at a particular point in history and within a particular

[1] Johannes Hofer first used the term in 1688 in his *Dissertatio Medica de nostalgia* – see Anspach (1934).

J. Malpas (✉)
School of Philosophy, University of Tasmania,
Private Bag 41, Hobart, TAS 7001, Australia
e-mail: Jeff.Malpas@utas.edu.au

H. Kenaan and I. Ferber (eds.), *Philosophy's Moods: The Affective Grounds of Thinking*, Contributions To Phenomenology 63, DOI 10.1007/978-94-007-1503-5_7,

technical discourse – it is an invented term, a technical neologism, belonging to the vocabulary of medical diagnosis – even though the experience of loss and estrangement that lies at its heart is ancient.

From its origins in the eighteenth to its usage today, the meaning of 'nostalgia' appears to have shifted. Part of that shift involves the disappearance of the term, along with other terms like 'melancholia' itself, from the language of medicine. Nostalgia, like melancholia, is no longer recognised as an illness to be medically diagnosed and treated. But a more significant, although associated shift, is in the way the term is seen as related to the spatial and the temporal. Understood precisely as a pain associated with desire for *home* – and as home is neither a space nor a time, but a place that holds a space and time within it – so nostalgia can never be understood as spatial or temporal alone (and this is a point to which I shall return in the discussion below).[2] Yet having originally referred to a condition resulting primarily from *spatial* displacement (the soldier serving in a foreign land),[3] 'nostalgia' has come instead to signify a condition usually taken to involve, first and foremost, *temporal* dislocation (our estrangement from our past, and especially our childhood) – (see Wilson 2005: 22–23), so that even the migrant who reflects 'nostalgically' on her homeland is typically reflecting back on memories of a place that, while perhaps spatially removed, is also more significantly and specifically temporally distant. One might say, then, that understood as a form of homesickness, nostalgia is that particular form of longing for home that arises in circumstances in which the return home is somehow made impossible, and in the contemporary world, in which, as the advertisements often tells us, the 'home' that is spatially distant is nevertheless only a flight or a phone call away, the only home that is rendered truly inaccessible is the home that lies in the past.

In addition to the shift from the technical to the commonplace and from the spatial to the temporal, nostalgia has also come to be viewed in contemporary terms in a way that effectively shifts the emphasis of nostalgia away from *algos* and towards *nostos*. Nostalgia is thus often associated, not with suffering and estrangement, but with familiarity and comfort. In terms of the history of 'nostalgia', it seems that what 'nostalgia' now refers to is not the *pain* that comes with the separation from

[2] This point is almost always overlooked in the existing literature. Place is typically opposed to time and treated as more or less identical with space. The conflation of space with place, and the opposition of both to time, is part of what underpins the view that nostalgia, in its contemporary form at least, is fundamentally temporal in character. On the nature and importance of the distinction, as well as the relation, between time, space and place that is at issue here see Malpas (1999: 9–30).

[3] Although Dylan Trigg argues that nostalgia and homesickness are *essentially* temporal in character (Trigg 2006: 54–55). The apparent shift here is presumably, on this account, a shift only in how nostalgia and homesickness are viewed, and not a shift in the character of nostalgia as such. Trigg cites Kant as having already recognised the temporal character of nostalgia when he writes that: "The homesickness of the Swiss…is the result of a longing that is aroused by the recollection of a carefree life and neighbourly company in their youth, a longing for places where they enjoyed the very simple pleasures of life" (Kant 1978: 69, quoted in Trigg 2006: 54). In fact, what Kant's comments as well as the position advanced by Trigg seem to indicate is the way space and time are both bound up with nostalgia through nostalgia's very relation to home and so also to place.

home, but instead that which was, in the past, often taken as its immediate cause, namely, the experience of familiar sounds, smells, sights that invoke the presence of home even in its absence. Such experiences, in which the longed for home reappears, briefly perhaps, but often with startling clarity, achieve a certain form of homecoming in which the pain of nostalgia may be temporarily assuaged, even though it may, as a consequence, also be exacerbated.[4] Contemporary nostalgia seems to involve just such a 'homecoming' as given in or evoked by some experience associated with home, and so we find a certain respite, or even pleasure, in re-experiencing the sounds, sights and smells of childhood or of some other place or world from which we are now irrevocably parted.

The 'mood' of nostalgia as it is most often manifest today is one in which we are overtaken by a sense of comfort and familiarity that comes from allowing the present to fade into the background as the past or, more specifically, some remembrance of the past, whether real or imagined, comes to the fore, and we allow ourselves to be overtaken by that remembrance almost as if at the edges of a dream. Yet even in this contemporary form, the mood of nostalgia is never taken up only with the sense of 'home', but always brings with it some element of pain. The memory of the past, as it is a memory, must always remain in contrast with the present, and so, even when experienced as pleasurable and comforting, it remains an experience tinged with a sense of loss and estrangement. The mood of nostalgia, so closely linked to memory, is thus always one that remains somewhere *between nostos* and *algos* – between the return home and the pain of its irrevocable loss.

The ambiguity or tension within the notion of nostalgia has not gone unnoticed (See Wilson 2005: 23). Nevertheless, the tendency in most contemporary treatments of nostalgia, in keeping with the shift in the meaning of the term that prioritises the notion of *nostos* or 'home', is to treat nostalgia in terms that elide this ambiguity. Rather than seeing nostalgia in terms that combine remembrance with loss, the usual understanding takes it to be little more than a form of escapist fantasy – a refusal of the demands of the here and now in favour of the seductive embrace of a glowing memory.[5] In the grip of nostalgia, it seems, we are like the Lotus-eaters of Homer's *Odyssey* – cocooned in a cosy dream-world that insulates us from the demands of the everyday. To refer to a view or attitude as nostalgic is consequently to condemn it as a form of passive and acquiescent immersion in remembrance, as unrealistic

[4]In her discussion of the early history of 'nostalgia', Svetlana Boym reports that "Swiss scientists found that rustic mothers' soups, thick village milk and the folk melodies of Alpine valleys were particularly conducive to triggering a nostalgic reaction in Swiss soldiers. Supposedly the sounds of 'a certain rustic cantilena' that accompanied shepherds in their driving of the herds to pasture immediately provoked an epidemic of nostalgia among Swiss soldiers serving in France. Similarly, Scots, particularly Highlanders, were known to succumb to incapacitating nostalgia when hearing the sound of bagpipes – so much so, in fact, that their military superiors had to prohibit them from playing, singing or even whistling native tunes in a suggestive manner" (Boym 2001: 4).

[5]From a Freudian psychoanalytic viewpoint, according to Dylan Trigg, nostalgia is "synonymous with regression", and the desire for home is "tantamount to a desire for parental supervision" (see Trigg 2006: 53–4).

and backwards-looking, and as privileging an idealised past in a way that cripples our capacity to respond to the present as well as the future.

Nostalgia is typically seen as a product of modernity, and, more specifically, of modernity understood as a mode of historical experience that is essentially given over to a process of unceasing change and renewal. On this account, it is not merely the present, but rather the modern, from which nostalgia attempts to escape. Nostalgia seeks a release from the impermanence and uncertainty of the contemporary world in a retreat back into the familiarity of a remembered time that remains always the same. As the fundamental experience of modernity is the experience of temporal discontinuity – in modernity, time itself appears to lose its constancy and connectedness – so nostalgia arises, in a form that seems quite different from its original sense, as a mood or disposition that is both provoked by that experience as well as being a counter to it. Thus the historian Peter Fritzsche writes that:

> … nostalgia is a fundamentally modern phenomenon because it depended on the notion of historical process as the continual production of the new… it was in the middle of the nineteenth century that nostalgia found a secure place in household vocabularies, its general usage made tenable by the massive displacing operations of industrialization and urbanization, which also standardized its meaning as a vague, collective longing for a bygone time rather than an individual desire to return to a particular place. Nostalgia retains this general and temporal meaning; it distills the 'dispirit of the age' (Fritzsche 2001: 5 & 9).[6]

The longing for home becomes, in the times with which we are familiar, a longing for a time of stability and security, a time that cannot be found in the present. It is almost, one might say, a longing for time itself – since, in modernity, it is as if time has become nothing more than a succession of disjoint moments, and in which there is no longer any more encompassing sense of time as that within which one could orient and place oneself.[7] It is easy to see how such nostalgia might indeed come to be seen (though not by Fritzsche) as entailing a denial of or blindness to the present, and as therefore inevitably given over to conservatism and self-delusion.

Within philosophy, in fact, the work of Martin Heidegger has frequently been treated as problematic precisely because of the way in which that work is supposedly given over to various forms of nostalgia: to a nostalgia for 'being as presence', as Derrida and many others following him (including, for instance, Baudrillard) would have it, to a nostalgia for the thinking of the Ancient Greeks, or a nostalgia for the pre-modern world of the Black Forest peasant. In Heidegger's case, the dangerously conservative character of such nostalgia is often taken to be given concrete demonstration by his problematic political involvement in the 1930s. Thus one writer has it that: "Heidegger's nostalgia for a *völkisch* past, which disposed him favorably toward the Nazis, constitutes a basic quality of his rhetoric and thought"

[6]Fritzsche draws upon a number of analyses of historical modernity, especially the work of Reinhart Koselleck – see Koselleck (1985).

[7]It is just such a more encompassing sense of time that is the object of Proust's search in *A la recherche du temps perdu* ('In search of lost time') – a work whose final book, *Le temps retrouvé* ('Time regained') ends with the reclamation of time understood as a form of encompassing place (see Proust 1954: 1048; see also Malpas 1999: 161–3).

(Ziolkowski 2001: 360). Alan Megill writes of Heidegger's nostalgia as "a longing for the immediate Dionysian presence of the origin, from which all division, all separation, all difference, is excluded" (Megill 1985: 125), and even such an otherwise sympathetic reader of Heidegger as Albert Borgmann can write that "an inappropriate nostalgia clings to Heidegger's account" and that the things he names are "scattered and of yesterday" (Borgman 1984: 196).

Both within philosophy as well as without, nostalgia is most often invoked as a term of critical opprobrium. Yet there is also a less common usage of the term that is more positive, and sees it as directing attention to a central and perhaps defining feature of philosophy. Heidegger, in particular, seems to view philosophical thinking as essentially tied to nostalgia, and frequently refers to his own thinking in terms of notions of home and homecoming. In one of his lectures on Hölderlin, for instance, he tells us that "[the]... nearness 'of' being, which is the *Da* of Dasein ... is called the 'homeland'" (Heidegger 2000: 42)[8] and he repeatedly talks of our modern predicament as one of homelessness (See, for instance, Heidegger 1993: 75; 1998a: 257–58). Moreover, Heidegger also famously cites Novalis' claim that "Philosophy is really homesickness, an urge to be at home everywhere. Where, then, are we going? Always to our home" (See Heidegger 1995: 5). Elsewhere, in discussing Nietzsche's identification of Zarathustra with 'the convalescent', Heidegger specifically refers to the Greek etymology of nostalgia: "But what does 'the convalescent' mean? 'To convalesce' (genesen) is the same as the Greek néomai, nóstos. This means 'to return home'; nostalgia is the aching for home, homesickness" (Heidegger 1967: 412). One might take Heidegger's own talk of nostalgia as merely confirming the views of his critics, and yet his emphasis on the Greek, and so on the importance of both *nostos* and *algos,* should also alert us to the possibility of a difference in the sense of nostalgia as Heidegger employs it from that employed by many of his critics.[9]

There can be no doubt that in both its philosophical and commonplace uses 'nostalgia' is usually taken as a pejorative term that refers, often quite generally, to any attitude that privileges the past over the present. But, as should already be evident from our brief explorations so far, nostalgia is more complex, and perhaps more significant, than this would imply. Nostalgia involves both the spatial and the

[8]See Heidegger's comments on this passage in Heidegger (1998a: 257–58).

[9]Dylan Trigg is especially critical of what he terms "Heidegger's spatial-centrism" (Trigg 2006: xvi), claiming that "Heidegger's musings on homelessness persistently reference the geometrical-spatial field, and so revert to the pre-reflective diagnosis of nostalgia as geographical displacement, and that alone. His failure to grasp homesickness in temporal terms is especially striking given the attention time receives in *Being and Time*. The omission is further heightened, since temporality is at the structural core of nostalgia" (Trigg 2006: 54), although Trigg's criticisms sit rather oddly with some of his discussion of Heidegger elsewhere in the book, especially in chapter 15, 199–207, where the issue of 'spatial-centrism' disappears, and there is instead a stronger appreciation (or so it seems) of the centrality of place in Heidegger's account. For a contrasting account of the way in which both space and time operate in Heidegger's thinking, and the problematic character of the emphasis on temporality in *Being and Time*, see Malpas (2006a).

temporal, both memorial recovery and loss, both a sense of home and of estrangement. Indeed, even the history of the term, as well as its contemporary meaning, are rather less straightforward than I have so far made explicit. Fritzsche, and other historians, have tended to emphasis the novelty of nostalgia and its direct link to modernity. Yet it should be quite clear that even though nostalgia may take on a different character in modernity, and may perhaps arise in a different form, there is a fundamental continuity between the sense of nostalgia that arises out of the experience of the loss of time in the face of the modern, and the ancient sense of nostalgia as the pain associated with the loss of home. Moreover, while Fritzsche talks of the way in which the experience of modernity led to a standardisation of the meaning of nostalgia "as a vague, collective longing for a bygone time rather than an individual desire to return to a particular place", that sense of nostalgia associated with the individual longing for home remains. Proust's *A la recherche du temps perdu*, for instance, which is one of the great works of modernity, and carries the imprint of modernity upon it, is nevertheless also a work that is centrally preoccupied with nostalgia understood precisely in terms of a return to, and recovery of, particular places (especially the village of Combray and the places that belong within and around it). Moreover, although that return is also construed explicitly in terms of time and memory, it is not independent, as Georges Poulet makes clear, of the spatial (see Poulet 1977).[10]

Nostalgia, refers to a mood or disposition that appears as both a generalized historical or cultural phenomenon - something *collective* – as well as a feature of *individual* personal experience (Davis 1979: 222). While historians and sociologists have tended to focus on the former, the latter has also been the subject of investigations – investigations that are often tied to particular culturally-specific forms. In Svetlana Boym's case, for instance, the primary focus is on the way in which nostalgia arises within the socio-political circumstances of Eastern Europe (where the Russian *toska* often stands in for the Anglo-Saxon 'nostalgia', although with some different nuances – see Boym 2001: 12 & 17), while in Fred Davis' early psycho-sociological investigation of nostalgia (Davis 1979), as well as in the more recent continuation of that work by Janelle L. Wilson (Wilson 2005), the focus is the appearance of nostalgia within, primarily American, popular culture, and its role as enabling the continuity of identity. In fact, none of the apparently different forms of nostalgia can be completely separated just as the different cultural manifestations of nostalgia nevertheless exhibit broadly similar features. The individual experience of nostalgia is inevitably entangled with forms of collective memory and imagining, as well as with nostalgia as a more generalized mode of historical experience, while the key features of nostalgia, even in its historically and culturally specific forms, overlap and connect with nostalgia understood more broadly.

[10] See also my discussion of Proust in Malpas (1999: 157–174). When I say there that Proust's work is "not primarily a work of nostalgic recollection, but is instead a project of recovery and reclamation" (159), I am employing a rather narrower sense of the nostalgic than I have used here, and the main point being that Proust's work is not oriented towards passive reminiscence, but is directed instead at a more active task of retrieval.

If we look to nostalgia specifically as a mood – a *Stimmung* as it would be put in the German of Heidegger's *Being and Time* – as well as a form of experience (for every mood brings a form of experience with it), so nostalgia is a certain mode of appearing of both self and world. That it should be so is characteristic of moods as such. Moods always involve, as Otto Bollnow points out, a common 'tuning' (as the German term suggests[11]) of self and world so that a mood is no mere internal feeling, but is always also externalised. Thus in boredom, for instance, we not only *feel bored*, but the world presents itself *as boring* – everything dissolves in the same lack-lustre meaninglessness in which we may even lose sight of ourselves. The way Bollnow puts this is to say that "in moods in the true sense there is no I, no objects, no border between I and object. One should rather say: the borders of the I fade away and disappear in a peculiar way. I and world are embedded in an undivided totality of experience. Mood is the feeling of I and world together" (Bollnow 1956: 40–41). Nostalgia exhibits the same encompassing character, and the same externalisation of the internal, as do other moods, and yet it also presents a more complex phenomenological structure. Although one of the characteristic features of moods is indeed a certain dissolution of the distinction between self and world, in the case of nostalgia, it is the relation between self and world that is brought to the fore as problematic – and together with that, the very relation of the self to itself. What is at issue in nostalgia is our own self-identity, but as the mood of nostalgia is no mere internal feeling, so the way in which identity appears as an issue here is precisely in terms of the way we find ourselves not at home in the world, as longing for home, as homesick.

The connection between nostalgia and the issue of self-identity is something that recurs frequently in discussions of nostalgia whether philosophical, sociological or historical, irrespective of whether it is the individual or collective sense of nostalgia that is at issue. It is, for instance, the central focus in the works of Davis and Wilson to which I referred earlier, and it is significant that both argue for a certain rehabilitation of nostalgia for just that reason. The direct implication of self-identity in nostalgic experience is shown by the way in which, as Edward Casey comments, nostalgia "cannot be sheerly fictitious (Kant would say 'creative') but must incorporate one's sense of being in a given place as conveyed by memories" (Casey 1987b: 368).[12] This comment draws attention, not merely to memory, as opposed to imagination, but to a certain sort of memory, namely, autobiographical memory. Autobiographical memory is that form of personal memory that is always self-referential and in which the 'I' is always involved. It is worth noting that the access to autobiographical memory becomes more common with age, and so too,

[11] *Stimmung* can mean 'mood', 'temper' or 'disposition', as well as 'tuning' or 'tonality', and comes from the verb *stimmen* (meaning 'to tune' – as in the tuning of an instrument – and to vote), as well as to *Stimme* (meaning 'voice' and 'vote' – the latter in the sense of that which one gives to a candidate), while it is also related to *bestimmen*, which means 'to will', 'to determine' or 'to decide'.

[12] Casey adds that, "on the other hand, it is not the simple summation of these memories" (Casey 1987b: 368).

of course, does the experience of nostalgia become more common as we get older – it is as if the past places that have formed important parts of our lives, and in and through which our lives have been formed, return to haunt us as our distance from them increases.

Autobiographical memory, inasmuch as it is tied to a sense of self, is also characteristically tied to a sense of place – autobiographical memories typically involve the remembrance of places no less than of events, people or experiences (indeed, one might say that in memory persons and events come to be inextricably bound up with the places in which they are encountered, in which they 'take place'). This is not merely an empirically contingent feature of the self as given in memory – so that autobiographical memories just happen always to be given in terms of the remembrance of our being in a place – but is a consequence of the very nature of experience and memory as such.[13] In Heidegger's *Being and Time*, this is captured through the explication of Dasein as being–in-the-world, and, more fundamentally, in the very concept of Dasein itself – Dasein is being-there/being-here, such that Heidegger can eventually say (even though it is not made explicit in *Being and Time* itself) that "'Dasein' names that which is first of all to be experienced, and subsequently thought accordingly, as a place – namely as the locality of the truth of Being" (Heidegger 1998b: 283). To be the sort of being that Dasein is – a being whose own being can be in question for it – is thus to be a being that finds itself only though its being already given over to a world, and its involvement in it, as that is articulated always in and through the singularity of place.[14]

Returning more specifically to the idea of autobiographical memory, and so also to nostalgia, one can say that it is the remembrance of oneself as a remembrance of one's own being-in-place (which is not the same as remembering a given location such that one could identify or re-identify it), that makes a memory an instance of autobiographical memory. Autobiographical memory is thus always a memory of self and world given as a memory of a specific being-in-a-place. Since nostalgia is itself a certain form of autobiographical memory – or, at least, incorporates autobiographical memory within it – so nostalgia takes the form of a remembrance of, and a longing for, a certain being-in-place that is also, of course, a certain being-at-home. On this basis, we can see why it is mistaken (quite apart from the very juxtaposition of the terms in this way) to treat nostalgia, as it so often is treated, as involving time as opposed to place. While it is true that there is a shift in the *conception* of nostalgia that prioritises the temporal, and that this has also been taken to involve a de-emphasis of the spatial as well as the topographic, this should not be allowed to obscure the nature of the nostalgic as such. Nostalgia remains, as it always was, a matter of our relatedness to place, even though that relatedness also involves, in different ways, both the spatial and the temporal.

---

[13]On the connection between memory and place, see Malpas (1999: 100–107); see also Casey (1987a: 181–215).

[14]See Malpas (2006a), for a fuller discussion of the topological character of Dasein and of the role of place in Heidegger's thought in general.

Nostalgia is essentially tied to place, then, and it is so tied in large part because of the self-referential character of nostalgia, because of the way nostalgia is connected with the sense of self that itself always implicates the sense of place. The self-referential character of nostalgia that is evident here, as well as its connection to place, is not peculiar to individual nostalgic experience, but also to nostalgia understood as a collective phenomenon. What we are nostalgic for as a society, and not merely as individuals, is always that which we already identify as belonging to us and to which we also belong, and that is articulated through characteristic places and landscapes that have collective resonance as part of collective memory. We are not, and cannot be, nostalgic for that which does not belong, or is not already taken to belong, to our own heritage and our own sense of identity.

Of course, this also means that precisely to the extent that collective nostalgia, and the past that is memorialised in it, is removed from the personal and the autobiographical, and so is more abstractly self-referential, so it already refers to a sense of nostalgia that is itself somewhat more abstracted and attenuated. This may turn out to be true of collective nostalgia, in particular, to the extent that it is more prone to deliberate manipulation – certain motifs or images that may draw on nostalgic associations may thus be deployed in order to advance particular collective self-conceptions that are seen as advantageous to certain social, commercial or political purposes, and yet may not be well-grounded in any collective experience or memory as such (although there will always be a certain degree of ambiguity here, since memory and imagination stand in such a close relation to one another) – but it can surely also apply in the individual case. In general, however, and to the degree that it is indeed more removed from our own memory and experience, from our own sense of self, so nostalgia can easily turn into, or perhaps be mistaken for, what should really be understood as a form of *mythophilia* – a longing not for what is remembered, but for what is known only through its retelling, through story and myth. Such longing falls short of nostalgia precisely because of the mythical character of that which it desires and valorises – a past of which we ourselves have no experience and in which we were never ourselves engaged. Such mythophilia is not nostalgic, even though it may share some features with nostalgia, and even though it may sometimes contribute to a nostalgic sensibility.

The distinction I have drawn here between the properly nostalgic and the mythophilic relates directly to a distinction Svetlana Boym draws between what she terms 'restorative' and 'reflective' nostalgia:

> Restorative nostalgia stresses nostos and attempts a transhistorical reconstruction of the lost home. Reflective nostalgia thrives in algia, the longing itself, and delays the homecoming – wistfully, ironically, desperately. Restorative nostalgia does not think of itself as nostalgia, but rather as truth and tradition. Reflective nostalgia dwells on the ambivalences of human longing and belonging and does not shy away from the contradictions of modernity. Restorative nostalgia protects the absolute truth, whereas reflective nostalgia calls it into doubt (Boym 2001: xviii, also 49).

Boym differentiates between these two forms of nostalgia partly in order to draw attention to what she clearly views as a productive mode of nostalgic experience in contrast to a mode that she viewed as unproductive. Yet one might argue that a mode of nostalgia that does not recognise itself as nostalgia, which is the characteristic feature of Boym's 'restorative' nostalgia, lacks what is essential to nostalgic longing, namely, its self-referentiality. This means that such 'nostalgia', if it is to be called that, not only lacks any sense of pain, of *algos*, but strictly speaking it also lacks any proper sense of home, of *nostos*, since it lacks any sense that what is at issue is what already belongs to it, and to which it might be said to belong, and so lacks any sense that what is at issue is its own sense of itself, its own sense of identity. Such 'nostalgia' is scarcely nostalgia at all, but corresponds instead to the mythophilia that remains fixated on a past of which it has no memory of its own, and that loses itself in the attempt to realise that mythical and unremembered past.

Part of what becomes evident here is that the sense of home that is so central to nostalgia only becomes evident to us in the pain of our separation from it. Nostalgia is thus both *nostos* and *algos*, and neither comes to presence without the other. Within the literature of nostalgia, this is most clearly evident in the emphasis on nostalgia as characterised by the experience of temporal discontinuity – which now has to understood as a discontinuity that is also a form of dis-placement – which nevertheless also invokes a form of continued connection. Thus Fritszche characterises nostalgia, in temporal terms, as involving both a sense of the ghostly presence of the past as well as its absence and loss:

> Nostalgia not only cherishes the past for the distinctive qualities that are no longer present but also acknowledges the permanence of their absence. It thus configures periods of the past as bounded in time and place and as inaccessible... What the ghostly remains of other pasts recall is the fact of other presents and other possibilities. It makes sense, then, to reconsider nostalgia not as blindness but as sightfulness, which completes the modern experience of time with its insistent perception of disaster and its empathy to strangers stranded in the present (Fritzsche 2001: 11).

Fritszche's characterisation of nostalgia, which focusses on nostalgia as a phenomenon of collective historical experience, closely matches the characterisation to be found in Wilson, who is concerned not only with the collective, but also the individual experience of nostalgia. Thus Wilson writes that "Nostalgia...is not simply a 'living in the past', but rather an active engagement with the past, and a juxtaposition of past and present" (Wilson 2005: 157).

The discontinuity that is encountered in nostalgia, and that gives rise to its pain, is a discontinuity that exists between the self and the world in which it presently finds itself. Thus the self finds itself out of place, estranged, homeless, and yearning for a home that it cannot reach.[15] Yet this should not be construed as a discontinuity that obtains between a self that is whole in itself and a world that appears to stand apart from it. Rather the discontinuity here is one that obtains *within the self as such*. This is inevitable given the character of the self as constituted in and through its involvement with the world and the places that make it up. The self is

[15]The discontinuity present here is thus an essential feature of our mode of being-in-the-world, and so of our mode of being-in-place, even though it is in the experience of nostalgia that it becomes most clearly evident. On the estrangement that is an inevitable part of our sense of self as well as our sense of place (see Malpas 2006b: 45–59).

always externalised (as Merleau-Ponty puts it "The world is wholly inside and I am wholly outside myself"– Merleau-Ponty 1962: 407), and so the discontinuity that appears between self and world, or between self and place, is also a discontinuity that must be internalised within the self just in virtue of that externalisation.

Focussing on the temporal character of nostalgia (and without relying on any problematic opposition of time to place), but also the way it implicates the issue of self-identity, Steve Crowell has explored the discontinuity at issue here in terms of a radical discontinuity within what he calls "the time of the 'I'". The self that is presented in nostalgic recollection is, for Crowell, a self that is at one and the same time my own and yet also a self that is irretrievably past – nostalgia is thus always, for Crowell, an encounter with the dead. As he writes:

> To see the way that I am present to myself noematically in nostalgic experience is to see that nostalgic yearning is not a function of the difference between past and present worlds, but arises from a radical disruption in the time of the I, a noncoincidence that thwarts every attempt to figure one's own past as narratively continuous with the present (Crowell 1999: 96).[16]

Crowell goes on to refer to Goethe's idea of nostalgia as an experience that brings something spectral into the present, concluding that although there is a certain connection between nostalgia and mourning, "Nostalgia does not mourn for what is dead and gone, but experiences the return of the dead." (Crowell 1999: 97). In this way Crowell connects nostalgia with the philosophy of death, and so also with the essential thinking of finitude. To experience nostalgia is to experience, in a very direct and immediate, although also problematic and uncanny way, a sense of our own temporality, our own mortality, our own strange finitude.[17]

Nostalgia, on this account, is thus a returning to self – a coming home to what one has been and so also to what one is, and yet a coming home that is fundamentally uncanny – so that what one encounters is a ghostly, spectral self. One might say that nostalgia, in this sense, is the direct re-encounter with one's own past, recognised as one's past (and always, I would add, in the manner in which that past is given as one's own in and through a remembered sense of being-in-place). It is this odd tension between the own-ness of what is recollected in nostalgia and the fact of its loss, its pastness, that renders nostalgia as characterised by both a sense of home and a sense of homesickness and loss of home. Such nostalgia is, once again, in marked contrast to what Boym calls 'restorative' nostalgia, which we can now characterise in terms of an experience, or attempted experience, of the past, not in terms of a uncanny or spectral presence, but rather as a reconstituted appearance in the present that denies the very pastness of the past – as if the dead could be returned to life through a refusal to recognise their deaths. Nostalgia, when understood in terms

---

[16]Crowell acknowledges that his approach follows that of Frank Ankersmit, quoting Ankersmit's claim that nostalgia represents "an authentic experience of the past in which the past can still assert its independence from historical writing" (Ankersmit 1994: 94 – quoted in Crowell 1999: 86).

[17]The strangeness at issue here is directly connected with the strangeness that is also encountered in the attempt to think the idea of our own mortality – see Malpas (2004: 34–6).

of the two elements that make it up – in terms of *nostos* and *algos* – is thus not a form of forgetting, but of remembering; not a form of escapism but of return; not a restoration of the past, but a reflective appropriation of the very temporality that encompasses present, past and future.

In looking to the character of nostalgia as a mode of temporal discontinuity within the structure of the self, Crowell is led to argue for nostalgia as a form of temporal experience that is nevertheless not an experience that can be structured in narrative terms. Nostalgic recollection does not itself depend on, nor carry within it, a narrativity of its own – nostalgic experience is thus not an experience of a story, but typically of a moment or an image – and it is this that partly explains its spectral and uncanny character. The experience of the self that is given in nostalgia is typically, therefore, an experience of the self, and of its past, that does not present itself in a way that is incorporated within an existing narrative of the self, or within an already articulated history. This coheres with Fritszche's emphasis on nostalgia, as it arises within the experience of modernity, as tied to an experience of historical discontinuity – a breakdown in the narrative of history itself. It also means that the discontinuity that is at issue in Fritszche's account, while it may be said to take on a more extreme form in the historical experience of the past 200 years or so, is nonetheless not a feature of nostalgia that is peculiar to historical modernity. The experience of discontinuity, and so also the breakdown of narrative articulation or integration, is at the very heart of nostalgic experience as such.

Although the experience of nostalgia involves a breakdown in the usual narrativity of time and of self, the response to that experience is often the attempt at a reconstituted narrative in which we try to find ourselves once again. Proust's great work is the classic example of such an attempt to overcome the discontinuity introduced by temporality, as that is given in nostalgic experience, and to use that experience as part of a retrieval of a sense of self that does not deny temporal discontinuity, nor the essential uncanniness of our being-in-the-world. One might even say that, in certain respects, all writing is directed at such retrieval. Writing, and so also narrative, is both the mark of our homesickness, and also the means by which we constantly attempt to come to terms with it. Writing is thus always an act of remembrance – a remembrance of the world in which we are always already placed, to which we belong, and yet from which we are always estranged. Moreover, the estrangement at issue here, while it is that to which writing may be said to respond, is also that in which the very possibility of writing, and indeed, of language and memory, is itself founded.

The connection between nostalgia and philosophy, or the possibility of such a connection, is reinforced by these considerations of the nature of nostalgia, but it is a connection that still remains to be elucidated, although the direction of that elucidation should already be clear. Of particular importance is the notion of remembrance – and not only because philosophy might be construed as a 'kind' of writing. As the epigram to his own essay on nostalgia Edward Casey chooses a line from Adrienne Rich: "Nostalgia is only amnesia turned around" (Casey 1987b: 361). Although it is not just this, nostalgia is, as we have already seen, fundamentally tied to memory. In this respect, the nature of Heidegger's thought as itself centrally concerned with overcoming *Seinsvergessenheit*, the forgetting of being, already suggests its nostalgic character. Moreover, Heidegger himself frequently speaks, not only of his own thinking, but of philosophy, as a kind of remembrance. Of such remembrance, Heidegger writes:

> Remembrance is no historiological activity with the past, as if it wanted to make present, from outside and from what is later, what earlier thinkers 'believed' 'about' being. Remembrance is placement into being itself, which still presences, even though all previous beings are past. Indeed, even talk about placement into being is misleading because it suggests we are not yet placed into being, while being yet remains closer to us than everything nearest and farther than all that is farthest... Hence it is not first a matter of being placed into being, it is a matter of becoming aware of our essential abode in being, and becoming genuinely aware of being beforehand (Heidegger 1993: 78).

On this Heideggerian conception, philosophy is itself, as a mode of *Seinserinnerung,* a mode not merely of abstract recollection of the thought or concept of being, but of our active re-emplacement into being. It is a return to our own experience of being, and one might say, our own experience of ourselves. It is also, it should be said, a remembering of place. Of course, the negative construal of nostalgia that is so widespread would suggest that it is precisely this idea of remembrance that involves the idea of a return to the past, or a desire to accomplish such a return, that is most problematic about nostalgia. It is problematic because it seems to imply a turning away from the present and the future, and so a deliberate remaining in and with the past that refuses change, and bases that refusal in an immersion in what is surely nothing but a form of self-obsession or self-contemplation. Indeed, one may argue that nostalgia is, on this basis, always given over to the contemplative, and the quietistic, rather than to activity and engagement – and this is, of course, precisely the argument that is often made, especially in regard to Heidegger.

Certainly the nostalgic does not entail any specificity of future action. Yet in being turned towards the uncanniness of our relation to self, time, and to place, it does not turn us only toward and into the past, but through the past, and the places from which we come, it also turns us into a future that remains open and unknown. Nostalgia can be seen as always predicated on, and always bringing home to us, our facticity, our uncertainty, and our freedom. Our freedom has its origins in our factical engagement which is always an engagement that has already been and to which we can return only in and through nostalgic recollection (nostalgic because it is a recollection that is predicated on our own capacity to re-appropriate our past as our own, and yet also set that past into question). Similarly, the experience of nostalgia need not constitute a form of self-obsession, since although that experience is an experience that is tied to who and what we are, nostalgia can itself be seen as disrupting and rendering such identity and self-identity uncertain. What is evident in nostalgia is precisely the loss of self and experience that occurs in time, even as that loss is also productive of self and of experience. What is experienced in nostalgia is not, and cannot be a return to something that renders us at home with respect to identity or to being. In Heideggerian terms, this means that the remembrance of being always has the character of nostalgia in that it remains a return that is never completed, but is essentially disjoint, *spectral* even. The homecoming that Heidegger so often evokes is thus a homecoming that is never completed, and that cannot be so completed. It is a homecoming that returns us to a questionability that is at the very heart of our being-in-the-world.

The ever-present estrangement that is characteristic of nostalgia, an estrangement that can never be satisfied or overcome, means that the mode of temporality that belongs to nostalgia, and to nostalgic experience, is one that exhibits an essential strangeness or discontinuity. Nostalgia is a certain sort of recollection or experience of the past – not any past, but a past that I recognize as my own through the way in which it is given always in terms of a remembrance of my own being-in-place. Yet that past, and the place with it, while it appears in the present, and so is present to me, is not a past that reappears in the fullness of presence – as simply present once more, complete and unaltered, a past in which I find myself once more back in the place I once knew. The past as given in nostalgia is always a past that, although present, remains past; the place is one from which I always find myself somehow displaced, a past that appears as mine, but as all the more strange in its very familiarity. While nostalgia, at least of the reflective sort that recognizes itself as nostalgia, may transport us back into our past, and into the places that belong to that past, it does so in a way that does not allow us to escape the present. In the nostalgic experience of the past we thus also experience something of the continuity and the discontinuity of temporality, and so of past and present. In the nostalgic experience of the past, we also experience something of the essential discontinuity, estrangement and uncertainty that is to be found in every place – the uncanniness and questionability that is to be found even 'at home'.

What is so often criticized in Heidegger's nostalgic thinking, and in the mode of philosophy to which his thinking directs attention, is not nostalgia in the sense I have defined it here, but rather what I earlier termed 'mythophilia' – the love of a mythical or imagined past. Admittedly, in Heidegger's case there is a genuine question as to what extent there are indeed elements of such mythophilia in his thinking (especially given the cultural and historical background against which he writes), yet perhaps this is something from which no philosophy is ever totally immune. Philosophy constantly retells its past in new mythic forms, and its relation to that past is often mythophilic whether or not the past it creates for itself is a past to which it would return or a past that it requires in order to legitimate its contemporary understanding of itself.

In the same passage in which Heidegger talks of nostalgia as a form of homecoming and of convalescence, he also writes that: "The convalescent is the man who collects himself to return home, that is to turn in, into his own destiny. The convalescent is on the road to himself, so that he can say to himself who he is" (Heidegger 1967: 412). Philosophy's nostalgia is not a nostalgia that removes us from the present nor the future; it is not a nostalgia that removes us from where or how we are, nor does it hide us from who we are. Yet at the same time it does not present us merely with a comfortable and comforting narrative. Nostalgia remains a form of longing rather than the assuaging of that longing, it retains a sense of home and of return, and yet does not achieve such a return nor realize that sense of home in any final fashion. Philosophy's nostalgia, simply, involves a sense of our own, and so of philosophy's, uncertain place in the world; of our own, and so of philosophy's, uncertain relation to being.

References

Ankersmit, Frank. 1994. "Historiography and Postmodernism: A Phenomenology of Historical Experience." In *History and Tropology: The Rise and Fall of Metaphor*. Berkeley: University of California Press.
Anspach, Carolyn Kiser. 1934. Translation of Johannes Hofer *Dissertatio Medica de nostalgia* (Basel, 1688). In "Medical Dissertation on Nostalgia," *Bulletin of the History of Medicine* 2: 376–91
Bollnow, Otto. 1956. *Das Wesen der Stimmungen*. Frankfurt-am-Main: Klostermann.
Borgman, Albert. 1984. *Technology and the Character of Contemporary Life*. Chicago: University of Chicago Press.
Boym, Svetlana. 2001. *The Future of Nostalgia*. New York: Basic Books.
Casey, Edward S. 1987a. *Remembering: A Phenomenological Study*. Bloomington: Indiana University Press.
Casey, Edward S. 1987b. "The World of Nostalgia." *Man and World* 20: 36–384.
Crowell, Steven Galt. 1999. "Spectral History: Narrative, Nostalgia, and the Time of the I." *Research in Phenomenology* 29: 83–104.
Davis, Fred. 1979. *Yearning for Yesterday: A Sociology of Nostalgia*. New York: The Free Press.
Fagles, Robert. 1997. *The Odyssey*. Trans. Homer. New York: Penguin
Fritzsche, Peter. 2001. "Specters of History: On Nostalgia, Exile, and Modernity." *The American Historical Review* 106: 1587–1618.
Heidegger, Martin. 1967. "Who is Nietzsche's Zarathustra?." Trans. B. Magnus. *Review of Metaphysics* 20: 411–431.
Heidegger, Martin. 1993. *Basic Concepts*. Trans. Gary E. Aylesworth. Bloomington: Indiana University Press.
Heidegger, Martin. 1995. *The Fundamental Concepts of Metaphysics*. Trans. William McNeill and Nicholas Walker. Bloomington: Indiana University Press
Heidegger, Martin. 1998a. "Letter on 'Humanism'". In *Pathmarks*, ed. McNeill William, 239–276. Cambridge: Cambridge University Press.
Heidegger, Martin. 1998b. "Introduction to 'What is Metaphysics'." In *Pathmarks*, ed. McNeill William, 277–290. Cambridge University Press: Cambridge.
Heidegger, Martin. 2000. "Homecoming/To Kindred Ones." *Elucidations of Hölderlin's Poetry*, 23–50. Trans. Keith Hoeller. New York: Humanity Books.
Kant, Immanuel. 1978. *Anthropology from a Pragmatic Point of View*. Carbondale: Southern Illinois University Press.
Koselleck, Reimnhart. 1985. *Futures Past: On the Semantics of Historical Time*. Cambridge: MIT Press.
Malpas, Jeff. 1999. *Place and Experience*. Cambridge: Cambridge University Press.
Malpas, Jeff. 2004. "The Discomfort of Strangeness." *The Philosopher's Magazine* 27: 34–36.
Malpas, Jeff. 2006a. *Heidegger's Topology*. Cambridge: MIT Press.
Malpas, Jeff. 2006b. "Philosophising Place in *The Joshua Tree*." In *U2 and Philosophy*, ed. M. Wrathall, 45–59. Chicago: Open Court.
Megill, Allan. 1985. *Prophets of Extremity*. Berkeley: University of California Press.
Merleau-Ponty, Maurice. 1962. *The Phenomenology of Perception*. Trans. Colin Smith. London: Routledge and Kegan Paul.
Poulet, Georges. 1977. *Proustian Space*. Trans. Elliott Coleman. Baltimore: Johns Hopkins.
Proust, Marcel. 1954. *Le temps retrouvé, A la recherche du temps perdu*, vol. 3. Paris: Gallimard.
Trigg, Dylan. 2006. *The Aesthetics of Decay*. New York: Peter Lang.
Wilson, Janelle L. 2005. *Nostalgia, Sanctuary of Meaning*. Lewisburg: Bucknell University Press.
Ziolkowski, Theodor. 2001. "Review of Five Portraits: Modernity and the Imagination in Twentieth-Century German Writing, Michael André Bernstein." *Modernism/Modernity* 8: 359–360.

Part IV
Anxiety

The Birth Pangs of the Absolute: Longing and Angst in Schelling and Kierkegaard

Bettina Bergo

Schelling's 1809 *Philosophical Investigations into the Nature of Human Freedom* is rooted in notes he took for a philosophy of nature. These notes first appeared in 1797 as preparation for *On the World Soul* and for a full-blown philosophy of nature. What we should keep in mind from Schelling's *Naturphilosophie* is its approach to existence, which starts from a thinking of the Absolute, instead of working up *toward* it. Further, the Absolute must be thought beyond antinomies and dialectics, which means that no dialectical method could claim to reach it without the *petitio* presupposing the Absolute even before the system unfolds. Schelling understood that teleological dialectical logics, like Hegel's, begin with a knowledge that they claim to reach, as a whole, at the end of their unfolding. I argue here that mood thus arises rather unexpectedly, in Schelling's idealism, as part of his rejection of teleological dialectics and his attempt to think life as immanence. Mood will be understood less as an emotion than as a kind of trembling, a tension that typifies absolute life, or the living Absolute. Schelling showed that a living Absolute—Nature or God—begins as the coexistence of two contraries, which cannot and do not pass over into each other. As a complex, almost unthinkable origin, Schelling referred to the tensed coexistence of contraries in "indifference." Although this coexistence resembles Aristotle's distinction between *dynamis* and *energeia,* in the Absolute it must be thought as proto-nature in which life is born out of itself. There would thus be no separation, of causality or temporality, between the constituent terms. Moreover, Schelling's Absolute is not ultimately a dualism, and nothing "contains" its two terms. In an effort to think something like absolute life—or a world soul, or again the ground of what-is, in terms of immanent emergence, Schelling argued for a twofold first principle whose existence is characterized by an imperceptible striving called *Sehnsucht.*

B. Bergo (✉)
Université de Montréal, FAS-Philosophie, CP 6128 Succ. Centre-ville, Montréal, Québec H3C 3J7, Canada
e-mail: bettina.bergo@umontreal.ca

H. Kenaan and I. Ferber (eds.), *Philosophy's Moods: The Affective Grounds of Thinking*, Contributions To Phenomenology 63, DOI 10.1007/978-94-007-1503-5_8,

Placing the term "God" in the place of the Absolute makes this logic appear uncanny. It is motivated by the just intuition that what is non-relative must be alive in and for itself. It would be alive before the phenomenal universe is alive, because out of it arises every process of generation and destruction. Alive, and giving birth to itself—nothing gives birth to God other than God—all things flow out of the Absolute, including the contraction necessary for "God" to "become" a being. From there, we begin to understand the origin of beings. *In fine*, the Absolute is absolute *and* relative; it is relative to itself and might be conceived as analogous to a cell that comes to divide through immanent forces existing in indifference to one another up to a certain point, until, for mysterious reasons, they enact *and* undergo fission.

The complexity of Schelling's system lies in his struggle to correct idealist philosophy by forcing it to think life according to a logic proper to life itself. Schelling found even Hegel's *Naturphilosophie* overly formalist on this point. That is why Schelling's *Philosophical Inquiries* turns on a principle already found in his philosophy of nature. He recognized that idealist dialectics had failed to grasp the becoming of nature from their starting point. Conceptualizing proto-forces coexisting in pure immanence without mediation or contamination, his path to a living Absolute—and one that exceeded Kant's formal temporality and categories—Schelling had recourse to a language of affects, despite their inevitable anthropomorphism: absolute life is affection and self-affection, simultaneously passive and active. Schelling deemed the inaugural indifference *Sehnsucht*, a sort anxious longing and striving. The activity-passivity of emotions and passions proved appropriate to the effort as it avoided more paltry anthropomorphisms implicit in the image of creation as *ratio*.

What, however, is the affect of *Sehnsucht*, and how does it serve Schelling's logic? The term itself belongs to the *Suchte* or passions, which eighteenth century German expressed as *Leidenschafte*, states of undergoing or suffering. As such, *Sehnsucht* is more than the "longing" of which English translators speak. Although "longing" is anthropomorphic, *Sehnsucht* denotes a striving alternately inertial, as in Goethe's "dreaming yearning (*träumende Sehnsucht*)," and intentional, as in Kant's observation that this yearning can have a distinct object ("[es] kann die Richtung auf ein bestimmtes Objekt sehr scharf hervortreten").[1]

In this context, *Sehnsucht* appears less anthropomorphic than would figures of reason, calculation or psychological motivation. We should note that Kierkegaard will later present a similar concept in his *Fear and Trembling*, when speaking of

---

[1] F. W. J. Schelling 1986. Hereafter NHF in the text. Also see Schelling 1980. For "*Sehnsucht*," see the entry in the *Deutsches Wörterbuch von Jakob und Wilhelm Grimm*, Vol. 16, 157. Here, "Sehnsucht" can evince a sharp orientation toward a determinate object, as Kant writes. The term was extensively employed in Romantic literature where it denoted a *Krankheit des schmerzlichen Verlangens, Liebeskrankheit, Liebesbegierde*—disorders of painful longing or hankering, a malady of love, amorous neurosis; in short, *Eros* as force and excessive passion.

the "movement of infinity."[2] We may assume that he borrowed this from Schelling. In the *Philosophical Inquiries*, *Sehnsucht* is, in any event, a restless yearning without an object, an *anxiousness* lying between an embodied sensation of disquiet and an affect that strives toward what it does not yet know. *Sehnsucht* bestrides sensation and sentiment, sensibility and affectivity. It is appropriate to understand it as *desiderium quo quis quasi morbo laborat*,[3] the unnamable process of desire "by or for which something strives, *quasi morbo*," almost morbidly. *Sehnsucht* permits Schelling to present, in their reciprocal contrast, power and suffering, against a horizon of unknowing. This passion describes pains of birth, the possibility of a proto-matter coexisting in place and time with an uncertain factor that initiates its own self-organization, the way a genetic code first 'manifests' itself in the movement of proteins.

In this figural depiction of incipient becoming, which is likely inspired by Luther's translation, among others, of Psalm 63 "*Sehnsucht nach Gott*," it is the indefiniteness of condition and tone that prevails.[4]

In developing his philosophy of life, Schelling proposed a mediation that combined the *vis inertiae* of mechanics and the virtuality of simple organization in the common form of a mood. As indicated, *Sehnsucht* was the tonality of the conjoined dualism, denoting a coexistence-in-tension of force and resistance, with neither conflict nor dialectic. This actually typified romantic biology's conception of life which invariably set out, as did Schelling, from the concept of a general organism and envisaged individual beings as so many halting-points in its universal unfolding. Unlike his contemporaries in zoology and embryology, notably Friedrich Tiedemann, Schelling carried the unity and parallelism of the living world into the Absolute.[5] It was to quite different ends that Kierkegaard—once profoundly influenced by Schelling—would extend the cosmological speculations of his erstwhile mentor, adapting them to an *existential* anxiety in his 1844 *The Concept of Anxiety* (*Angest*).

---

[2] Kierkegaard describes the movement of infinite resignation by the Knight of Faith as rooted in the only authentic "mediation" possible: passion. "Every movement of infinity is carried out through passion, and no reflection can produce a movement. This is the continual leap in existence that explains the movement, whereas mediation is a chimera..." In *Repetition*, the author of letters to his "silent confidant," struggles to be rid of the "infinite striving of my soul"; to no avail. See Søren Kierkegaard 1983: 42n. 214.

[3] "*Sehnsucht*" in *Grimm*, 157. Thanks to David Piché, Université de Montréal, for his assistance.

[4] Kant spoke of *Sehnsucht* as "*der leere Wunsch*," the empty wishing that corresponds to the "*unbestimmtheit des Gemütszustandes*," the indeterminacy of mood. When Luther writers of *Sehnsucht* it is in experiencing a lack; his soul thirsts after something, after God....Lacking a concrete object, *Sehnsucht* functions anti-teleologically, as indeterminate hope.

[5] Tiedemann published his respected *Zoologie* between 1808 and 1810, precisely around the year that the *Philosophical Inquiries* was published (1809). Criticized by French materialists, German biologists shared a metaphysical concern with, in the words of Pierre Flourens, "a general organism, which [they] postulated as a real being: [thus] particular beings were no more ... than simple ... *arrests of development* of this organism. Apart from their (degree of) complication, all beings are similar; the different classes are nothing but different ages of a single (being)." See Clarke and Jacyna 1987: 40–41. Hereafter NCO.

Therein anxiety, again as tension and striving, argued in favor of a *spiritual* evolution for humans and nature. In the former, anxiety was the symptom of self-consciousness in light of the sinfulness "of the race," even as anxiety could motivate the overcoming of sin. Kierkegaard wrote, "Because in innocence [a state of nature] spirit is qualified only as dreaming spirit, the eternal appears as the future, for this is…the first expression of the eternal, and its incognito. Just as…the spirit, when it is about to be posited in the synthesis [of body and psyche], or---when it is about to posit the synthesis as the spirit's (freedom's) possibility in the individual, expresses itself as anxiety, so here the future in turn is the eternal's (freedom's) possibility in the individual expressed as anxiety. As freedom's possibility manifests itself for freedom, freedom succumbs, and temporality emerges in the same way as sensuousness in its significance as sinfulness" (COA: 91).

For Kierkegaard, humans are the synthesis of two incompatible principles, provided what effectuates the synthesis—"spirit"—is not repelled by excesses on the material or sensuous side. The work of spirit, whose "translation" as freedom echoes both Hegel and Schelling here, is expressed as a two-sided anxiety that drives humans forward *and* exhausts them. Kierkegaard's adaptation of Schelling is evident in his insistence on a subjective, psychological anxiety and a natural or objective anxiety, both of which denote the tensions and possibilities of mortal life.

Before proceeding to examine Schelling's *Philosophical Inquiries* more closely, I want to cast light on mood in Schelling as opposed to mood in relation to Hegel's concept. Without this, it is difficult to understand Schelling's innovation. In the *Phenomenology of Spirit*, which appeared 2 years before the publication of the *Philosophical Inquiries* (1809), Hegel argued that absolute knowledge culminates in the spirit assuming all the various shapes and modes of its historical unfolding. As a "self" (*Selbst*), spirit has fully externalized itself in the world and its *Gestalten* can be known thanks to the history of culture. Through philosophical science, spirit is aware both of its evolving forms and it "philosophizes" with them in ascending orders of self-consciousness. The evolution of these forms will be called a "restless activity" that "consists in cancelling and superseding itself," or again, a "negativity."[6] Spirit as negativity is the accompaniment and the end of a process of temporal unfolding: "in thus concentrating on itself, spirit is engulfed in the night of its own self-consciousness….Here it has to begin all over again at its immediacy, as freshly as before" (PM: 807). Nevertheless, "the goal of the process is the revelation of the depth of the spiritual life…the Absolute notion" (PM: 808). In Hegel, the quality characteristic of the movement of reason into spirit—through its various formations in self-consciousness—is restless activity. The ambiguity of a mood like *Sehnsucht* is not evident here. Restless activity, or negativity, represents a *telos*, or fragile culmination, which presumably begins again repeatedly, but which is nevertheless a logical *terminus*. For Schelling, who begins with the Absolute and thinks it *physiologically*, mood bespeaks the *Gemütszustand*[7] or 'state' of a pre-spiritual duality

[6]Hegel 1967: 807. Hereafter PM.

[7]*Gemützustand* or *Gemütsanlage* would denote state of mind.

able to give birth to itself. The birth or self-generation strikingly resembles the path of Hegel. Both philosophers employ distinctly Lutheran concepts of restless immanentization or *Insichgehen*, and *kenosis,* or externalization in the world. For all that, the *Philosophical Inquiries*—whose general arguments Hegel certainly knew from his collaboration with Schelling, and which Hegel had anticipatively stood on their head—place a particular emphasis on mood and desire. Straightaway equated with negativity, Hegel's restlessness appeared formalist (*and* anti-romantic) by comparison. Now, because he strove to surpass Fichte and Kant, Schelling's Lutheran *Sehnsucht* found itself playing the uncanny role of expressing a logic as old as Gnosticism and Kabbalah,[8] reviving a (Christianized) version of *Tsim-tsum*, the kabbalistic self-contraction of Absolute to make way for creation. Here, however, the contraction of the Absolute is a birth, and in no way the product of Hegel's dialectical, and historical, unfolding. In Schelling, the first creation is God as One. That means that the first creation is the same as that from which it arose, distinguishable only as a sort of intensification relative to its ground or base.

In this metaphysics of life, whose influence on Nietzsche and later strains of vitalism should not be underestimated,[9] Schelling merged mystical speculation on a living divinity with a physiology of forces in conflict and balance. Nineteenth century German biology engulfed French materialism, setting it into vitalisms that conceived life force as overarching characteristic. But Schelling will reject the notion of 'life-force' itself as contradictory: in a logic of immanence, forces come from forces and produce concrescences, or intensifications. All forces we can know are finite, which means that some aspect of the living Absolute itself will prove to be somehow finite. However, because limitation is present in the Absolute, limitation must be in relation with something such that there are always at least two forces, and never simply one extrinsic "life force."

> Where we think of force (as in matter)…we must also presume a force *opposed* to it. Between opposing forces…we can only conceive a double relationship. Either they are in *relative* equilibrium[10]…then they are thought of as at *rest*, as in matter…[and] said to be inert. Or one thinks of them as in perpetual, never-settled conflict, where each in turn prevails and submits. (IPN: 37)

While relative equilibrium is a state that characterizes life in Schelling's proto-universe, it promises to reemerge with the ultimate self-realization of that universe, at a metaphoric point where the two inaugural grounds prove to be part of a single totality. Even then, equilibrium may not wholly supplant conflict. And, while we discern ongoing conflict, or resistance, throughout nature as well as in humans, it is

---

[8] Schelling credits Marcion with this logic; he reads Kabbalah through Franz Baader.

[9] Despite his derision of the "theologians," Hegel, Schelling, Kant, and despite the laughter that rings in *Beyond Good and Evil* (§11) about Schelling's baptism of the "Übersinnliche," Nietzsche pondered Schelling's (and the German romantics') philosophy of nature, and may have returned to it for his multifaceted *Wille zur Macht*. See Nietzsche (1967–1988), Vol. 3, 163 and Vol. 5, 25.

[10] "(In absolute equilibrium, they would both be completely eliminated)." See Schelling 1988: "Introduction," 37.

not the fundamental characteristic of the world—or not the sole characteristic, as that would lead to one of two things: the destruction of one of the terms, and therefore both ultimately (since the one depends on the other), or to an oscillation of dominations from which nothing new could arise. For this reason, the Absolute holds together two modalizations of its "self," whose symptom or expression is the troubled *Sehnsucht*. In the Absolute, the presence-in-indifference of these two processes generates their own third term in the contraction of the Absolute into the One. In nature, too, the tension between material and form-giving forces likewise produces a third term. Schelling argues that this third term cannot itself be a force, lest it join or replace one of the other two. Instead, we find at work a third term analogous to the relationship between the dualist base and its contraction into the One. For his natural philosophy Schelling proposes to call this third term "soul" or "principle of life," because the separation of thinking and extension is a difference of *expression*. In this, he is a Spinozist. More importantly perhaps, he understands that any logic that separates the concept from what it collects and specifies, will prove as inadequate to grasping life as the vitalism that imposes life-force extrinsically.

> In order to comprehend [the] union of concept and matter, you assume a higher divine intelligence…who designed his creations in ideal forms and brought forth Nature in accordance with these ideals. But a being in whom the concept *precedes* the act, the design, the execution, cannot *produce*, [it] can only form or model matter already there, [it] can only stamp the impress of the understanding and of purposiveness upon the matter from without. What he [the higher divine intelligence] produces is purposive, not *in itself*, but only in relation to the understanding of the artificer… only contingently. Is not the understanding [thereby made into] a dead faculty? (IPN: 33)

When Schelling thinks a third term in nature, not as force but as soul, he is working out of a coherent spiritual vitalism: nothing self-animates from without. There is no divine artificer in Schelling. God and nature are processual, and both arise from themselves, although *de facto* nature appears to stand in a relation of analogy to the emergence of the Absolute. This has led commentators like Werner Marx to argue that when Schelling investigates human freedom starting from the Absolute, he could just as well be starting from life itself.[11] It is a matter of a difference of

[11]For Werner Marx, this equivalence, God and Nature, is clearest in the young Schelling of the "Philosophy of Identity." "In view of Spinoza's system, Schelling recognized quite clearly that the proof of freedom's predominance in both realms, in nature and in spirit, can be convincing only if the appearances of finite freedom are founded in divine freedom. Therefore, Spinoza's *causa sui*, the freedom of the absolute as absolute 'groundlessness', must previously have been conceived of as such if freedom within the finite realm is to be secured….Schelling had taken great pains to model himself after Spinoza and to conceive the absolute, God, as the unity of mind and nature, as the unity between the ideal and the real….[It] is obvious that both these aspects are 'not actual' [*wirklich*] in God's essence…[but] at the same time, divine Being is the 'universe', 'absolute totality'." After works like the *Presentation of My System*, the dialogue *Bruno* (1802), and the *Philosophy of Nature* (1805–1806), the diremptions inherent in according a positive reality to evil, or 'non-being', shifted the emphasis of Schelling's system, and freedom had to be thought in light of the freedom to enact evil. See Marx 1984: 60ff.

levels, here, between life as observable, and life as its own genetic condition and self-production. This difference of levels would be pure transcendentalism were it not for the fact that Schelling above all strives to hold together the speculative and the empirical.

Nature, in its dual aspects—the seen and the unseen—thus unfolds everywhere in the same way. In the Absolute, the birth of God to itself from itself may be likened to the emergence of two cells out of one, or the emergence of a definite entity out of the indeterminacy of a seed or droplet condensing from a cloud. The best example is Schelling's own, which speaks of the emergence of light, drawing away from dark gravity but carrying with it the resistant inertia of its own obscure ground.[12]

> We must imagine the primal longing [or desire] in this way—turning towards reason, indeed, though not yet recognizing it, just as we longingly desire unknown, nameless excellence. This primal longing moves in anticipation like a surging, billowing sea... following some dark, uncertain law, incapable in itself of forming anything that can endure. But in response to the desire, qua still obscure depths, *the first emotion* of the divine Being is formed as a reflective internal representation taking shape in God himself, thanks to which God perceives himself as in an image (*Ebenbild*), since there can be no other object here than God. (NHF: 35, trans modified)[13]

The dynamic *ground* of this total life called "God"—which evolves by ec-stasis throughout the natural world—is thus anxious desire without an object. Facing the conundrum of rendering this "primal longing" and "anticipatory surging," Schelling's French translators proposed *désirement* (process of desire) and *angoisse* for the notion. It is after all the first "emotion of divine *Dasein*," where emotion must be understood as *e-movere* or a moving outward. The zero degree of phenomenalization—that is, of a *speculative*, genetic self-phenomenalization—is an absolute mood, prior to any understanding and accompanying both the *stasis* that surrounds birth and the process by which difference emerges from sameness, without becoming alienated from it. It is not hard to see why readers like Slavoj Žižek find in Schelling a precursor to the psychoanalytic drives-unconscious, much less why Deleuze illustrates his concept of minimal difference, i.e. "contrariety," using Schelling's example of lightning that stretches

[12]Compare Deleuze 1994: 28–31. Deleuze recalls a scale of differences the minimal conceivable being "contrariety"—as in contrariety in the species or the genre. Here, difference is not the difference called "opposition," it "alone expresses the capacity of a subject to bear opposites while remaining substantially the same (in matter or in genus)." He concludes, in a Schellingian tone, "Thought 'makes' difference, but difference is monstrous. We should not be surprised that difference should appear accursed...There is no sin other than raising the ground and dissolving the form" (29).

[13]Schelling 1980 is the source of the modification. The Grimm Brothers dictionary provides the following examples of the use of *Ebenbild*, all of them Neo-testamentary: (*Christus*) ist das Ebenbilde Gottes" 2 Corinthians 4:4. "Welcher ist das Ebenbilde des unsichtbaren Gottes. Colossians 1:15.

outward from the dark ground that accompanies it without engulfing it.[14] These are Schelling's thematic debts to Aristotle and above all to Spinoza. As he says of God's first contraction:

> This image is the first in which God, viewed absolutely, is realized, though only in Himself... This image [or re-presentation, a return at a different level] is at the same time understanding—the Word, the "logos" of this desire, and the eternal spirit that feels in itself the word and at the same time ... infinite desire. (NHF: 36)

Schelling can call this 'precipitate' or concrescence "understanding" for the simple reason that it corresponds to a primitive *Vor-stellung*, which is emotion and sense, *not* an idea; comparable to an intensification of the initial *Sehnsucht.* At this level, *Vorstellung* and passion correspond like passivity and activity, as something crystallizes out of its own ground yet is different from that ground insofar as virtuality precedes and produces actuality, although not in a singular "time." Nothing external is superadded and there is no higher temporal framework. As flow and counter-flow, this is the structure of representation or *Vorstellung*, the *inadæquatio* that contracts into a temporary *adæquatio*, or the excess whose concentrations mirror it to itself. If we are inclined to say that Schelling is naïvely projecting the model of thought onto something he has called the Absolute, we need not long await his reply. For we must begin with something that is "neither a subjective nor an objective Idea" (IPN: 46), above all not the production of scholastic casuistry.

Schelling will argue cogently that there is no way to objectify subjective universality or subjectivist formalism, other than by a further (human) insight that redoubles and limits the initial subjectivism. The problem is not solved by enlisting a community of external observers and Schelling is not pleading for the objectivity of his system. He is urging that we approach thinking as the spontaneous ordering of differentiated miasmas, which do not persist in *stasis* and should never be limited to *human* subjectivity. We would do much better to see, in the work of understanding, complex combinations and oppositions that are also found in natural processes. Because the hypothetical paradigm of natural processes will be called the Absolute, Schelling will argue that here we have the possibility of approaching being and becoming *before* they are conceptually, or even ontologically, separated. At the level of phenomenality, whereby we imagine this process, a conception of time, qua

[14]Deleuze 1994: 31. "Indifference has two aspects: the undifferentiated abyss, the black nothingness, the indeterminate animal...but also the white nothingness, the once more calm surface upon which float unconnected determinations like *membra disjecta*....Is difference intermediate between these two extremes? Or is it not rather the only extreme....[I]nstead of something distinguished from something else, imagine something which distinguishes itself—and yet that from which it distinguishes itself does not distinguish itself from it. Lightning, for example, distinguishes itself from the black sky but must also train it behind....*It is as if the ground rose to the surface, without ceasing to be the ground*," (28). The example comes out of Schelling. And Deleuze would add: "The most important aspect of Schelling's philosophy is his consideration of powers...*it is Schelling who brings difference out of the night of the Identical*, and with finer...more terrifying flashes of lightning than those of contradiction: with *progressivity...not from a negative or a non-being* (*ouk on*) but from a problematic being" (190–191). This recapitulates Schelling's thinking of the gestating oppositional yet undifferentiated Absolute.

accompanying-duration or succession, cannot be avoided and therefore the unity seems more dynamic than static. Yet in Schelling, it is really as if the phenomenal level existed together with its own possibility—which is the case with life, as well. Unity is never completely dissolved, "but ... because ... Nature and the ideal world each contains a point of absoluteness, where both opposites flow together, each must again, if it is to be distinguished as the *particular* unity, contain the three unities distinguishably in itself ... we call them potencies" (IPN: 49). The three unities in question are: being as production and dynamism, the dissolving of dynamism into static form, and those states of affairs where the first two exist conjoined in indifference.

To return, now, to the *Philosophical Inquiries*, if we take what Schelling calls "understanding"—that first metaphoric fold of desire—whereby the Absolute mirrors itself, or stands as if facing itself, we can also trace this "understanding" in nature. What follows is a structuralist account of this so-called understanding.

> The first effect of understanding in nature is the fission of forces, which is the only way in which understanding can unfold and develop the unity which was held in it unconsciously, like a seed, and yet, necessarily. Just as in humans there comes to light, when in the dark longing to create something, thoughts separate out of the chaotic confusion of thinking, in which all were connected but each one prevents the other from coming forth—so the unity appears which contains all within it and which had lain hidden in the depths. Or it is as in the case of the plant which escapes the dark fetters of gravity only as it unfolds and spreads its powers, developing its hidden unity as its substance becomes differentiated. For since this Being (*Wesen*) of primal nature is nothing else than the eternal basis of God, it must contain within itself, locked away, God's essence, as a light of life ... but longing or desire, roused now by the understanding, strives to preserve this light of life ... within [the base], and to close up in itself so that they always remain [together in the] ground. (NHF: 36)

Sehnsucht, or the anguished yearning intrinsic to virtuality, carries a disturbing, dual movement. As a symptom and as the medium of the trembling of birth out of itself, *Sehnsucht* characterizes a temporary *stasis* that is both absolute, simple, and becoming-relative as two. Unity must unfold itself in order ultimately to return to itself with internal differentiations. In the "dark longing to create something," separation occurs as a leap; however, the intensification of unity that produces two entities is not sublimation. The ground, being itself alive, exerts a force on the new entity, whether this is light, a plant, or a complex body. In the speculative recapitulation of the emergence of God out of itself, the base can be seen as the very being of all that will unfold from it. As such, impelling yet resisting the intensification through which it becomes two, the base protects itself by "striving to preserve this light of life within it." And the erstwhile student of Schelling, Kierkegaard, will extend this to human *angst* and speak of "in-closing reserve." He too distinguishes between an objective and a subjective anxiety, although his project turns from Schelling's speculative physics explaining positive evil to a psychology that justifies Christian theology's approach to evil as "sin."[15]

---

[15]When Kierkegaard adapts *Sehnsucht* to his perspective, he will distinguish between a subjective anxiety and anxiety in nature. Objective anxiety is the finitude and incompleteness of nature itself, the chasm. See Kierkegaard 1983: 61.

> Anxiety may be compared with dizziness. He whose eye happens to look down into the yawning abyss becomes dizzy. But what is the reason for this? It is just as much in his own eye as in the abyss, for suppose he had not looked down. (COA: 61)

Kierkegaard deliberately inflects Schelling, recoiling from what he conceives as Schelling's "vigorous and full-blooded anthropomorphism" (COA: 59n). Above all, Kierkegaard focuses on anxiety as preceding the creative leap, which in humans is freedom enacted and in nature points to the struggle to self-transform.

> Schelling's main thought is that anxiety ... characterizes especially the suffering of the deity in his endeavor to create.... The mistake, however, is a different one...Here is an example of how strange everything becomes when metaphysics and dogmatics are distorted by treating dogmatics metaphysically and metaphysics dogmatically. (COA: 59n)

For Kierkegaard, the interest of Schelling's work lies in its conceiving the ways in which evil can be positive—thus something more than mere privation. Nevertheless, Schelling failed to consider the way in which evil passes into *human* history and into the psychology of cultures themselves ("the history of the race") as a growing *gravitas*, to be understood as anxious melancholia *and* as a capacity for spiritual discernment.

> [A]nxiety is of all things the most selfish, and no concrete expression of freedom is as selfish as the possibility of every concretion. This again is the overwhelming factor that determines the ... ambiguous relation [to anxiety as] sympathetic and antipathetic. In anxiety, there is the selfish infinity of possibility, which...ensnaringly disquiets. (COA: 61)

What occurs in Schelling's God or Absolute life, plays itself out at the psychological level for Kierkegaard, where it is precursive to any spiritual awakening. Schelling might well have accepted such a variation in perspective, though his ends—and his approach to belief—remain more formal and idealist.

Nevertheless, because Schelling too works perspectivally, anxious longing shows us that the Absolute is invariably but never dialectically two-in-one. And what goes for vegetal life is also the case for human existence. We speak of entities as unities containing plurality because, in their respective existence, their inner multiplicity holds together. For Schelling, the ultimate sign of the simultaneous presence of unity through the diversity of natural and spiritual history will be illustrated by what looks like a final unification; final because indemonstrable and non-chronological. Unity, whose pluralist aspects express themselves in nature and in humans, must be viewed as 'holding', sometimes even in-closing, as in Kierkegaard's psychological inclosing reserve (COA: 123–135). In the Absolute, the dynamism of unity is both force and "love," by which Schelling refers to something not unlike Freud's *Eros*, which draws together: "for there is love neither in indifference nor where antitheses are combined, which require the combination in order to be; but rather ... this is the secret of love, that it unites such beings as could each exist in itself and nonetheless neither is nor can be without the other" (NHF: 89). This is why we must consider absolute unity according to two perspectives, while understanding that the two original forces are in a sense one. At the end of their cosmological pluralization—following the trials of positive evil and freedom in the world—we can imagine either a return to the state in which "neither is nor can be without the other" or acknowledge that this unity is present throughout the ages of the cosmos, as virtuality.

The dualist and monist perspectives are co-present and co-necessary. They can hardly be envisioned at the same time, however. For human understanding, the explication of the duality makes possible a final approach to its fundamental unity, which is not a Hegelian *telos* to be attained.[16] Moreover, there is a processual quality already in the initial fission because, without the emergence of the first intensification, Schelling's "the One," emerging out of itself, out of the base, there could be no further development and therefore no way in which to see the unifying efficacy of *Eros*. The unity is invariably there, virtual; love does not come from the outside to reconcile the anxious dualisms spread across natural or cultural history. Love and desire are aspects of the same dynamism, although their relation to each other, as emotions, or moving powers, is unclear. Schelling suggests that we consider this through the example of meaning, produced by actual words: morphemes constitute phonemes thanks to voiced and non-voiced components guided by intrinsic invisible rules; substantives take on attributes, and verbs are adjoined thanks to higher levels of combinatorial rules. Sounding again like Deleuze to post-modern ears, Schelling refers to vowels as light elements and consonants as dark ones, against which what is voiced stands forth.

These are all approaches to the same fundamental question: How to conceive the co-originarity of the simplest meaning and life, in and for themselves? Schelling no doubt represents the ultimate idealist attempt to think life without falling into vitalism *or* mechanistic physics. He opposed the physicalist reductions of his age (like Franz Joseph Gall's work on the origin of the nervous system in 1809),[17] just as he opposed grounding "rational philosophy by means of [mere] physiology." The whole subsequent school of thought, inspired by Schelling, urged that "in the universe there was no absolute distinction between the material and the spiritual: mind was immanent in all matter and particular natural objects could be regarded as thinking beings" (NCO: 272, 82).

Following a logical strategy as ancient as Philo's pre-Plotinian emanations, Schelling argued that out of the intensification, which breaks free from and concentrates the base into the one, there also emerges meaning. He called meaning "*das Wort*." It denoted the productiveness of what Schelling characterized as the divine fold or mirroring "understanding." This will ultimately be the model of human reason. Yet the ground is also differently productive. From it arises what we call "matter" in the world. In nature, matter and form, inertia and dynamism coexist with a stability that resembles the indifference of the principles in the divine *Grund*. Therefore, nothing in nature ever enduringly disrupts the order of its cycles of becoming. If the divine Word phenomenalizes naturally as light—a light that breaks free of that attractive, basal force devoid of illumination, i.e. gravity— meaning in the human

[16]Hegel is speaking, in 1807, of the *phenomenalization* of spirit in history, not of the a-chronic logic that presides over the process: "Spirit externalized and emptied into Time…This way of becoming presents a slow procession and succession of spiritual shapes (*Geistern*), a gallery of pictures, each of which is endowed with the entire wealth of Spirit, and moves so slowly just for the reason that the self has to…assimilate all this wealth of substance," in Hegel 1967: 807.

[17]See Clarke and Jacyna 1987: 274–280. Gall's most important contribution was a monist conception of mind.

being is an illumination of a different sort. Predictably, the dualism of principles is united in humanity as well, but understanding does not always coexist well with the drive-ground that Schelling calls *ipseity*, or self-will when speaking of humans. It happens that self-will enters into conflict with understanding or the light principle, or spirit; in this case the natural relationship of the two principles gets reversed, and a hypertrophy of drives results.

> Man's will may be regarded as a nexus of living forces; as long as it abides in its unity with the universal will [Love], these forces remain in their divine measure and balance. But hardly does self-will move from the center which is its station, than the nexus of forces is also dissolved; in its place a merely particular will rules which can no longer unite the forces among themselves … but must therefore strive to form or compose a … peculiar life out of the now separate forces, an insurgent host of desires and passions. (NHF: 41)

This is Schelling's account, both of the positivity of evil and the necessary resistance opposed by self-will to human freedom; no force being what it is, virtually, unless it can act against a limiting counter-force. The positive account of the origin of evil and the effectivity of freedom is aligned with Schelling's major *élan* which extends out of his "identity philosophy," first formulated in the 1800s, and into his philosophy of nature as a concern that ultimately guided his whole philosophical endeavor. The positive account of evil is faithful to his early conception of intellectual intuition, or the tension he maintained between a pre-conscious and a conscious activity, out of which creation arises spontaneously and unfolds humans' mental powers. In regard to nature, Schelling kept a similar, structural transcendentalism, distinguishing between empirical nature and its deeper conditions of possibility. Consequently, he was able to develop the outlines of a chemistry and physics of finite forces that were not reducible to mechanical necessity or to an anti-mechanistic vitalism. Each level of his thought mirrors the other by placing emphasis on grounds, consisting of degrees of inertia and activity. The higher-level intensities explain the effectivity or "mind," which works like a genetics of life and reason. This becomes particularly important insofar as what we call evil is often the result of a positive choice, of enthusiasm, even intense pleasure. The drive of the pre-conscious center to extend itself throughout the periphery, usurping the place of reason, is Schelling's conception of a recurrent tendency in human beings, whose outcome is not determinable in advance, though it explains the embrace of cruelty. This does not, however, define the essence of a human being. For Schelling, we are simply our acts. The motor of our choices are passions. These are not intrinsically evil; rather they express the drives. In privileging our narcissism, whose attractive force functions like the gravity that dogs the emergence of light, we give weight to what Schelling called a "false imagination" of outcomes. At the drive level, a collection of impulses is thus privileged, which comes simultaneously to resemble profound anxiety and one dimension of Plato's *Eros*: "The general possibility of evil … consists in the fact that, instead of keeping his selfhood as the basis or the instrument, man can strive to elevate it to be the ruling and universal will, and, on the contrary, try to make what is spiritual in him into a means" (NHF: 68). With this, the balance of forces in us becomes skewed and incomprehensible.

> [If] the two principles are at strife, then another spirit occupies the place where God should be. This, namely, is the reverse of God, a being which was roused to actualization by God's revelation but which can never attain to actuality ... which indeed never exists ... and which, like the 'matter' of the ancients, can ... never be grasped as real by ... reason but only by false imagination. (NHF: 68)

False imagination thus realizes, in an image or an aspiration, a *stasis*, an uncanny fullness and a sort of rest, resulting from sur-potency. We might speak here, in Freudian terms, of the duality of drives coming apart, and of the base drives pursuing their course alone. It remains that the imbalance is a passage from being into a kind of non-being, and its enactment is *de facto* evil. "There springs the hunger of selfishness, which, in the measure that it deserts ... unity becomes ever needier and poorer; but just on that account, more ravenous, hungrier, more poisonous. In evil there is that contradiction which devours and always negates itself, which just while striving to become creature destroys the nexus of creation and ... falls into non-being" (NHF: 69).

An intuitive representation of these movements—or disruptions—is given to us as *mood*. Moreover, it is mood that remains with us, semi-consciously, in the perverse fullness of the expanded drives-base. It is mood that indicates that psychic harmony has been broken, just as a mood precedes creation. "True freedom is in accord with a holy necessity of a sort which we feel in essential knowledge, when heart and spirit, bound only by their own law, freely affirm that which is necessary" (NHF: 70). Schelling's "necessity" is one that unfolds; one that moves through time at the empirical level. However, for love to triumph, the inertial and the intensified principles, body and mind, drives and rationality, must remain together and balanced in their difference. It is precisely this that Kierkegaard will glean from Schelling.[18]

> The synthesis of psychical and the physical [must] be posited by spirit; but spirit is eternal and the synthesis is, therefore, only when spirit posits the first synthesis along with the second synthesis of the temporal and the eternal.... Just as ... the spirit ... when it is about to posit the synthesis as the spirit's (freedom's) possibility in the individuality, expresses itself as anxiety, so here the future in turn is the eternal's (freedom's) possibility in the individuality expressed as anxiety. As freedom's possibility manifests itself for freedom [in a decisive act], freedom succumbs, and temporality emerges in the same way as sensuousness in its significance as sinfulness [in persons and over time]. (COA: 91)

Kierkegaard's aforementioned concern to connect the individual and the human race—while insisting upon each person's freedom to leap freely into action—obliges him to work out various dialectics between individuals and groups ("the race"). In this way, anxiety denotes the possibility of freedom, and anxiety expresses the weight of *phylogenetic* sin or evil. The Kierkegaardian dialectics depend on the preservation of unity between body and mind: spirit. Desire, affect and reason are for him the work of spirit as an evolving, moral self-consciousness. Thus Kierkegaard's

---

[18] See also Schelling 1986: 96: "The nexus of our personality is the spirit."

"spirit" reproduces Schelling's "love," at a level where history and psychology unite in single individuals. For his part, Schelling always remained closer to the structural conditions of possibility of freedom, a choice resulting from his enduring engagement with post-Kantian idealism.

In fact, Schelling inherits significant aspects of Kant's conception of evil, as seen in the latter's essay "Religion in the Bounds of Mere Reason." For Kant, radical evil was more structural than positive, in the sense that we are never able consistently to determine our will according to a maxim in harmony with the Categorical Imperative. Kant nevertheless refrained from determining *why* we are unable to hold fast to our practical maxims. He acknowledged that "the ultimate ground of the adoption of our maxims, which must itself lie in free choice, cannot be a fact revealed in experience, [and therefore] the good or evil in man … is … posited as the ground *antecedent to every use of freedom in experience*."[19] This innate ground was as far as human understanding was permitted to go in tracing the origin of evil. Indeed, Kant's transcendental empiricism explains why Schelling first developed his philosophy of identity, which first focused not on evil but on the pure, spontaneous upwelling of *creative* thought or intellectual intuition. Schelling's original point of departure held consciousness and pre-consciousness, activity and passivity, in correlation, and in a state of indifference. As the condition of possibility of intellectual intuition, it is redolent of the spontaneity psychoanalysis, notably Lacanian, pinpoints, "Ça parle tout seul." Something *means* by itself, spontaneously. Something unfolds, limiting itself and its world, in what is called, at the empirical level, the "discovery of the not-I" or exteriority. I cannot explore Schelling's identity philosophy in depth, here. It is crucial to note however that, rather than dismissing affect and passion as proper merely to a pragmatic anthropology or a reflection on everyday psychological states (Kant's position), Schelling employed a speculative philosophy to explore the indeterminacy that preceded self-differentiation and autonomy in all life forms.

In the place of Hegel's "work of the negative," Schelling, and Kierkegaard after him, placed a passion: restless desire for the one, anxiety and earnestness for the other (COA: 15). Only an affect that was *both* passive and active could precede founding distinctions between necessity and freedom. The affect had a specific relationship to human motivation and acts, whether for good or for evil. If freedom could be evinced as real for humans, thanks to the possibility of positive evil, the unfolding of evil had to be tied to a drives conflict, whose corollary was, in turn, an indeterminate passion.

> For it is not the passions that are in themselves evil, nor are we battling merely with flesh and blood, but with an evil … which attaches to us by our own act, [and] does so from birth … and it is noteworthy that Kant, who did not in theory rise to a transcendental act determining all human being, was lead in later investigations, by sheer … observation of the phenomena of moral judgment, to the recognition of a subjective basis of human conduct … which preceded every act within the range of the senses. (NHF: 66–7)

Schelling's project requires that this subjective basis be structural rather than corporeal or psychological—much the way early psychiatry and psychoanalysis had

[19] Immanuel Kant 1960: 17, emphasis added.

to point to inherited predispositions to ground their etiology of psychic disorders attached to circumstantial trauma. I will not decide, here, whether Schelling's *Philosophical Inquiries* are a treatise of theology or a new transcendental exploration of the perversions of the drives-core in humans and its relationship to freedom. For Schelling, human freedom is best illustrated starting from the origin of the Absolute, whether that is God or life, or both at once. As the end of the essay makes clear, the best *revelation* of the structure of the Absolute, with its base of forces existing in tension and fundamental indifference to each other, is indeed nature. The unfolding of God is thus the unfolding of empirical natural being and its condition of possibility. The contraction of the divine base explains how an entity that is simultaneously natural and cosmological, immanent and transcendent (as love), is possible. Humans thus arise, in and like nature, from and with God. However, humans' emergence comes from the aspect of the Absolute which has already undergone a fundamental precipitating change with the emergence of the One and the Word that is active signification. We should pause here and observe that, in order to explain evil as a reality, and as pleasure and enthusiasm, Schelling declares:

> It would require nothing less than … a … thoroughly developed philosophy to prove that there are only two ways of explaining evil—the dualistic, according to which there is assumed to be an *evil basic being* … alongside the good; and the Kabbalistic, according to which [positive] evil is explained by emanation and withdrawal…. Every other system must annul the difference between good and evil. (NHF: 93)

If we are to understand the importance of mood in nineteenth century post-Kantian philosophy, we should note that moods arise at the point where dialectics proves too formalist, thereby threatening immanent self-development or life. Mood arises with the difficulty of justifying freedom and evil in a system where practical and pure reason stand divided. Schelling attempted to read life into Hegel's dialectic of history through Spinozism. He had recourse to kabbalistic imagery as he attempted to surpass Kant's antinomies of freedom and necessity, practical postulates *versus* pure impossibilities (God, the soul, freedom). Schelling knew that "a transcendental act determining all human being (*alle menschliches Sein*) could only be realized intuitively through images. At the heart of this work, then, we "perceive" a base inhabited by the strange movement called *Sehnsucht*, which seeks to denote unrest without concepts. If longing seems closer to desire than to anxiety, we might note the futility of proposing a single noun to characterize a *motion* that engenders but "goes" nowhere. What arises out of the base *is* the base precipitated, just as understanding concentrates indeterminate experiences into concepts. For Schelling, something comparable occurs in nature, and it is fair to regard the sprout as belonging to its seed, light as belonging to gravity as well as resisting it. These images present the unfolding of what does not express itself directly in the seed or the gravitational field.

Between 1841 and 1842, Kierkegaard was impassioned by Schelling's lectures on the philosophy of mythology. By 1844, when he published *The Concept of Anxiety*, he was convinced that Schelling's fidelity to idealist logic meant that he would theorize life without ever reaching existence. Thus, Kierkegaard—and Heidegger after him—would take up anxiety as the true opposite of necessity, the corporeal precursor of freedom, and the sign of power—that concomitant excitation and exhaustion that accompanies our striving to create.

Within the framework of the meaning of moods for philosophy, the concept of *Sehnsucht*, which in Schelling occasionally slides into *Angst*,[20] is both anthropomorphism and an attempt to show something fundamental. From a dynamic perspective, which attempts to get past the fixity of idealist formalism, *there is no simple origin of life*, much less of freedom and consciousness. By extension, there is no pure foundation, even of God. Life is characterized by the curiosity of arising in and of itself, without remaining recognizably what it first was, and without being able to endure eternally in a developed form. When God is thought on the basis of life, as Schelling does, God becomes finite—from one perspective. However, even if a species of life proves to be finite, something about the organization called "life" is not similarly limited by mortality. For Schelling, the duality of finitude and infinity had to be thought metaphysically, as genesis and reconciliation. This characterized German-language post-Kantian thought after him, from Schopenhauer to Nietzsche—at least in the concept-experience of "Eternal Recurrence." Hence Schelling urges, late in the treatise, that this God of two principles is also one. Grasping this primordial unity means thinking the anti-ground, which borders on absurdity.[21] We may imagine this through a change in perspective, which required the entire foregoing analysis of cosmos and nature. Love, naming the "neither-nor" logic of divinity as two *and* one, is related to the *Sehnsucht* that characterized divine duality-in-indifference. A mood thus names the impossible "movement," which we know only because we *feel* it at the human level. Vigorously anthropomorphic, as Kierkegaard would say, *Sehnsucht* registers affectively the two ambiguous potencies in relation. The core of Schelling's philosophy, like that of Cohen, Rosenzweig, and Levinas after him, turns on the ways that fundamental relationality passes through modes and moods. If the origin lies in the indifference and indistinctness of the base, the base nevertheless contains forces in relation. Before their relation evolves into a generative tension, it is dynamic coexistence.

The same is true of the embodied human being. How could we know such a thing? We can observe those who derive positive pleasure from evil; we may also

[20] In Sect. I, Part 7, Schelling writes of human striving: "Die Angst des Lebens selbst treibt den Menschen aus dem Zentrum, in das er erschaffen worden; *denn dieses als das lauterste Wesen alles Willens ist für jeden besondern Willen verzehrendes Feuer; um in ihm leben zu können, muss der Mensch aller Eigenheit absterben*." Thus anxiety drives life as the conscious cognate of instincts, but it must be surpassed, because nothing in creation can remain ambiguous. This Schelling argues about the evolution of the ground. Kierkegaard picks it up in a logic of the either/or. Schelling 1986.

[21] Schelling 1986: 86–87. "Here at last we reach the highest point of the whole inquiry….What is to be gained by that initial distinction between being insofar as it is basis, and being insofar as it exists? For either there is no common ground for the two…absolute dualism; or there is such common ground—and in that case…the two coincide again… *there must be a being before all basis and before all existence*…before any duality; how can we designate it except as…the 'groundless' [*Ungrund*]?"

observe creative spontaneity—the sign of Schelling's freedom. The artist reveals at least that much to us. In nature, the dual principles never separate. They remain in a relationship of equilibrium. In humans, the mood of anxiety shifts our focus onto the relation between our own drives-base, and the understanding, which can either move past the inclinations of the drives or raise them into prominence. As Heidegger realized, using different language, Schelling's *Sehnsucht* points us precisely toward the question that we *are* and, beyond this, to the one that asks, Why is there is being instead of simply nothing? Schelling, however, preferred to ask, 'Why is there life instead of nothing?' As historians of philosophy, we might observe, here, that idealism moved toward vitalism and gnosticism as Kant's successors strove to simplify or amend his system. This motivates a more contemporary question as well: Toward what will the grand "idealism" of the twentieth century, phenomenology, move?

References

Clarke, Edwin, and L.S. Jacyna. 1987. *Nineteenth-Century Origins of Neuroscientific Concepts.* Berkeley: University of California Press.

Deleuze, Gilles. 1994. *Difference and Repetition.* Trans. Paul Patton. New York: Columbia University Press.

Grimm, Jakob, and Wilhelm. 1854–1960. *Deutsches Wörterbuch von Jakob und Wilhelm Grimm.* Leipzig: Hirzel. Universität Trier for the online edition. On-line: http://germazope.uni-trier.de/Projects/DWB

Hegel, G.W.F. 1967. *Phenomenology of Mind.* Trans. J.B. Baillie. New York: Harper and Row.

Kant, Immanuel. 1960. *Religion Within the Limits of Reason Alone.* Trans. Theodore Greene. New York: Harper and Brothers.

Kierkegaard, Søren. 1983. *Fear and Trembling/Repetition.* Trans. Howard Hong and Edna Hong. Princeton: Princeton University Press.

Marx, Werner. 1984. *The Philosophy of F. W. J. Schelling.* Trans. Thomas Nenon. Bloomington: Indiana University Press.

Nietzsche, Friedrich. 1966. *Beyond Good and Evil: Prelude to a Philosophy of the Future.* Trans. Walter Kaufmann. New York: Vintage Books.

Nietzsche, Friedrich. 1967–1988. *Kritische Studienausgabe*, vol. 3. ed. Giorgio Colli and Mazzino Montinari. Berlin: Walter de Gruyter.

Schelling, F.W.J. 1980. *Oeuvres métaphysiques (1805–1821).* Trans. Jean-François Courtine and Emmanuel Martineau. Paris: Gallimard-NRF.

Schelling, F.W.J. 1985. *Friedrich Wilhelm Joseph von Schelling, Ausgewählte Schriften*, 6 vols. ed. Manfred Frank. Frankfurt: Suhrkamp.

Schelling, F.W.J. 1986. *Philosophical Inquiries into the Nature of Human Freedom.* Trans. James Gutmann. LaSalle: Open Court Publishing (First published 1936).

Schelling, F.W.J. 1988. *Ideas for a Philosophy of Nature.* Trans. Errol Harris, Peter Heath, and Robert Stern. Cambridge: Cambridge University Press.

Attunement and Disorientation: The Moods of Philosophy in Heidegger and Sartre

Stephen Mulhall

On the early Heidegger's understanding of the ontological significance of moods, any proper philosophical grasp of their nature is inseparable from the realization that a proper philosophical grasp of the nature of anything will inevitably be itself subject to or informed by specific moods. For according to the existential analytic developed in *Being and Time*,[1] Dasein is thrown projection – a being whose existence is a matter of realizing one amongst the range of existential possibilities available to it in its present situation, a situation for which it is necessarily not itself entirely responsible. Heidegger explicitly associates the projective dimension of Dasein's existence with understanding: for to choose to realize a particular possibility necessarily involves understanding it and its alternatives in their relation to the situation in which they are confronted, and so also involves an implicit understanding of the particular Dasein who is confronting them. In this sense, every projection reveals an implicit commitment to a particular comprehending grasp of self and world, of our being-in-the-world – it is, as Heidegger would say, essentially discursive.

But Dasein's thrownness is no less internally related to comprehension, and so to the structures of discourse; or to put it another way, human discursive understanding is as much a matter of thrownness as it is one of projection. For the primary ontic trace of Dasein's ontological thrownness (the existentiell register of our ontological *Befindlichkeit*) is, according to Heidegger, our vulnerability to moods. His term for these affective inflections of our worldliness is *Stimmung* – literally, attunement. We always find ourselves already suffering a certain mode of receptivity to the world, in a situation at once determined by and determining a sense of the world as mattering to us in a certain way – as fearful, boring, hateful or cheering. And for Heidegger,

[1] Heidegger (1962), hereafter BT, followed by page number.

S. Mulhall (✉)
New College, Oxford, UK
e-mail: stephen.mulhall@new.ox.ac.uk

H. Kenaan and I. Ferber (eds.), *Philosophy's Moods: The Affective Grounds of Thinking*, Contributions To Phenomenology 63, DOI 10.1007/978-94-007-1503-5_9,

such moods are not purely subjective distortions of an inherently meaningless world, but rather ways of revealing something about that world that would otherwise be missed – genuinely cognitive achievements.

Take fear. This mood is a subjective state, and its focus or internal object is the well-being of the person undergoing it; but it is also a response to something in the world – it has an external as well as an internal object – and it can be evaluated as appropriate or inappropriate to that object. Someone who fails to feel fear in the face of a rabid dog is missing something important about the dog – something that makes it genuinely fearsome; whereas someone who fears house-spiders is either lacking critical knowledge about the nature of house-spiders or ought to take steps to recalibrate her responses to them. The fact that a proper explanation of the dog's fearsomeness will inevitably make reference to human subjects and their physiological vulnerabilities to certain viruses does not make it any less the case that rabid dogs possess the power to harm human beings; their possession of that power is as much a matter of fact about them as their possession of teeth and a tail.

For Heidegger, then, thrownness and projection are internally related structures of Dasein's modes of being. Any concrete projection of Dasein's is always from a situation into which it is thrown, and every situation into which it is thrown is one from which a projection is required of it. Hence, the comprehending grasp implicit in any such projection is itself conditioned or inflected by the particular mood in which the projecting Dasein is situated, by the particular mode of attunement to its world that partly constitutes that situation. And if this is true of Dasein in general, then it must be true of Dasein insofar as it engages in philosophizing: insofar as Dasein projects itself into the existential possibility of philosophical investigation, and so attempts to render concrete some specific comprehending grasp of the phenomena under investigation as well as of the one investigating those phenomena, it must always do so out of some particular mode of attunement to its world. Accordingly, if Heidegger's existential analytic of Dasein as living out a discursive understanding that is always both thrown and projecting is correct, it follows that any philosophical understanding of phenomena must always be similarly conditioned. If we are properly to understand that understanding, therefore, we must ask ourselves not only what comprehension of the world it articulates, but also what affective inflection of the world's significance it embodies. Iris Murdoch once suggested that it was always illuminating to ask, of any given philosopher, what he or she was afraid of; Heidegger's analysis suggests that some particular mood (if not fear, then some other mode of attunement) will always lie at the heart of any philosopher's attempts to grasp beings in their Being, and so should always lie at the heart of any critical evaluation of those attempts.

Moreover, if this point applies to philosophers in general, it must also have a specific, reflexive application. In other words, it is not so much advisable as essential, in any attempt to understand the philosophical significance of Heidegger's writing, to identify its mood. Indeed, if a comprehending grasp of the mood of *Being and Time* were not internal to a properly critical evaluation of it, then that text would amount to a concrete falsification of the existential analytic it contains – its form would invalidate its philosophical substance. What, then, is *Being and Time*'s mode of attunement?

I. Anxiety

The pivotal example of a mood in *Being and Time* is Angst. It is introduced towards the end of Division One to perform a twofold function: it is the means whereby any Dasein mired in 'das man' might free itself for the possibility of realizing its mineness, and it is also the means whereby the analytically distinguished elements of Heidegger's analysis of Dasein as Being-in-the-world might be re-combined or re-membered in such a way as to reveal the underlying articulated totality of the care-structure. Just as undergoing angst gives an individual Dasein the ontic opportunity to overcome its dispersion into inauthenticity, so the phenomenological investigation of angst gives Heidegger the opportunity to overcome the necessary initial disarticulation of his existential analysis of Dasein.

It is the objectlessness of angst that allows it to perform both functions simultaneously. For whereas fear is responsive to (a specific aspect of) a specific entity or situation in the world, angst in this respect lacks an object. The distinctive oppressiveness of angst originates in this fact about it, because its lack of a specific object deprives those undergoing it of any specific way of responding to it (and thereby making it manageable). If we are afraid of our final university examinations or of an approaching job interview, there are particular courses of action that might legitimately diminish our fears, but if we feel anxious about them in Heidegger's sense, those courses of action will ultimately fail to engage with whatever it is about the examination or the interview to which we are responding. If, for example, we are anxious as opposed to afraid about the examination, that is because – beyond the specific difficulties inherent in doing well in such examinations – it recalls us to the fact that they herald the rest of our life; they reveal our lives as something for which we must ultimately take responsibility (or fail to), and so reveal our recent lives, lived out unquestioningly within the expectations of the university and our fellow-students, as having amounted to a way of avoiding that responsibility. As Heidegger puts it, the inherently non-specific object of angst is Being-in-the-world as such: being-in-the-world is that about which we are anxious, and that in the face of which we are anxious.

There is thus inherently something more or other to us than the present, particular worldly situation in which we find ourselves, with its particular array of entities and possibilities; for beyond every specific situation that makes up our existence is the ontological reality of our situatedness – our Being as thrown projection, as inherently finite or conditioned freedom. And, shifting from the message to the medium, what this reveals about Division One of *Being and Time* is that, beyond the particularities of Heidegger's necessarily sequential analysis of worldliness, Being-oneself, Being-with, and Being-in, there lies the ontological unity of Being-in-the-world understood as care. As existing individuals, we must relate to each situation we encounter in the light of our situatedness if we are to relate authentically to our own existence; and as individual readers of Division One, we must relate to each chapter in the light of the articulated textual whole it constitutes. Being-in-the-world is the background condition of our existence, and hence of any authentic existentiell projection; so it must also be the background condition of any attempt to exist authentically as readers of *Being and Time*, and the author of that text has done what he can to acknowledge that reflexivity in his composition of it.

But just as fear of an examination can occasion an anxiety that exceeds its specific situation, so the textual function of angst exceeds its apparent limits in *Being and Time*. For no sooner has it served its exemplary purpose of allowing us to sight through the specific analyses that make up that Division in order to grasp the whole that they make up than it recurs, unpredictably but decisively, and in both textual directions (as it were) – back into Division One and forward into Division Two. In so doing, it illuminates both the philosophical mood specific to Heideggerian phenomenology at this stage of its development (going forward), and the moods that Heidegger takes to be characteristic of specifically modern philosophy and then of philosophy as such (going back). I shall approach these ramifications, in authentic Heideggerian style, by going forward in order to go back.

The critical role of angst in Division Two of *Being and Time* of course includes its continuing significance in Heidegger's characterization of a genuinely authentic mode of human existence – as anxious, resolute anticipation. But given the reflexive point made earlier, one should then expect anxiety to have a constitutive role in authentic philosophizing, and so in Heidegger's conception of what an authentic phenomenological approach demands of him. And such is the case: but the precise way in which angst pervades Heidegger's composition of *Being and Time* turns out to have surprising implications.

Heidegger begins Division Two of *Being and Time* by, in effect, expressing a certain anxiety about the completeness of the analysis of Division One. Most obviously, it has omitted any detailed ontological analysis of authenticity (as opposed to the inauthenticity of das man); but more importantly, one element of the care-structure itself implies a certain lack or inadequacy in its own articulation. For the projective dimension of care – Dasein's Being-ahead-of-itself – suggests that, insofar as Dasein is always necessarily oriented towards the future and so towards that which is not (yet), it is always essentially incomplete; and yet it does come to an end, and so in a sense completes itself, insofar as Dasein necessarily dies. The difficulty is that death is not an event in life, not even the last. And what makes Heidegger anxious is that this suggests, first, that no Dasein can comprehend its own existence as a whole, and second, that his phenomenological attempt to comprehend the ontological structure of Dasein is similarly doomed, since the phenomenological method necessarily analyzes phenomena (whatever discloses itself to Dasein as it is in itself) and death appears in this respect not to be a phenomenon. The opening of Division Two thereby suggests that there is something beyond the articulated unity of the care-structure without which Heidegger's existential analytic of Dasein would remain inadequate, but which cannot itself be regarded as a specific, overlooked element of that structure. What mood other than angst, with its distinctive objectlessness, its inherent impulse to exceed specificity, would be the appropriate mode of attunement to such a threat?

In Division One, Heidegger defines the inherently non-specific object of angst as 'nothing and nowhere' (BT: 231). It would be no exaggeration to say that this is a perfectly precise specification of the object of the analysis throughout Division Two, and hence to conclude that angst is the only mood out of which a proper philosophical appreciation of the human relation to negation, nullity and nothingness – to the 'not' – might emerge. This tone, or attunement, is set in the opening chapter on death, in which (as I have argued in detail elsewhere[2]) Heidegger acknowledges death not as a distinctive kind of existential possibility (for an impossible – unrealizable, unprojectable – possibility is not a kind of possibility at all) but rather in terms of an ontological structure – Being-towards-death – that signifies the internal relation of every aspect and element of our existence to that which necessarily exceeds our comprehension. Precisely because death must be characterized as Dasein's ownmost, nonrelational and not-to-be-outstripped possibility, and hence as an omnipresent, ineluctable but non-actualizable possibility of its Being, at once undeniable and ungraspable, Dasein can only relate to it in and through its relation to what *is* graspable in its existence – that is, by relating to those genuine existentiell possibilities that constitute it from moment to moment, and so to its life, as its ownmost, nonrelational and not-to-be-outstripped possibility.

For Heidegger, the mortality of our existence is a matter of there being no moment of it in which our Being as such is not at stake, of our being unable to slough off responsibility for it, and of our being unable to deny its utter non-necessity (since it need not have been, and none of its constituent moments need have been what they in fact were) or ultimately to avoid its utter annihilation. In other words, we have to understand it in relation to nullity or negation. But that is not to say that we thereby grasp our mortality, that we can make sense in our individual lives of the 'possibility' of its utter impossibility; it is precisely to say that a proper comprehension of mortality is a matter of comprehending its essential incomprehensibility. The omnipresent, undeniable possibility of my own utter annihilation – the reality that every moment might be my last – is not something that I can grasp or accommodate or master: *that* is precisely its significance in and for my individual existence.

But in establishing that point, Heidegger precisely attains a properly phenomenological grasp of death – by acknowledging that fully to understand Dasein's Being is to understand that it is internally related to that which lies beyond phenomenological representation. Death shows up in his analysis as the ungraspable ground against which all the other features of that analysis configure themselves – as the self-concealing condition for Dasein's capacity to disclose its own existence (and so the existence of any phenomenon) to itself as it really is. Heidegger thereby invokes a new horizon or broader context for the whole of his existential analytic of Dasein as presented in Division One – the requirement to relate every element of it to that which is neither a phenomenon nor of the logos, to that which cannot appear as such or be the object of a possible discursive act. For nothingness is not a representable something, and not an unrepresentable something either; hence it can be represented only as beyond representation, as the beyond of the horizon of the representable – its self-concealing and self-disrupting condition.

[2]Cf ch 5 of Mulhall (2005).

In one sense, then, every phase of the analysis in Division Two contributes to the phenomenological task of representing Dasein's existence as internally related to nothingness. Beyond the analysis of death, we have the notions of guilt (defined as the null Being-the-basis of a nullity) and conscience (the voice of which speaks by being silent, and speaks thereby of Dasein's necessary non-self-identity – its failure to coincide with its past or present situation); and the tripartite structures of temporality are notoriously inter-defined by negation (each internally related to that which it is not, thereby ensuring Dasein's non-self-coincidence).

But it would be misleading to think of each of these phases of Division Two as adding specific elements to the analysis of Division One – as if the initial definition of the care-structure had unaccountably omitted certain specifiable elements of Dasein's ontological structure. Division Two is rather a re-reading of Division One which relates each element of that care-structure to 'the nothing' – and so to nothing specific, nothing in particular. In this respect, it would be more accurate to say that Division Two adds nothing to Division One – it adds, precisely, an internal relation to 'nothing' to every element of that earlier analysis, and so it alters everything in it.

One might say: if 'the nothing' really is the self-concealing and self-disrupting condition of Dasein's comprehending and questioning relation to Being, then phenomenological philosophy can only acknowledge it as such (that is, allow it to appear as it really is) by allowing 'the nothing' first to conceal itself and then to disrupt its concealment in the phenomenological analysis itself – that is, to appear within the analysis as that upon which the analysis as a whole is shipwrecked. Only in this way could an existential analytic of Dasein achieve the kind of completeness that its condition allows and its object discloses – by presenting itself as essentially incomplete, as beyond completion, as completed and completeable only by that which lies beyond it. This is the philosophical significance of the internal division of *Being and Time*, the gap at its heart around which everything pivots, and its consequent failure to coincide with itself as an analysis and as a text. The function of Division Two is to disrupt the apparent completeness of Division One, thereby allowing *Being and Time* as a whole to represent the self-concealing and self-disrupting condition of Dasein's Being, and so its relation to Being as such. The peculiar way in which Division Two alters nothing and everything in Division One is Heidegger's anxious and angst-inducing way of ensuring that *Being and Time* successfully represents Dasein's essentially enigmatic and anxious relation to 'the nothing'.

If, however, angst is the mood orienting and pervading everything in *Being and Time*, this casts a rather different light on another element of the analysis in Division One, and so on the relation between the mood of Heideggerian phenomenology and that characteristic of philosophy in the modern era. This is the element of scepticism, and its connection with angst is not far to seek: for, insofar as we are prepared to imagine scepticism as an existentiell possibility (as opposed to a sketch in epistemology textbooks), then it must be, and is, pervaded by a distinctive, doubting, uncertain mood – one that precisely matches Heidegger's analysis of angst. And since Heidegger characterizes angst as 'one of the most far-reaching and most primordial possibilities of [Dasein's] disclosure' (BT: 226), in which Dasein reveals itself as a worldly being whose Being is an issue for it, then the implication is that sceptical anxiety must embody exactly that illumination. But doesn't Heidegger decisively dismiss scepticism as a philosophical phenomenon in Division One of *Being and Time*?

Heidegger famously claims that the true scandal concerning scepticism is not our failure to refute sceptical doubts but rather our repeated attempts to construct such refutations. And one reading of that claim is strongly suggested by his attempt to reorient our understanding of human existence as inherently worldly. For in the course of analysing that worldliness, Heidegger shows two things. First, if we conceive the relation between subject and world as both cognitive and external, and thereby leave room to articulate a sceptical doubt about the reality of the world, we also deprive ourselves of any way of rejecting that doubt and so of any grounds for believing ourselves capable of genuine knowledge (for if the ground of our claim to apprehend its reality is a sensory or intellectual modification of the subject, the possibility that nothing in reality corresponds to the representational content of such modifications is ineliminable). Second, if we begin by assuming an internal relation between subject and world, sceptical doubts become inarticulable, and so in no need of refutation. Precisely parallel points are also made in the course of his analysis of Being-with, in relation to scepticism about other minds. The first point implies an internal incoherence in the position of Heidegger's opponents; the second demonstrates a strength of his own. Taken together, they suggest that scepticism is simply an incoherent position derived from a misunderstanding about the discursive underpinnings of our grasp of the world – a confusion of discourse rooted in a confusion about discourse.

But Heidegger's sense of the scandalous in our attempts to refute scepticism might also be read as suggesting that we ought not to attempt to refute scepticism because it does not, or at least need not, misdirect us, philosophically speaking. To be sure, taken as an intellectual hypothesis against the background of an assumption that our primary relation to the world is cognitive, it lacks any substance open to refutation; but what if it is differently understood – what if we look beyond the sceptic's intellectualized self-understanding and examine the mood that is orienting his sense of the world's significance?

The 'external world' sceptic feels an abyss to open up between herself and the world, a sense of its insignificance or nothingness, of its recession beyond our grasp; she experiences a hollow at the heart of reality, and an essential uncanniness in her own existence – a sense of herself as not at home in the world. The 'other minds' sceptic feels an abyss to open up between herself and others, as if their thoughts and feelings were withdrawing unknowably behind their flesh and blood, as if she were truly confronted by hollowed-out or infinitely dense bodies, mere matter in motion; she experiences a sense of herself as alone in the world. In either mode, scepticism finds itself opposed to common sense, to the truths that average everyday human existence, with its absorption in phenomena and the opinions of others, appears to confirm us in taking for granted; and in this opposition the sceptic both falsifies and discloses the underlying realities of human existence. For on Heidegger's account, we are essentially worldly, but we are also uncanny; we are essentially Being-with, but we are also individuated – marked or branded with mineness. Hence the intellectual expression of scepticism conceals the truth of Dasein's Being; but the anxiety of which it is the expression, in its aversiveness from worldly absorption and its existential solipsism, reveals that truth.

Furthermore, the inarticulacy to which the sceptic's thwarted desire for connection with reality drives her makes manifest both the fundamentality and the contingency of the discursive attunements upon which Dasein's capacity to grasp beings in their Being depends. For the fact that the sceptic can unknowingly repudiate criteria shows that human attunements to discourse can become discordant, that they exist only if Dasein continues to invest its interest or concern in them, and that Dasein can effect such withdrawals of interest in the guise of the most passionate investment of that interest. In this way, we can come to see that human responsiveness to the articulations of discourse is not something to which we are fated, but rather an inheritance for which we must take (or fail to take) responsibility.

What one might call the truth in scepticism – its sense of uncanniness and aloneness, together with the eloquence of its inarticulacy – finds its emblematic expression in the words that come most easily to the lips of one in the grip of angst, when she declares that what she is anxious about is 'nothing and nowhere'. But to appreciate the truth in scepticism is not a matter of endorsing its expressions and mood, but rather of subjecting them to question, making an issue of them. In particular, the phenomenologist must not accept scepticism's own interpretation of its significance; for the disclosures that it makes possible are graspable only by wresting them from its self-concealments and dissemblings – by overcoming scepticism from within, or one might say by dwelling in this mode of Being-in-the-world without being at-home in it. Is this a way of inheriting the sceptical tradition of modern philosophy, as epitomized by Descartes? It is certainly a way of finding fruitful philosophical re-orientation within what might seem the most fruitless and perverse forms of Dasein's capacity to alienate itself from itself and its world; and in this sense, it fits very well within Heidegger's introductory emphasis upon phenomenology as making progress by deconstructing the Western philosophical tradition (which means allowing oneself to be constantly responsive to and so oriented by it).

II. Perplexity

But of course, the Western philosophical tradition does not begin with Descartes, but with Plato; and whilst *Being and Time* persistently orients itself to Cartesian and post-Cartesian modernity, it presents itself as finding its own origin in the Platonic origins of the subject – more specifically, as a response to a specific moment in Plato's dialogue the *Sophist*. For the book's introduction is itself prefaced by the following quotation from that dialogue, which is itself followed by a sequence of rhetorical questions and answers whose style is simultaneously reminiscent of numerous exchanges between Socrates and his interlocutors, and of liturgical exchanges between priest and congregation:

> 'For manifestly you have long been aware of what you mean when you use the expression "*being*". We, however, who used to think we understood it, have now become perplexed.'
>
> Do we in our time have an answer to the question of what we really mean by the word 'being'? Not at all. So it is fitting that we should raise anew *the question of the meaning of Being*. But are we nowadays even perplexed at our inability to understand the expression 'Being'? Not at all. So first of all we must reawaken an understanding of the meaning of this question. Our aim in the following treatise is to work out the question of the meaning of *Being*, and to do so concretely. (BT: 19)

In this highly condensed opening, Heidegger invites his readers to recognize themselves as presently standing in the position of those addressed by the Eleatic Stranger, but as needing to take up his position instead. He wants us to recognize that we not only do not have an answer to the question of the meaning of Being, but that we do not really understand the question; so his primary task is to engender a mood of perplexity in his readers about that question, and thereby get us to see that there is a difficult question to ask here. In other words, what he needs to do first of all is to bewilder or disorient us – leave us at a loss.

But it is not as if this mood of perplexity is one that the reader of *Being and Time* is in a position to leave behind by the end of the book – perhaps a necessary precondition for acquiring philosophical insight, but one which that insight will necessarily dissipate. For even though the most that its author aspires to do with respect to the question of the meaning of Being is to work it out concretely – that is, not to answer the question but to get us in the position of being able to ask it in a way that is sufficiently clear or intelligible for us to be able to seek an answer – he all-but-declares on the final page of his book that it has failed to achieve even this apparently minimal aspiration: 'And can we even *seek* the answer as long as the *question* of the meaning of Being remains unformulated and unclarified?' (BT: 487). In effect, then, the mood of bewilderment that Heidegger aims to create is one that never dissipates; it is rather the mood in which the book as a whole maintains its readers at every point. So unless we wish to deny that *Being and Time* enacts any genuinely philosophical work, seeing it simply as engaging in endless preparatory, pre-philosophical manoeuvres, the implication seems to be that genuine philosophizing requires that mode of attunement throughout its labours, that the sign of the authentic philosopher is his ability to live within perplexity from first to last. But why and how can philosophizing finds its way by maintaining itself in a state of disorientation? What makes bewilderment or perplexity essential if the philosopher is to be properly attuned to his subject-matter?

Etymologically speaking, perplexity is not just a condition in which human beings might find themselves, it is also a condition that objects and situations might manifest. Someone can be perplexed; but if so, that is because something or someone is perplexing them – confusing, bewildering, or tormenting them; and in at least some cases, they will be having that effect precisely because they are themselves entangled, involved or complicated. The Latin term 'perplexus' derives from the verb 'plectere', which means plait, interweave or involve. In sixteenth century English, one could talk of a perplexed object – one whose parts were intricately intertwined.

Textually speaking, Heidegger's invocation of the *Sophist* points us towards the Eleatic Stranger's famously perplexing conception of Being and non-Being as intricately interwoven – his solution to the problem of saying of that which is not that it is not. We have already seen that Heidegger's anxious engagement with nullity is not very distant from that of the Stranger. But what his invocation of the *Sophist* also prepares is Heidegger's own initial characterization, in his first introductory chapter, of what the term 'Being' might mean – a characterization without which his inquiry could not possibly begin, and which presents Being as something plaited or interwoven in a rather different (although not unrelated) sense.

Heidegger's characterization is implicitly oriented by an apparently passing reference to Aristotle's idea that the universality of Being is transcendental – that is, that it consists in a unity of analogy, in what Heidegger calls the 'categorial interconnectedness' holding between the various ways in which beings can be grasped as existing and as manifesting a particular kind of existence. The idea is more fully and explicitly developed in his analysis of what he calls the ontological priority of the question of Being.

He begins by pointing out that our pretheoretical comprehension of the phenomena of everyday life is never absolutely final or complete, but rather always capable of being further refined or developed, even of being radically revised or reconceived; in this sense, our everyday grasp of things is inherently open to question. I may have a good understanding of our cat, Jemima, and hence of certain kinds of animal life, and nonetheless be deeply surprised on occasion by something Jemima does; I may be forced to revise my sense of the general character of cats by the particular temperament of my neighbour's animal; and of course, such surprises might lead me to pursue a more systematic understanding of that species, and of animal life more generally. We might accordingly think of disciplinary practices such as biology, zoology and anthropology (Heidegger calls them ontic sciences) as what results from making an issue of this everyday understanding; we rigorously thematize it with a view to systematically interrogating it, and develop thereby a body of knowledge which may surpass or even subvert our initial understanding, but which is made possible by it and which is no less open to further questioning.

After all, what we learn reveals what we don't yet know; it orients our attempts to acquire that further knowledge; and it may also lead us to question the assumptions that governed our initial theorizing. Moreover, everything we come to know in this manner takes for granted certain basic ways in which this ontic science demarcates and structures its own area of study – conceptual and methodological resources which can themselves be thematized and interrogated (when, for example, biology was revolutionized by Darwinian theories of natural selection, or physics by relativity theory – or when a philosopher of science inquires into the validity of inductive reasoning). Such inquiries concern the conditions for the possibility of such scientific theorizing, what Heidegger calls the ontological presuppositions of ontic inquiry; and whether one inquires into them as a practitioner of the discipline or as a philosopher, the subject-matter could not be within the purview of a purely intra-disciplinary inquiry (which would necessarily presuppose what is here being put in question). It is, in short, the business of philosophy.

The object of investigation here is thus a regional ontology; every domain of ontic knowledge presupposes one, and thus invites this kind of philosophical questioning. And the results of that questioning themselves provoke further inquiry: given that each ontic region discloses an ontology, the relations between the various regional ontologies inevitably become a matter for philosophical inquiry. For on the one hand, each ontology will differ from others, as each ontic region has its own distinctive nature. But on the other, each region may open up onto cognate regions (as chemistry might shed light on biology and zoology, or as Heidegger thinks theology has deformed anthropology, psychology and biology [BT: 10]), thus revealing that its ontology bears upon those others; and of course each regional ontology is an ontology – each performs the same determinative function with respect to its region (determines the Being of a certain range or domain of beings), even if differently in each case. How, then, is this synthesis – this plaiting or interweaving – of categorial diversity and categorial unity to be understood? What is it for beings to be? This is the question of fundamental ontology.

The universality of Being is thus manifest in a threefold categorial interconnectedness. First, there is the internal articulation of philosophy, or ontological inquiry. To engage properly in any regional ontology, one must acknowledge not only that region's distinctiveness, but also its context – the way in which its ontology is located amongst and hence related to others, as well as the way in which the diversity-in-unity of regional ontology invites the question of fundamental ontology (since to thematize that diversity-in-unity just *is* to ask the question of fundamental ontology). Hence, any authentically penetrating exercise of philosophy in any of its regions must bear in mind its place in, and hence its bearing upon, the broader articulated unity of philosophical inquiry as such. In short, there can be no properly rigorous philosophy of science or philosophy of literature in the absence of a properly rigorous inquiry into the question of the meaning of Being; and that inquiry necessarily involves reflecting upon the diversity-in-unity of philosophy.

The second level concerns the ontic sciences upon whose existence and nature distinctively philosophical inquiry is focussed. Philosophy is thus parasitic upon the existence of ontic sciences; hence, insofar as regional ontological inquiries hang together with one another in the articulated unity of philosophy (qua intellectual discipline or tradition), then so must the ontic sciences from which those inquiries take their bearing and motivation. Philosophy makes sense (can be seen to hang together as an intelligible, interwoven whole) only insofar as regional ontologies do so; and for regional ontologies to hang together just is for individual ontic sciences to do so. Their results hang together internally (making it possible to form coherent bodies of knowledge, as opposed to accumulations of purely local data) and externally (insofar as the understanding they systematize has a bearing upon other such forms of understanding – whether by complementing, qualifying, challenging or otherwise putting it in question).

If the ontic sciences did not manifest such an articulated unity, then to precisely that extent the idea that reality is an articulated unity would lack any genuine substance; for each regional ontology is not only the basis upon which we construct an understanding of the entities of a particular ontic domain, it is also that which determines those entities as the distinctive kind of entities they are. The fact and nature (the Being) of ontology is thus Janus-faced in the familiar Kantian way, looking at one and same time towards our mode of comprehension of things and towards the nature of the things thus comprehended. In this respect, it reflects Heidegger's provisional understanding of Being, which refers both to that which determines entities as entities and to that upon the basis of which entities are understood (BT: 25-6). For of course, if we really do understand entities, then we understand them as they really are. And this means that to think of the question of Being as a genuine question (which means to think of philosophy as a genuine mode of understanding) is to think of our ontic sciences as genuine modes of understanding – as ways of disclosing how things really are, of getting at the truth of things; it is to think of them as discursive articulations that are also articulations of reality.

The third level of Heidegger's picture concerns the domain from which both ontic knowledge and ontological inquiry emerge, the domain embodying those pretheoretical modes of questioning comprehension whose reflexive radicalization generates the systematic forms of human understanding of the world – the domain of everyday human existence. For, of course, the pursuit of ontic and ontological knowledge is itself an achievement of human beings, hence an aspect of their comprehending, questioning mode of existence. And whilst such modes of comprehension might embody radical revisions and subversions of our pretheoretical grasp of things, they must also be essentially continuous with that understanding: they must be made possible by it and the resources it makes available; and the ways in which the various aspects of this understanding implicitly hang together must be such that their rigorous thematization is possible in an articulated, unified way. In short, if philosophy makes sense only if ontic science makes sense, then both make sense only insofar as the everyday ways in which Dasein grasps and interrogates its world make sense. Thus, for Heidegger, the question of whether living makes sense, the question of whether our ways of understanding the world have any genuine substance, and the question of the meaning or point of philosophy, have to be seen as three internally related questions – even as three aspects or dimensions of one and the same question: whether the human form of life has sense or meaning.

The human way of being is thus not just the origin and condition for the possibility of all forms of discursive understanding; its articulated unity as a being (its Being), the articulated unity of the discursive fields of our culture, and hence the particular articulated unity of philosophy, stand or fall together. They are simply different ways of disclosing the same phenomenon, the categorial interconnectedness of Being. And Heidegger sees this diversity-in-unity on the model of a conversation or a dialogue, of the kind exemplified in the Platonic origins of the subject and recapitulated in Heidegger's immediate, opening dialogic response to that exemplar. In other words, he is implicitly conceiving not just of Being, and of philosophy, but of the Being of Dasein itself, as comprehensible only in those terms – quite as if Dasein's distinctive way of being is to converse (with its world, with other Dasein, and with itself).

But here we need to recall that the mode of attunement Heidegger implicitly recommends as appropriate for any proper acknowledgement of the categorical interconnectedness of Being is perplexity – which means not just being impressed by the overwhelming intricacy of these dialogical interweavings, but apprehending them as convoluted, tormenting and disorienting. If perplexity is the appropriate mood, then the plaiting of these structures of Being must be constitutively bewildering – say, riddling or enigmatic. And we can best see how Heidegger's initial sketch of the field of Being accommodates this essential feature by asking how that sketch invites us to think of the place of philosophy in the conversation of human culture.

For on the one hand, philosophy is one more field of discourse – hence one more domain or region of intelligibility, one potential conversation partner in the ramifying dialogical inter-relations of the human form of life. But on the other hand, philosophy's subject-matter is the possibility of discourse as such – that is, the sheer possibility of human discursive understanding of reality; and so it necessarily aspires to take in or survey the whole field of possible discursive interchange, including presumably its own place in that field, as specified by its own distinctive capacities for questioning and being questioned by other discursive enterprises (science, literature, history, and so on). But can the place from which any such survey might conceivably be made also be a place within that which is being surveyed? Can the possibility of intelligibility as such ever be properly encompassed by one concrete instance of intelligible discourse, however self-aware and self-questioning? Does philosophy's defining aspiration therefore place it within the field of culture, or must any such suggested placement inevitably undermine itself, so that philosophy no sooner finds itself (somewhere in particular) than it is obliged to displace itself – as if endlessly fated to lose any specific orientation it manages to acquire? What exactly is the place of philosophy in the conversation of humanity?

One might say: its place is nothing and nowhere – and that would reconnect philosophy with the mood of anxiety and skeptical doubt. Or one might say: its place is to torment itself about its own, inevitable but ultimately bewildering, entanglement within the phenomenon it aspires to acknowledge as a whole, to enact its self-subverting drive to place itself beyond the discursive field of culture, as if at once yearning to inhabit what it thinks of as a wilderness (essentially beyond cultivation) and reluctantly recognizing that each such self-displacement – being itself more discourse – simply amounts to a further extension of the field of discourse that culture is (as if demonstrating that there is no wilderness for it to inhabit, since if its inhabitation is even conceivable, then it is within the reach of culture). Then one might say that the perplexing involutions of Being are crystallized in the perplexing unlocatability of philosophy in relation to those involutions; for if philosophy cannot be placed either within or without the categorical interconnectedness of discourse, then the simple fact of philosophical discourse – the sheer existence of philosophy as a cultural enterprise – indicates that the field of human discourse as such is inherently, enigmatically self-transcending and so fated to place itself beyond its own grasp, since the position from which alone it might be comprehended, and so the possibility of such comprehension, cannot itself be comprehended. Little wonder, then, that the authentic philosopher will find himself undergoing the self-inflicted torment of disorientation and bewilderment; for only that mood bears genuine witness at once to the nature of his subject-matter and the nature of his own enterprise.

III. Boredom and Shame

In the final part of this essay, I want briefly to examine the ways in which the range of moods appropriate to specifically Heideggerian phenomenology were expanded in later work in that tradition – some by Heidegger, and some by Sartre; for it turns out that this expansion both confirms and casts new light on the ways in which (as we have already seen) the moodedness of the human subject and of the subject of philosophy as such are internally related, in their distinctive ways of suffering dislocation or not-at-homeness in the world.

Heidegger's own first expansion of this range occurs in his 1929–30 lecture series on *The Fundamental Concepts of Metaphysics*.[3] Like *Being and Time*, this text falls into two parts – an analysis of the mood of boredom, followed by an analysis of the mode of existence of nonhuman animals; and again like *Being and Time*, each must be understood in the light of the other. More specifically, Heidegger's notorious claim that animals are world-poor must be understood as articulated from within a mood or state of boredom.

This internal relation between the text's content and mode of attunement is easier to see if one notes that central to Heidegger's understanding of animality is the claim that it is 'essentially a potentiality for granting transposedness, connected in turn with the necessary refusal of any going along with' (FCM: 211). In other words, animals neither simply lack access to objects in their own right, nor do they simply possess such a mode of access; their singularity in our experience lies in their having a mode of access to and dealings with the world from which we are excluded. Animal dealings with objects are accessible to humans, but only as resistant to human accessibility; hence, properly to grasp animal modes of existence is to grasp them as essentially beyond our grasp.

This apprehension of animality as enigmatic, insofar as it involves a mode of access to the world that neither is nor is not simply comparable to the human, naturally reminds us of Heidegger's opening declaration in *Being and Time* that the human modes of existence in the world is essentially enigmatic to itself (BT: 23). After all, human beings are animals too; so perhaps we should align our own animality with all the other aspects of Dasein's Being that turn out to exceed its grasp – as one more aspect of our own nature that actively resists comprehension. On this reading, whereas the primary focus of that resistance to comprehension was the projective dimension of Dasein's Being, in this text it turns out to be our thrownness, and in particular our thrownness into embodiment.

[3]Heidegger (1995), hereafter FCM. All citations refer to section number, followed by page number.

This is the point at which Heidegger's declaration that contemporary society discloses its world through boredom, and hence that 'we constantly already question concerning the essence of world [and thus the essence of animality] from out of this attunement' (FCM: 272) becomes critically important. For Heidegger characterizes this mood as 'Dasein's being delivered over to beings' telling refusal of themselves as a whole' (FCM: 139); it is a disclosure of beings in general as indifferent to us, and so of us as indifferent to them – not so much lacking a world of existential possibilities from which to choose, but rather lacking any desire or drive to realize them, as if fundamentally not drawn or gripped by those possibilities.

In this sense, Heidegger's characterization of nonhuman animals as responsively refusing our interest in them is both symptomatic and revelatory: symptomatic, in that it corresponds to the way we find ourselves attuned to all beings in boredom, and revelatory, in that it projects upon nonhuman animals an aspect of Dasein's real state – its relation to its own animality (the affective, desiring, passive dimension of its thrown projectiveness) as enigmatically refusing itself. This aspect of Dasein's emptiness is not exactly nothingness; more precisely, it is nothingness disclosed under the aspect of lack, deprivation or need. It is not that we lack the means to satisfy specific desires, but rather that we lack any sense of ourselves as experiencing specific lacks or needs that we feel it worth while satisfying.

What we lack is neediness as such, Heidegger claims; and this needy deprivation of need can be disrupted only through a moment of vision that discloses '*that Dasein as such is demanded of man, that it is given to him – to be there...to let the Dasein in him become essential*' (FCM: 165-6). In this context, the idea of liberating the humanity in man (as if from his animality), need not imply a simple opposition between humanity and animality; it rather envisages a disruption of animality from within. For the situatedness from which Dasein's projections always emerge is a modification of desire or need, hence of Dasein's embodiedness or animality. Realizing my mooded comprehension of the world thus neither negates nor simply reiterates my animality; it is a demand made upon a particular species of animal, a radicalization of animality as such, a mode in which it transcends itself. To let Dasein be is to do the most intimate, uncanny violence to one's animality, but thereby to answer the most originary demand that our particular inflection of embodiedness (our form of subjection to desire) makes upon us. To understand the root of this discontinuous continuity is to grasp that it is – to grasp it as – constitutively resistant to our grasp.

The role of boredom in *Fundamental Concepts of Metaphysics* suffices to show that Angst is not the only significant mood for Heideggerian phenomenology; and I want to end by suggesting that a text not authored by Heidegger but evidently deeply inspired by it suggests one other candidate for such a mood that Heidegger himself does not (I believe) ever consider – that of shame, which has a famously pivotal role in Sartre's *Being and Nothingness*.[4]

Sartre's primary aim is to show that the experience of shame gives us phenomenological access to the reality of other persons in our world in a form so direct and

[4] Sartre (1958), hereafter BN.

penetrating that it obviates the need to validate the 'hypothesis' that there are such others, and indeed to show that any philosophical attempt to treat the matter as a primarily cognitive one (whether by pressing skeptical doubts about it, or by affirming its truth in the face of such doubts) is fundamentally misbegotten. So this claim about the nature of interpersonal relations already has a certain philosophical edge or function. But that edge can be further sharpened, if viewed against our Heideggerian background.

For what, more precisely, does the experience of shame reveal? To begin with, our embodiedness or animality: the characteristic desire of the ashamed person is to remove themselves from sight, and so is generally recognized to declare the body's visibility – its revelation of itself as an element in the field of another's vision. And Sartre reinforces this general point by placing his ashamed man at the keyhole of a hotel room, moved by 'jealousy, curiosity or vice' (BN: 259): in other words, he stresses not only the human animal's subjection to want or desire, but also its specifically sexual dimension.

But for Sartre, it is not just that one's embodiment renders one material, and so visible; for of course, an individual can see his own body, and so apprehend himself as material and visible, without the intervention of another. Shame requires the intervention of a viewer other than the person viewed – a subject or centre of consciousness who is himself embodied, and so possessed of sense organs as well as the motive (if not jealousy or voyeurism, then at least curiosity) to use them. To apprehend the existence of such another is not something that a simple awareness of oneself as Being-for-self in relation to Being-in-itself, however deeply explored and appreciated, could confer. It is rather an essentially unforeseeable shock: a brute recognition of oneself as both facticity and transcendence that is conferrable only by the felt presence of another who is similarly facticity and transcendence.

What Sartre stresses about this asymmetric reciprocity is (in increasing order of importance for our purposes) its instability, its incomprehensibility and most specifically its perplexity. Sartre's famous diagnosis of interpersonal relations as endlessly reversing asymmetries of mastery and subjection depends upon the fact that seeing oneself as looking/looked-at by encountering another looking/looked-at involves understanding the nature of both in terms that essentially resist comprehension.

In recognizing the existence of another for-itself, one is confronted with the necessity of thinking of the world (of which one was hitherto the centre, the point from which everything radiated and to which everything converged) as having another centre (one into which everything now converges, drains and vanishes – a black hole, a place that is no longer simply a place but the ungraspable point in relation to which everything, including oneself as placer, is now itself placed). And in recognizing oneself as so placeable, one must cede one's previous exclusive role as the unlocatable locator – a displacement to which we will never fully reconcile ourselves, in part because we cannot make sense of being both. Thus shame reveals to us not only that we are not alone and embodied, but also that we are, incomprehensibly, not God (even though we are fated endlessly to renew our aspiration to be God).

And insofar as our recognition of ourselves as always already shamefully displaced from the centre of the universe is a function of our shameful apprehension of others like us in that universe, Sartre conceives of this apprehension of our Being-with as an apprehension of something internal to us that is not us – our body, and our finitude, certainly, but also others. Part of our shame is thus that what it is to be a self comes from without, not only from what is not us but from what is another us – from beings just like us except for the fact that they are not us. Their reality is always already constitutive of our own reality, not just for them but for us as well. In this sense, selfhood is always open to inhabitation by others, and so amounts to relating to oneself as another. The self's failure to coincide with itself here reveals the self's ineliminable indebtedness, and so openness to, other selves.

One might say: shame is philosophy's best way of attuning itself to that aspect of the internal relation between nothingness and human existence that is manifest in the body's non-identity with the mind, both one's own mind and those of others. For if the idea that a creature in one's world is also a creature possessed of a world is inherently enigmatic, then so is its inevitable complement – the idea that my world is one that I am in just as much as one upon which I have a point of view. The shame of it all thus teaches us that it is not just philosophy that both is not and must be placeable within its world: it is also the self, the subject, the existing human being that both is and is not its world, and so is and is not its body. At least this shame is impersonal, the inheritance of any thinking being – is it not?

References

Heidegger, Martin. 1962. *Being and Time*. Trans. J. Macquarrie and E. Robinson. Oxford: Blackwell.

Heidegger, Martin. 1995. *The Fundamental Concepts of Metaphysics*. Trans. W. McNeill and N. Walker. Bloomington: Indiana University Press.

Mulhall, Stephen. 2005. *Heidegger and Being and Time*, 2nd ed. London: Routledge.

Sartre, Jean-Paul. 1958. *Being and Nothingness*. Trans. Hazel Barnes. London: Routledge.

Anxiety and Identity: Beyond Husserl and Heidegger

Yaron Senderowicz

I. Introduction

Anxiety, in Heidegger's analytic of Dasein, is characterized as a unique type of state-of-mind, [*Befindlichkeit*]. It is connected to Dasein's authentic ability-to-be. In anxiety one feels uncanny, not at home. Everyday familiarity is lost (Heidegger 1962: § 40). The concealed grounds of Dasein's fall that motivate one's flee in the face of oneself are unmasked. But anxiety is above all an *individuating* state-of-mind, and it has this nature due to the features noted above:

> Anxiety takes away from Dasein the possibility of understanding itself, as it falls, in terms of the 'world' and the way things have been publicly interpreted. Anxiety throws Dasein back upon that which it is anxious about – its authentic potentiality-for-Being-in-the-world. Anxiety individualizes Dasein for its ownmost Being-in-the-world which as something that understands, projects itself essentially upon possibilities. Therefore, with that which it is anxious about, anxiety discloses Dasein as *Being-possible*, and indeed as the only kind of thing which it can be of its own accord as something individualized in individualization. (Heidegger 1962: 187).

Let it be noted that the term 'individualization,' as it is used in the present context, is ambiguous. Anxiety, in one sense, individualizes Dasein as a *kind* of being. It discloses Dasein as something that understands, as something that projects itself essentially upon possibilities, as "*being-possible*." In this sense, it individuates the being of *anything* that is Dasein. According to the second sense of 'individualization,' anxiety individualizes Dasein as a *particular* being-in-the-world, by throwing Dasein back to what he or she is anxious about, that is, his or her own being in the world. 'Being-possible' cannot be interpreted in this context as being open to possibilities in the generic sense of the term, but rather as being open to *one's own* real possibilities.

Y. Senderowicz (✉)
Department of Philosophy, Tel-Aviv University,
P.O. Box 39040, Ramat Aviv, Tel-Aviv 69978, Israel
e-mail: yaron.senderowicz@gmail.com

H. Kenaan and I. Ferber (eds.), *Philosophy's Moods: The Affective Grounds of Thinking*, Contributions To Phenomenology 63, DOI 10.1007/978-94-007-1503-5_10,

My main concern in the present article will be with difficulties connected to the second sense in which anxiety individualizes Dasein. How can anxiety individualize Dasein as a *particular* being in the world? The answer seems straightforward: Anxiety *discloses* one's own authentic ability-to-be. Yet, this could hardly be the basis of an account of the individualizing nature of anxiety. 'Authentic' does not express some secret inner properties of Dasein, but rather a type of understanding that is connected to a mode of action. Anxiety is the mood that corresponds to this type of understanding. Nevertheless, it seems that if Dasein's authentic ability-to-be is *disclosed* by anxiety, anxiety individualizes Dasein only derivatively, that is, by *disclosing* Dasein's essential ability-to-be.

It would not be unfair to maintain that Heidegger's account of anxiety and its role in the hermeneutics of human existence presents a problem to his reader rather than a theory or a solution. One way of grasping the problem begins by noticing that anxiety is in fact a mode of *self-awareness*. Heidegger does not explicitly state this feature of anxiety. Yet, what one is anxious about is *one's own* being-in-the-world (Heidegger 1962: 186). Similarly, "with that which it is anxious about, anxiety discloses Dasein" (to oneself, we may assume) as "being-possible" (Heidegger 1962: 187–188). Bearing this in mind, the question is whether the various features that Heidegger ascribes to anxiety cohere. How can a mode of self-awareness individualize *and* disclose Dasein in its ownmost being? The problem persists even if one distinguishes self-awareness from self-knowledge, and in addition views the relevant mode of self-awareness as having a practical sense. It seems that one could be disclosed (to oneself and to other persons) only if one is "already there" before being disclosed. But if anxiety individualizes Dasein, if it is the innermost ground that constitutes its individuality, *what* anxiety discloses cannot be something that was "already there."

One way of avoiding this problem is to point out that authentic ability-to-be is *always* a genuine *possibility* of Dasein, and that anxiety is involved in *actualizing* the possibility of being authentic, and, therefore, of being a particular individual. Yet, this response unjustifiably places the individualizing character of anxiety on the same level with other possibilities. But, the possibility that anxiety actualizes is the possibility of *being an individual*. In other words, anxiety conceived as an ontological mood that discloses Dasein seems to rule out the possibility that it individualizes Dasein.

Things are even more complicated when one considers the other features that Heidegger assigns to the phenomenon which anxiety belongs to. In anxiety, the fleeing of Dasein in the face if itself, that is, of its authentic ability-to-be, becomes manifest (Heidegger 1962: 184). Yet, when one is confronted with "*that in the face of which that one has anxiety,*" with one's "Being-in-the-world as such," it is "the nothing and nowhere within-the-world" that becomes manifest (Heidegger 1962: 186–187). It is not as if anxiety reveals one's secret hidden self to oneself. When one is confronted with that in the face of which one has anxiety, "the nothing and nowhere within-the-world" is disclosed.

The difficulty is therefore to conceive how a mode of self-awareness could individualize the very same individual that is thus aware of herself. This is not a distinctive feature of Heidegger's early philosophy. In fact, in endorsing one version of the link between individuality and self-awareness and its paradoxical results, the early Heidegger continues to be part of the transcendental tradition. This link is similar to that expressed in Kant's account of self-consciousness, in Fichte's doctrine of self-positing, and in Husserl's paradox of subjectivity. Nevertheless, Heidegger's position in *Being and Time* significantly differs from that of Kant, Fichte, and his teacher Husserl. While Husserl assigned a fundamental role to the pure 'I' in constituting the link between individuality and self-awareness, a notable feature of Heidegger's partial departure from this tradition consists in the denial that the notion of the transcendental 'I' is part of the link between individuality and self-awareness.

As I will demonstrate below, in spite of their manifest differences, there are surprising similarities between the role that the pure 'I' has in Husserl's mature phenomenology and the role of anxiety in Heidegger's hermeneutical ontology. These similarities raise the question regarding the reasons that motivated Heidegger to place anxiety at the heart of the link between individuality and self-awareness. I will attempt to respond to this question by clarifying the way in which placing anxiety qua ontological mood at the depth of the link between selfhood and self-awareness could be viewed as a response to a problem implicit in Husserl's account of individuality.

Replacing the pure 'I' with anxiety affects the whole structure of selfhood and self-awareness. Moreover, it affects the foundations of phenomenology. The pure 'I' and the ontological mood of anxiety both involve the idea that an account of individuality and selfhood cannot merely be based on intentional experiences (Husserl) or on the features of the world (Heidegger). They both express the idea that particular conscious individuals transcend the world in which they live. Nevertheless, in contrast to Husserl's disinterested gazing 'I' that is detached from the stream of experiences (and the experienced world), the transcendence of Dasein consists in an ontological *mood* that is rooted in *care*. Although anxiety is a mode of self-awareness, it is not a *representation* of the anxious self. As a result, anxiety qua transcendence loses the epistemic and foundational role that the pure 'I' has in Husserl's theory. Anxiety is not a resting place. In being anxious, Dasein is inevitably thrown back to his or her real worldly possibilities, though in a transformed way.

Did Heidegger succeed in his attempt to avoid positing a pure *representation* of the self similar to the pure 'I'? In the final section I will claim that the elimination of the pure 'I' from Heidegger's account of selfhood leaves a gap that affects the coherence of Heidegger's position. This gap is ignored rather than resolved. There are reasons to suppose that the representation of a pure 'I' cannot fulfill its individuating function. But given the phenomenological background of this debate, and in particular the idea that individuation involves some mode of transcendence, there are also reasons to suppose that anxiety or any other mood cannot fulfill this function either. These are reasons to the effect that any form of individuation that is based on a temporal structure similar to that of anxiety and authenticity is bound to involve a representation of the self that is similar to the pure 'I.' I will not attempt to resolve this puzzle in this context.

II. The Transcendental 'I' in the *Logical Investigation*

As is well known, in the *Logical Investigations* Husserl denied that the transcendental 'I' is a part of our cognitive lives. His view is based on two suppositions. First, conscious experiences are inherently intentional. If an entity could be *given* to thought, the entity must be conceived as an object (in the broad sense of the term) (LI, II: 92).[1] It should be noted that Husserl does not claim that all the features involved in an intentional experience have the role of objects while one 'leaves in the act,' but rather that they have the role of objects when one reflects upon them. This feature is connected to the second reason that explains why the early Husserl thought that the pure 'I' is an empty notion. According to Husserl, intentionality does not consist in *real relations*. An intentional act of 'meaning something' is an act in which an *object* is meant. Yet, in Husserl's theory the object meant is identical to the object given in the intuitive act that fulfills the 'meaning intention.' In particular, the fact that not all acts of meaning are fulfilled or satisfied does not entail the existence of inner objects of thought distinct from real objects.

A question that a theory that posits a pure 'I' faces concerns the reasons that establish why it is required as part of a theory of intentional experiences. The denial that intentionality consists in real relations challenges at least one type of such reasons: The pure 'I' is not needed in an account of intentionality by virtue of the fact that the content of intentional experiences involves a relation between subjects and objects. The inherent intentionality of experiences, and the denial of the claim that intentional acts consist in *relations between subjects and objects* therefore imply the groundlessness of the pure 'I.'

III. The Shortcomings of Husserl's Early View

One of the most striking transformations that distinguish Husserl's early and transcendental positions consist in the rediscovery of the transcendental 'I.' What were the reasons that motivated this change? In trying to respond to this question it should first be noted that the fact that the pure 'I' had no role to serve in *the theory of intentionality* presented in the *Logical Investigations* does not entail that it was not required by an account of *self-awareness*. Indeed, Husserl's early account of self-awareness contained some flaws that his matured position attempted to remedy.

In the *Logical Investigations*, Husserl explicates the notion of the ego as follows:

> The Ego in the sense of common discourse is an empirical object, one's own ego as much as someone's else's and each ego as much as any physical thing, a house, a tree etc. Scientific elaboration may alter our ego concept as much as it will, but if it avoids fiction, the ego

[1]Throughout this essay I will refer to Husserl's writings immediately following the quote by way of the following abbreviations: LI II - *Logical Investigations* (Husserl 2001); Hua - the Husserliana edition of Husserl's Collected Works followed by the volume number: Hua1 - *Cartesian Meditations* (Husserl 1960); Hua3 - first part of *Ideas pertaining to a pure phenomenology and to a phenomenological philosophy (Ideas 1)* (Husserl 1982); Hua4 - second part of *Ideas pertaining to a pure phenomenology and to a phenomenological philosophy (Ideas 2)* (Husserl 1989).

> remains an individual, thing-like object, which, like all such objects, has phenomenally no other unity than that given it through its unified phenomenal properties, and which in them has its own internal make-up. (LI II: 85)

The ego is not merely a physical body but also as a phenomenological ego. Cutting out the physical body from the empirical ego leaves one with "the phenomenologically reduced ego" (LI II: 85). In the *Logical Investigations*, the phenomenologically reduced ego is conceived as identical to the interconnected *unity* of intentional experiences (LI II: 85–86).

In the first edition of the *Logical Investigations*, Husserl's view was that awareness of the unity of phenomenal experiences is the grounds of first-personal self-awareness. How does Husserl explain the self-evidence of 'I am'? In that period his view is that what 'I' in 'I am' stands for, that is, what is *meant* by it, could be specified in each context by *a certain kernel of an empirical ego-notion* that is not bounded by a clear concept (LI II: 87).

In a footnote added to the second edition of the *Logical Investigations* (first published in 1921), Husserl comments on his earlier position as follows:

> The text as here set forth is taken over without essential changes from the First Edition. It fails to do justice to the fact that the empirical ego is as much a case of transcendence as the physical thing. If the elimination of such transcendence, and the reduction to pure phenomenological data, leaves us with no residual pure ego, there can be no real (adequate) self-evidence attaching to the 'I am.' But if there is really such an adequate self-evidence – who indeed could deny it? – how can we avoid assuming a pure ego? It is precisely the ego apprehended in *carrying out* a self-evidence *cogito,* and the pure carrying out *eo epso* grasp it in phenomenological purity, and necessarily grasp it as the subject of pure experience of the type *cogito*. (LI II: 352)

According to Husserl's earlier position, the phenomenological ego is *abstracted from* the empirical ego. This seems to have two undesired results. The first concerns the possibility of a science of phenomenology in Husserl's mature sense. If the empirical ego is the primordial ground for intentional experiences, the science of pure phenomenology is jeopardized. Cutting the physical body does not put out of action the positing involved in the notion of an empirical ego as required by the phenomenological *epoché*.

Why, however, does Husserl believe that *the self-evidence* of the *cogito* is undermined by his previous position? We may answer this question by first noting that the self-evidence of 'I am' implies the self-evidence of 'I am identical to myself.' The identity of what one is conscious of when thinking the self-evident thought 'I am' does not consist merely of this or that particular intentional experience or even of a collection of such experiences. Here one may wish to argue that even if the stream of appearances changes continually, the self *given* in it does not change. This is admitted by Husserl with regard to perception, which involves a perceptual horizon that includes the awareness of the identity of the *perceptual object* given in the various (possible and actual) modes of givenness in the perceptual act. Yet, Husserl's theory rules out a similar type of account of what 'I' stands for in 'I am.' The claim that one is *given* to oneself (as in perception) as *the self-identical subject* that has the manifold of intentional phenomena that are one's own implies that the *content* of intentional phenomena involve modes of givenness of the phenomenological subject and not merely of their intentional objects. In other words, it implies that intentional phenomena involve *relations* in which objects are meant *and* a subject that is given as in perception, that is, the subject that has the experiences.

Husserl explicitly denies that self-awareness has the character of perception:

> The ego, however, does not appear, does not present itself merely from a side, does not manifest itself merely according to discrete determinations, aspects, and moments, which, moreover, for their part merely appear. Instead, the pure ego gives itself in absolute selfhood and a unity which does not present itself by way of adumbrations. (Hua4: 104–105)

If it is not possible to constitute one's own identity in a way that parallels the constitution of the identity of a perceptual object, the self-evidence of 'I am' seems to be inexplicable in the *Logical Investigation*.

IV. The Pure 'I' as a Pole of Identity

After his transcendental turn, Husserl conceives of the pure ego as *a pole of identity*:

> The ego is himself *existent for himself* in continuous evidence; thus in himself, he is continuously constituting himself as existing. Heretofore we have touched on only one side of this self-constitution, we have looked only at the *flowing cogito*. The ego grasps himself not only as a flowing life but also as *I* who live this and that subjective process, who live through this and that *cogito as the same I*. (Hua1: 100)

In some of his writings, Husserl tends to view the relation between the *unity* of a given stream of consciousness and the *identity* of the pure ego as a relation of reciprocal dependence. Yet, the relation is not a symmetrical relation of epistemic dependency. We may assume that the unity of the experiences of the stream of consciousness involves not merely past and present experiences but also future experiences. These are not *intuited* by subjects entertaining *cogito* thoughts at a given moment. Hence, if consciousness of identity *is determined by* consciousness of unity, the possibility of self-evident consciousness of one's own identity seems to be ruled out. The self-evidence of the *cogito* requires one to conceive of first-personal consciousness of identity as criterionless consciousness of identity.

This line of argument underlies Husserl's account of the self-evidence of the *cogito* in the *Cartesian Meditations*. Husserl distinguishes there between apodictic evidence and adequate evidence. Adequate evidence is the corresponding idea of *perfection* (Hua1: 55). If evidence is adequate, there cannot be *unfulfilled components* connected to it (Hua1: 55). As Husserl notes, evidence "is a grasping of something itself that is, or is thus, a grasping in the mode "itself," with full certainty of its being" (Hua1: 56). Nevertheless, "it does not follow that full certainty excludes the conceivability that what is evident could subsequently become doubtful" (Hua1: 56). By contrast, apodictic evidence "discloses itself, to critical reflection, as having the signal peculiarity of being at the same time the absolute *unimaginable* (inconceivability) of their *non-being*" (Hua1: 56).

Evidence could be apodictic and *not* adequate. As Husserl notes:

> Perhaps this remark was made precisely with the case of transcendental self-experiencing in mind. In such experience the ego is accessible to himself originaliter. But at any particular time this experience offers only a core that is experienced 'with strict adequacy' namely the ego living present (which the grammatical sentence, *ego cogito*, expresses); while beyond that, an indeterminately general presumptive horizon extends, comprising what is strictly non-experienced but necessarily also meant (Hua1: 62).

Evidence is apodictic if the *non-being of the intended entity* is inconceivable. In the *Cartesian Meditations,* the *cogito* is characterized as apodictic and *not* adequate. Husserl's departure from his earlier position is most notable in this context. In his earlier position, "self-evidence attaches to a certain kernel of our empirical ego-notion" (LI II: 87). In contrast to that, the core that is experienced with strict adequacy does not ground the apodicticity of the *cogito.* Since to each *cogito* "an indeterminately general presumptive horizon extends, comprising what is strictly not experienced but necessarily also *meant*" (LI II: 87) the type of evidence related to this act is not adequate evidence.

Each *cogito* is carried out at a given point in time. Each such act is connected to a core of experiences. Why, however, is it inconceivable that what is meant by tokens of 'I' in tokens of 'I am' is determined *only* by this core of experiences? To be sure, the relevant core of one's own experiences progressively changes in the course of time. Nevertheless, one may wish to maintain that what tokens of 'I' in 'I am' mean changes in a way that corresponds to the changes in the core actually experienced. Yet, the coherence of this account requires that the different acts of 'I am' are not *linked by virtue of their content* in a way that involves their being the *intentional acts* of *one and the same individual.* What Husserl realized after his transcendental turn is that *a precondition* of intentional experience is that the (implicit or explicit) acts of 'I am' related to such experiences must be the acts of one individual. The 'I' must be conceived *now* as having a horizon of future experiences. It follows that uses of 'I' in 'I am' must include a representation of the self. The content of this representation cannot be specified by means of the continually changing core of strictly adequate experiences. The referent of 'I' is not given in these experiences as a perceptual object. Hence, the identity of the 'I' cannot be constituted in the same way in which the identity of a perceptual object is constituted. This criterionless consciousness of self-identity expressed by tokens of 'I' in tokens of 'I am' is the pure 'I.'

The pure 'I' is not merely required for the account of the self-evidence of 'I am.' It is also required as part of the foundations of Husserl's phenomenology and, in particular, for reasons related to the phenomenological *epoché.* An act of bracketing suspends the positing that belongs to the natural attitude. It suspends the existence of the physical world or the life-world, including the psychophysical subject. Yet, it cannot put the phenomenological ego that carries out the act out of action. 'Carrying out an act' does not indicate any feature of the *content* of the act but rather of the *being* of the act. Nevertheless, although "the pure ego belongs to each coming and going lived experience... ", "...after carrying out the reduction we shall not encounter the pure ego anywhere in the flux of manifold of lived experiences" (Hau3: 109).

The stream of pure consciousness that results from the phenomenological reduction does not contain the pure ego. Nevertheless, the pure ego as a pole of identity is involved in *the individuation* of the stream. Stated differently, the identity of the stream of conscious experiences presupposes the identity of the subject that is not part of the stream itself. In contrast to Husserl's position in the *Logical Investigations,* the phenomenological 'I' cannot be identified with the interconnected unity of the experiences or with a *certain kernel of our empirical ego-notion*. Nevertheless, the transcendental 'I' is disclosed *within* what is left by the bracketing.

V. The Problem

On the basis of the above clarifications, I will now try to spell out the problem involved in Husserl's theory that is relevant to the issues discussed here. We may begin by presuming that there should be as many pure egos as there are persons. In thinking the self-evidence thought 'I am,' one *ipso facto* grasps one's own identity, that is, the identity of the subject that thinks that thought. The capacity to think *cogito* thoughts is not a contingent feature of the ego. "*The essence of the pure ego thereby includes the possibility of an originary self-grasp…*" (Hua4: 101). It is therefore natural to suppose that originary self-grasp involves the ability *to distinguish oneself from other egos*.

But how exactly can one distinguish oneself as a pure ego from other pure egos? As noted above, the consciousness of identity linked to the pure 'I' does not consist in the singularity of a stream of consciousness. Rather, the pure ego as a pole of identity is a precondition that determines the singularity of one stream.

Phenomenology qua science of essences requires a procedure for uncovering the *individual essences* of pure egos. The procedure by which the essence of an entity is revealed is 'eidetic reduction.' It is carried out by abstracting from the *particularity* of the given entities. In the case of the individual pure egos, one might assume that the particulars are the variety of particular conscious mental acts each of which is referred back to the same pure ego pole. The relevant procedure by which the individual essence is uncovered is presumably *imagining* oneself in counterfactual situations, that is, as having intentional experiences different than those actually included in one's own stream of consciousness. When the pure ego conceives of herself in counterfactual situations, she need not conceive of herself as being a different 'I.' Since the pure 'I' *is not part of* her own of stream of experiences, she *can* imagine herself as the *same 'I'* connected to a *different stream*.

According to Husserl, all individual pure egos *share an essence*. How is it possible to reveal the essence 'pure ego'? In the case of perceptual objects such as tables and chairs, eidetic reduction is carried out on a variety of particulars that are given in perception. Similarly, in order to reveal "the all-embracing eidos transcendental Ego" (Hua1: 105–106), one must abstract from *the particularity of the pure ego*. Given the differences between perception and self-awareness, how can one perform eidetic reduction on the transcendental ego? Husserl's contention is that the idea of an ego different from 'me' is based on an intentional act of imagining 'myself' having different experiences. Since the mode of awareness of a pure ego differs from that of a perceptual object, the particular/universal distinction requires one first to represent to oneself *other* pure egos. Indeed, according to Husserl, a possible pure ego is "a pure possibility variant of my *de facto* ego" (Hua1: 105). Imagining a variant of my *'de facto* ego' would not have been possible if the *content* of experiences entailed the identity of the subject that has them. But, in Husserl's theory, the essence of an experience consists in its intentional character. No feature of the intentional character of particular experiences indicates the identity of a particular pure ego.

Here, however, the following problem is revealed: If one conceives other pure egos by counterfactually imagining *oneself* having different experiences than those one actually has, in what sense does one imagine *a different ego* when one imagine *oneself* having different experiences? The fact that one *can* imagine oneself having different experiences at least indicates that one *could have had them.* As noted above, this is how one distinguishes between the individuality of the pure ego and the particularity of its stream of consciousness. But the same procedure by which the pure ego may be distinguished from its stream of consciousness is the procedure by which one abstracts the "all-embracing eidos" 'pure ego' from the particular pure egos. In other words, the procedure by which the individual essence of a particular pure ego is constituted as distinct from its stream of consciousness renders it indistinguishable from *all other* pure egos. This need not entail that Husserl's theory does not allow one to *conceive* of the existence of other pure egos. But, the indistinguishability of the pure ego and "all-embracing eidos transcendental ego" that is due to the identity of the phenomenological procedure by which they are both uncovered entails that the *self-awareness* of self-identity of a particular pure ego *converges with the awareness* of the essence of all egos. The self-conscious 'I' that thinks the thought 'I am' is certain of her own identity. This was one of the main insights that motivated Husserl's transcendental turn. Nevertheless, it appears that Husserl's theory lacks the means to point out what distinguishes the pure ego that one is from all other pure egos.

VI. Anxiety and the Transcendental Ego

As many have argued, Heidegger's ontology appears to be a reversed picture of Husserl's transcendental phenomenology. Streams of consciousness, unity of consciousness, immanency and the related features of Husserl's transcendental phenomenology are not part of Heidegger's analysis of Dasein. Nevertheless, traces of Husserl's legacy appear in the depth of Heidegger's account of human Dasein. There are at least five points of similarity between Heidegger's analysis of Dasein and Husserl's phenomenology that are relevant to the present context: (a) the impersonality of the background of individuality; (b) the ambiguity of what is meant by 'I'; (c) the world-(experience)-transcendence character of the innermost ground of individuality; (d) the contingency of the relation between the condition that constitutes individuality and the background in which individuals exists; (e) projectiblility and temporality qua constitutive features that determine human selves as a "being-possible".

Although each of the two philosophers provides a different account of these features, this hardly indicates that Heidegger has abandoned Husserl's philosophical project. Rather, their points of divergence may clarify the reasons that motivated Heidegger to transform his teacher's theory.

The Impersonality of the Background of Individuality

In the exposition of the tasks of the analysis of Dasein qua 'Being-in-the-world', Heidegger separates between three questions: (1) the question that concerns the world in which Dasein 'is'; (2) the question as to who is in the world; and (3) the character of 'being-in' as such. The world, in which Dasein 'is' is the everyday world, the "'public' we-world or one's 'own' closest (domestic) environment" (Heidegger 1962: 65). 'Environment' is the ontical sense of 'world.' It is distinguished from the ontological sense, the world designated by the ontological-existential concept 'worldhood' (Heidegger 1962: 65). In Heidegger's case no less than in Husserl's case, the concept of the world in which Dasein exists involves reference to an *understanding individual*, and yet, all the features of the world, including the entities that are in it, are impersonal. No feature that 'world,' 'worldhood,' 'significance,' or the 'ready-to-hand' possess bounds them to this or that particular individual. Indeed, in anxiety Dasein is uncovered as detached from the world. Yet, as noted above, it is uncovered as "the nothing and nowhere within-the-world," and if it conceives herself as 'something,' it must be interpreted in terms of the world and the worldhood of the world, that is, in terms of entities that are not bound to a particular individual.

The relation of 'worldhood,' 'world,' and the entities involved in it to Dasein's understanding is expressed in Heidegger's account of the nature of the entities that are in the world, the nature of the world, and of worldhood. As noted above, entities that are encountered within the world are entities whose mode of being is that of 'readiness-to-hand,' that is, of equipment. These are entities "that stand in some ontological relationship towards the world and towards worldhood" (Heidegger 1962: 83). As Heidegger notes "…there is no such thing as *an* equipment. To the Being of any equipment there always belongs a totality of equipment" (Heidegger 1962: 68). A totality of equipments "is constituted by various ways of "in-order-to," such as serviceability, conduciveness, usability, manipulability," (Heidegger 1962: 68) and so forth. In the in-order-to as a structure "lies an assignment or reference of something to something" (Heidegger 1962: 68). It presupposes a "toward which," or "for-the-sake-of-which." Heidegger's response to the question regarding the meaning of 'reference' and 'assignment' is the following:

> To say that the Being of the ready-to-hand has a structure of assignment or reference means that it has in itself the character of *having been assigned or referred* (*Verwiesenheit*). An

entity is discovered when it has been assigned or referred to something, and referred as that entity which it is. With any such entity there is an involvement which it has in something. The character of Being which belongs to the ready-to-hand is just such *involvement*. If something has an involvement, this implies letting it be involved in something. (Heidegger 1962: 83–84)

An entity that possesses the mode of being of involvement is an entity that was "freed for its Being" (Heidegger 1962: 84). "Letting something be" does not mean "to produce it" but rather to discover it in its readiness-to hand. (Heidegger 1962: 85) Heidegger sums up the relations between 'readiness-to-hand,' 'world,' 'world-hood,' and 'understanding' in the following passage:

Dasein always assigns itself from a "for-the-sake-of which" to the "with-which" of involvement; that is to say, to the extent that it is, it always lets entities be encountered as ready-to-hand. *That wherein* [Worin] Dasein understands itself beforehand in the mode of assigning is *that for which* [das *Woraufhin*] it has let entities be encountered beforehand. *The "wherein" of an act of understanding which assigns or refers itself, is that for which one lets entities be encountered in the kind of Being that belongs to involvement; and this "wherein" is the phenomenon of the world.* And the structure of that to which [Woraufhin] Dasein assigns itself is what makes up the worldhood of the world. (Heidegger 1962: 86)

In spite of the fact that the being of entities involved in the world essentially involves Dasein's understanding, the impersonal character of the world, the world-hood of the world, and, therefore, the entities that are encountered in it are not affected by their relation to Dasein's understanding. Dasein does not arbitrarily invents or produces, but rather finds or discovers structures of significance that are not determined by her or his existence as a particular being.

The Ambiguity of 'I'

According to Heidegger, Dasein's world is a 'we-world,' that is, a 'with-world.' The features of the 'with-world' are determined by the nature of those that are in the world, that is, the 'they-self.' Dasein's everyday mode of involvement consists in doing and thinking that conveys no individual characteristics. In a sense, it is impersonal doing and thinking. Nevertheless, the 'they-self', is not disconnected from the first personal mode in which one is *given* to oneself. The others with whom Dasein is in the world do not stand out against the 'I':

To avoid misunderstanding we must notice in what sense we are talking about 'the Others'. By 'Others' we do not mean everyone else but me —those whom over against the 'I' stands out. They are rather those from whom, for the most part, one does *not* distinguish oneself —those among whom one is too. (Heidegger 1962: 118)

Nevertheless, what 'I' means cannot be merely 'they-self':

Proximally, factical Dasein is in the with-world, which is discovered in an average way. *Proximally*, it is not 'I,' in the sense of my own Self, that 'am', but rather the Others, whose way is that of the 'they.' In terms of the 'they' and as the 'they,' I am given proximally to 'myself' [mir "selbst"]. (Heidegger 1962: 129)

One cannot distinguish *one's own self* from the they-self merely on the basis of the first personal mode of givenness. Nevertheless, this does not entail that one cannot distinguish between the two meanings of 'I.' As in Husserl's case, 'I' is *systematically ambiguous*. It means a worldly person, a pure ego, or both. Although a worldly person is distinct from a pure ego, in Husserl's view, one cannot be a worldly person without being a pure ego. Yet, mere first-personal givenness cannot distinguish between the two. In Heidegger's case, the ambiguity of the 'I' concerns the 'they-self' and the 'authentic-self,' that is, *'my own self.'*

The World-Transcendence of the Innermost Grounds of Individuality

According to Husserl the transcendental ego is a pure subject and not an object, although the transcendental ego is connected to an embodied human person. Similarly, what anxiety reveals is "the nothing and nowhere within the world." The authentic self is not an *object* revealed by anxiety. It is not, properly speaking, *part* of the world. Although the 'they-self' is distinct from the 'authentic-self,' an ontological bond ties them together:

> *Authentic being-one's- self* does not rest upon exceptional condition of the subject, a condition that has been detached from the "they;" it is rather and existentiell modification of the "they" – of the "they" as an essential existential. (Heidegger 1962: 130)

Each Dasein is essentially opened to the possibility of existence, that is, the possibility of being an authentic self. In Husserl's case the pure ego is revealed against the background of the stream of intentional experiences. In Heidegger's case, the authentic mode of being is possible only against the background of the we-world, that is, the world of the 'they'.

VII. Anxiety as a Transformation of the Pure Ego

The similarities and differences between Husserl and Heidegger's respective accounts provide reason to suppose that Heidegger's account was at least partly motivated by the attempt to overcome the above noted problem in Husserl's theory. To the extent that anxiety individualizes Dasein, it does so in a way that radically differs from the individuating role assigned by Husserl to the pure 'I.' Let us begin by noting that anxiety expresses the awareness of the ontological difference between 'one's own self' and 'the world' that is covered up by the everyday mode of involvement. Transcendence is presupposed by the ontological difference. No feature of the familiar world—of the background of individuality—can fully determine one's own individuality. It is 'me,' the unique individual that 'I am,' that transcends 'this world.' This feature of Heidegger's ontology is apparently similar to the status of the pure 'I' in Husserl's phenomenology. Yet, the individualizing function assigned to the pure 'I,' renders it a pure epistemic category. The individual subject is at least partly individuated by means of a unique *type of representation* that does not lead to any type of *action*. Individualizing oneself by first-personally conceiving oneself as a pure ego leaves everything that is in the world as it is. By contrast, anxiety is an ontological *mood* and not a representation of a subject. I suggest that the "nothing and nowhere within-the-world" revealed by anxiety can be correlated with Husserl's aforementioned failure to grasp what constitutes the identity of a particular self-conscious individual and distinguishes her from other individuals. Anxiety expresses the acknowledgment of this failure. It is a mode of self-awareness that inherently involves the practical dimension. In other words, in contrast to Husserl, the fact that the authentic self is revealed by an ontological mood indicates the limits of the *purely epistemic* attempt to uncover the grounds of the individuality of human persons that led to the positing of a pure 'I.'

As noted above, in emphasizing the individualizing character of anxiety, Heidegger continues to be part of the tradition that endorses the link between individuality, self-awareness and selfhood. Yet he significantly transforms this tradition when he assigns to anxiety the revealing role in self-awareness. In particular, self-awareness in this context cannot be viewed as a mode of *self-knowledge*. Anxiety reveals the features that motivate one's fleeing in the face of oneself and, consequently, "the primordial individualization of the reticent resoluteness" (Heidegger 1962: 322) that constitutes "being authentically oneself." The individuality of a human person is not constituted on the basis of a distinction between two spheres of entities, an inner sphere and an outer sphere. Here one could also point out the uniqueness of Heidegger's position. In Husserl's phenomenology, the transcendence of the pure 'I' has a *binding* function. Anxiety does not bind but rather *separates*. Individuality is not based on a pure 'I' that binds experiences, but, rather, on being thrown to concrete real world-situations that are one's own and on resoluteness.

Heidegger's transformation of Husserl's pure ego seems to respond to the problem hidden in the grounds that, according to Husserl, constitute the individuality of self-conscious subjects. Nevertheless, something is missing in Heidegger's account; something that essentially belongs to the ontological character of Dasein. Heidegger's avoidance of inner self-awareness is motivated by the shortcomings of the approach that connects the individuality of human beings merely to the content of self-conscious *cogito* thoughts. Mere first-personal givenness covers up one's individuality rather than disclosing it. But can anxiety, conscience, resoluteness and guilt be instantiated by a creature deprived of self-consciousness of identity? That is, can it be detached from the fundamental feature of Husserl's transcendental ego? Here is what Heidegger has to say about this matter:

> With the 'I,' what we have in view is that entity for which the issue is the Being of the entity that it is. With the 'I' care expresses itself, though proximally and for the most part in the 'fugitive' way in which the 'I' talks when it concerns itself with something. The

> they-self keeps on saying 'I' most loudly and most frequently because at bottom it is not *authentically* itself, and evades it's authentic potentiality-for-Being. If the ontological constitution of the Self is not to be traced back either to an 'I'-substance or to a 'subject,' but if on the contrary, the everyday fugitive way in which we keep on saying 'I' must be understood in terms of our *authentic* potentiality-for-Being, then the proposition that the self is the basis of care and constantly present at hand, is one that still does not follow. Selfhood is to be discerned existentially only in one's authentic potentiality-for-Being-ones-'self —that is to say, in the authenticity of Dasein's being *as care*. In terms of care the *constancy of the self*, as the supposed persistence of the *subjectum*, gets clarified... Existentially, '*self-constancy*' signifies nothing other than anticipatory resoluteness. (Heidegger 1962: 322)

Presumably, Heidegger's concern in this passage is with the same problem that motivated Husserl's transcendental turn: What constitutes the self-constancy of 'I' in 'I am'? It might be supposed that if being an authentic self is, as Heidegger maintains, an *existentiell modification* of the 'they self', 'I' in 'I am' must refer *both* to the 'they-self' and to the 'authentic-self.' Indeed, this is precisely the basis for the ambiguity of the 'I' discussed above. Yet Heidegger denies here that this is entailed by his account. Such a view amounts to tracing the ontological constitution of the self to an 'I'-substance or a 'subject.' The self that is "constantly there" does not constitutes the basis for care but is, rather, constituted by care. 'Self-constancy' is not eliminated from Heidegger's account, but is rather claimed to be based on anticipatory resoluteness. Husserl's *cognitive* account of the self-constancy of the self is replaced with a practical model of self-constancy.

But can this move avoid the positing of a *subjectum?* There are several reasons for suggesting that Heidegger failed to achieve this goal. In particular, although the possibility of being an individual (in the authentic sense) essentially belongs to man's existence, to the kind of being that Dasein is, one is not born an authentic self but rather becomes one. The authentic-self is an existentiell modification of the they-self. It therefore appears that the authentic-self and the they-self must be somehow bound together, that is, that there must be a binding ground that makes it possible to refer to oneself without depending merely on what determines the they-self or the authentic self. What could be the basis of this unified mode of self-reference and self-awareness? One such candidate seems to be ruled out in advance—the human body. Even if the leaving body is identical with the everyday self, it cannot be identical with the authentic self that presupposes its own transcendence. In anxiety, what one is conscious of *is not* in the world as bodies are. This clarifies why in this context Heidegger appeals to the self-constancy of *anticipatory resoluteness* and not of a leaving body. But can an account of practical constancy, that is, of the kind of practical constancy related to an authentic self, avoid positing a pure 'I'? The main feature that needs to be addressed in this context is *the conception of Dasein as essentially 'being-possible.'* 'Being projected upon possibilities,' the feature of Dasein that Heidegger identifies with 'understanding,' involves the idea that Dasein is always what it is "not yet." When one is aware of oneself as 'being possible,' one's attitude towards oneself is not to something that 'is there.' This mode of awareness involves the capacity *to represent oneself* as *the selfsame individual* of a manifold of possibilities that await one's own resoluteness. This type of representation of oneself seems to be equally related to the self-conscious they-self and the self-conscious authentic-self. Its content is not determined by the indeterminate horizon of possibilities or by the concrete events in which one is involved. The representation of oneself as self-identical, a representation that does not involve any worldly property, object or event, is, therefore, required by one's authentic ability-to-be. It is a condition of possibility of Dasein's essential features even if it does not constitute the overall unity of the self.

VIII. Conclusion

The link between the pure ego and 'being possible' is central to Husserl mature account of the 'I am'. It forms the basis for his contention that 'I am' has the *apodictic* but not *adequate* type of evidence. No less than Husserl's ego, Heidegger's Dasein is linked to an indeterminate opened horizon of possibilities. As in Husserl's case, the self-evidence of 'I am' must be distinguished, in his case from all type of contentful grounds. What 'I' stands for involves transcendence in his case no less than in Husserl's case. Husserl posited a transcendental ego. Heidegger wished to avoid the pure 'I,' but he does not provide any alternative account that can meet the demands of self-awareness that led Husserl to posit a pure 'I.'

Anxiety reveals nothing, neither objective-like property, nor subjective property. But it cannot separate and individuate without involving the awareness of *one's own self* as being anxious; resoluteness is inexplicable without self-awareness of taking responsibility. This type of self-awareness tacitly involves the awareness of self-identity required for the self-evidence of 'I am.' This does not entail that one's individuality can merely be based on self-awareness. But, it is questionable whether selfhood and self-awareness are possible without *involving* the binding function of the 'I.' As I read Heidegger, he responds to what he considers missing in Husserl's account by spelling out the way in which individuality is bound to one's being in the world. Yet, Heidegger seems to confuse the *insufficiency* of the pure 'I' with the *dispensability* of self-awareness of self-identity.

Although I believe it is implicit in Heidegger's account that the features that constitute Dasein's individuality are connected to inner self-awareness of identity, this supposition is never made explicit in his ontology. Heidegger prefers to *avoid* inner self-awareness rather than *face the problems that it involves*. The required emendation cannot consist in a naïve return to the old form of the inner. If Heidegger and the philosophers that share his views have taught us anything, they have taught us that this is a hopeless move. Nevertheless, the need to address the blind spot in the implicit connection between self-awareness and selfhood is unavoidable. It requires a novel account of the way in which selfhood and inner self-awareness are related.

References

Allison, E.H. 2004. *Kant's Transcendental Idealism. An Interpretation and Defense*, Revised and enlarged ed. New Haven: Yale University Press.

Bernet, R., I. Kern, and E. Marbach. 1993. *Introduction to Husserlian Phenomenology*. Evenston: Northwestern University Press.

Carr, D. 1999. *The Paradox of Subjectivity*. New York/Oxford: Oxford University Press.

Gallagher, S. 1998. *The Inordinance of Time*. Evenston: Northwestern University Press.

Heidegger, M. 1962. *Being and Time*. Trans. J. Macquarrie and E. Robinson. New York: Harper & Row Publishing.

Husserl, E. 1960. *Cartesian Meditations*. Trans. D. Cairns, The Hague: Martinis Nijhoff.

Husserl, E. 1970. *The Crisis of the European Sciences*. Trans. D. Carr. Evenston: Northwestern University Press.

Husserl, E. 1982. *Ideas Pertaining to Pure Phenomenology and to a Phenomenological Philosophy, First Book* (Ideas I). Trans. F. Kersten. The Hague: Martinis Nijhoff Publishers.

Husserl, E. 1989. *Ideas Pertaining to Pure Phenomenology and to a Phenomenological Philosophy, Second Book* (Ideas II). Trans. R. Rojcewicz and A. Schuwer. Dordrecht: Kluwer Academic Publishers.

Husserl, E. 2001. *Logical Investigations*, 2 vols. Trans. J.N. Findlay. London/New York: Routledge.

Senderowicz, Y. 2005. *The Coherence of Kant's Transcendental Idealism*. Dordrecht: Springer Academic Publishers.

Shoemaker, S. 1996. "Self Knowledge and Inner Sense I-III." In *The First Person and Other Essays*. Cambridge: Cambridge University Press.

Shoemaker, S. 2003. "Self-Reference and Self-Awareness." In *Identity, Cause and Mind*. Cambridge: Cambridge University Press.

Smith, D.W. 2007. *Husserl*. London/New York: Routledge.

Smith, D.W., and R. McIntyre. 1982. *Husserl and Intentionality*. Dordrecht: Reidel Publishing Company.

Strawson, P.F. 1966. *The Bounds of Sense*. London: Routledge.

Zahavi, D. 2005. *Subjectivity and Selfhood*. Cambridge: The MIT Press.

Part V
Otherness

Kant on the Affective Moods of Morality

Ido Geiger

Attempts to employ the categorical imperative to derive the substantive moral laws it seems to promise are very often the first task readers undertake in their work on Kant's moral philosophy. For this reason, so it seems, Kant's moral philosophy is more often charged with emptiness than for its complete and utter austerity. It is perhaps because many readers are so invested in the idea of a purely formal and thus objective procedure for the derivation of moral duties that the price of a theory of moral agency which allots no place for feelings seems reasonable to pay. Indeed, the choice might seem to be a necessary one: It is either reason or feelings that drive agents. But from the very first, readers have pointed out that a theory of moral agency should not be made to choose between reason and feeling. Famous is the pithy caricature drawn in *The Philosophers* (1796).[1]

> Scruples of Conscience
> Gladly I serve my friends, but I do it, unfortunately, by inclination,
> And so it often bothers me that I am not virtuous.
>
> Decision
> There is no other counsel, you must strive to feel contempt for them,
> And with utter dislike then do what duty commands.[2]

The principal philosophical concern here as well as in Schiller's *On Grace and Dignity* (1793) and the *Letters on the Aesthetic Education of Man* (1795) is that Kant's conception of rational moral agency might seem to leave feelings no role to play in dutiful action. This purported absence is parodied as a hatred of all feelings

[1] For the circumstances surrounding the composition and publication of the *Xenien* by Goethe and Schiller see, Safranski 2004: 440–443.

[2] Schiller 1869: 467.

I. Geiger (✉)
Department of Philosophy, Ben-Gurion University of the Negev,
P.O. Box 653, Beer-Sheva 84105, Israel
e-mail: geigeri@bgu.ac.il

H. Kenaan and I. Ferber (eds.), *Philosophy's Moods: The Affective Grounds of Thinking*, Contributions To Phenomenology 63, DOI 10.1007/978-94-007-1503-5_11,

and indeed as a recommendation of affective self-mortification. It is not that Schiller thinks that feelings and, more broadly, human nature should alone govern our lives. Indeed, he absolutely agrees with Kant that rational legislation is a necessary condition of moral action.[3] His claim is that commitment to this position does not entail an utterly dispassionate picture of moral agency. Ideally, reason would harmonize with inclination and dutiful action would be guided by feeling.

My claim in this paper is that Kant does not at all exclude feelings from the realm of moral action. Unlike Schiller, Kant does not think that inclinations can (at least ideally) be shaped by reason and then guide moral agents. But he does hold, or so I will argue, that there is a whole host of rational feelings that are indeed necessary conditions of moral agency. In the first section of the paper I will examine the one feeling Kant is famous for discussing, namely, respect for the moral law. It suggests that for Kant reason and feeling do not necessarily contradict each other but are rather different necessary aspects of moral agency. Kant does claim in the *Critique of Practical Reason* (1788) that respect for the moral law is the only moral feeling. Almost a decade later, however, in the *Metaphysics of Morals* (1797), he claims that there are other moral feelings that are necessary conditions of morality. I will examine Kant's discussion of these affective capacities in the *Metaphysics of Morals* and try to explain what he means by the categories of moral feeling, conscience, love of human beings and self-respect and how these affective capacities are related to each other and to respect for the law. Finally, I will make Kant's theory of affective moral attunement more concrete by examining some examples of moral feelings in the *Metaphysics of Morals*. Coupled with Kant's illuminating discussions of the phenomenology of respect and of conscience, these examples suggest that the affective palette with which our moral lives are painted is rich and diverse. For Kant, this variegated affective attunement to the rational claims of morality is a necessary condition of moral agency. This attunement is what I shall call in this paper the affective moods of morality.

I. The Feeling of Respect for the Moral Law

Although Kant is often charged with leaving feeling no part to play in moral action, there is one notable and well-known exception, namely, the feeling of respect for the moral law. Kant devotes to this feeling a whole chapter of the *Critique of Practical Reason*, entitled On the Incentives of Pure Practical Reason (CPrR: 71–89).[4] Although the focus of this paper is Kant's discussion of moral feelings in the

---

[3]This point is emphasized by Beiser. See, Beiser (2005: 81–84, 172–175) and *passim*.

[4]I will use the following abbreviations: **CPrR**: *Critique of Practical Reason* in Kant (1996a). **Gr**: *Groundwork of the Metaphysics of Morals* in Kant (1996a). **MM**: *The Metaphysics of Morals* in Kant (1996a). **R**: *Religion Within the Boundaries of Mere Reason* in Kant (1996b). **TSP**: "On a Recently Prominent Tone of Superiority in Philosophy" in Kant (2002).

Metaphysics of Morals, it is important to consider the discussion in this earlier text for two main reasons. First, this singular feeling is an essential part of the affective life of moral agents and any discussion of this topic must examine it. Second and even more important for our concerns is the controversial question of the role that the feeling of respect plays in moral motivation. It is not my aim here to contribute directly to this debate. Rather, I will present the reading of the second *Critique* that I think meshes with the view of moral feelings later developed in the *Metaphysics of Morals*.[5]

As a way into the matter before us it is useful to consider the following fundamental dilemma concerning moral motivation. According to the empiricist view of motivation, our desires are both the reason for which we act and what actually moves us to action. Desires give action both its direction and the force it harnesses. According to the rationalist or cognitivist view, it is reasons that both direct our action towards the good and somehow move us towards it. On the first view, acting against all inclination is inconceivable. Yet in certain situations morality seems to many of us to demand precisely such actions. For the second view it is hard to explain how grasping intellectually that something ought to be done actually moves us to do it.

The question then is the question of what force moves agents in doing their moral duty. In Kant's own terminology, the topic is what is usually translated as the incentive (*Triebfeder; elater animi*) of pure practical reason, defined as "the subjective determining ground of the will of a being whose reason does not by its nature necessarily conform with the objective law" (CPrR: 72).

Now Kant might seem obviously to represent the cognitivist horn of the dilemma I just sketched. It is beyond doubt that for Kant the moral law is the reason of the moral agent. To act morally is to do what morality demands, *because this is what morality demands*. Thus Kant says emphatically that "the incentive of the human will (and of every created rational being) can never be anything other than the moral law" (CPrR: 72). It seems then that intellectual recognition of the authority of the moral law is also what moves moral agents in doing their duty. But Kant also says, apparently at least in contradiction to the last assertion, that the singular *feeling* of respect for the moral law is "the sole and also the undoubted moral incentive" (CPrR: 78). What then is the role of the feeling of respect in Kant's theory of moral motivation? What actually drives or moves the moral agent, intellectual recognition of the moral law and its authority or the feeling of respect for the moral law?

According to what might be called the conative interpretation of respect, the moral law is the reason for action, while the feeling of respect for the moral law is the force driving moral action. The main task this interpretation faces is reconciling the cognitive and conative aspects of moral action, without compromising the central commitment of Kan's moral theory: To act morally is to obey the moral law of reason. If a feeling is to play an essential part in Kant's view of moral agency, it must do so without compromising this central commitment. Kant must then put forward the notion of a rational moral feeling.

[5] See, Beck (1960: 209–236). For a different and influential view see, Reath (2006: 8–32).

Kant's discussion can be read as contending with the question of the transcendental conditions of moral agency: How can the noumenally free subject act morally in the phenomenal world? How does the moral law actually move agents to action? The moral law gives us an objectively or categorically compelling reason to act. But we need a further explanation of how this single objective reason becomes, in Kant's words, the subjective determining ground of the will. By what force or capacity does reason drive our action? Kant assumes that the effective forces driving naturally affected beings – what actually moves us to action in the phenomenal world – are feelings. This is the insight that Kant, surprisingly enough, takes from the empiricist view of agency.[6]

Kant does not intend to dispel the mystery of noumenal agency. Rather, he assumes its possibility and investigates the capacity that enables the noumenal self to trigger an action of the phenomenal self. In other words, he is searching for the affective capacity of the phenomenal self that is responsive to the rational command of the moral law. In this way, he will be able to maintain that in moral action reason alone is practical, while still attributing to the feeling of respect a necessary role in fulfilling the commands of reason.[7]

Now the answer to the question of what incentives drive heteronomous action is quite simple. When an inclination determines our will – perhaps in transgression of our duty – it is the feeling that underlies it that is our incentive, our desire for some object, say fame or wealth. According to Kant, inclinations never immediately move us to action. We freely choose to act on an inclination. But when we do choose, there is, so to speak, a mainspring we need only release in order to act, namely, the desire for the object. The difficult question to answer is what kind of feeling could possibly drive autonomous moral action.

According to the conative view of respect, it is the moral law (the objective ground of action) that causes the feeling of respect for the moral law (the subjective determining ground of the will). The law is the cause; the feeling of respect for it – its effect.[8] Thus, feeling is not the objective determining ground of the will of the moral agent. It is not the feeling of respect that gives us a reason to act: "It does not serve for appraising [*Beurteilung*] actions and certainly not for grounding the objective moral law itself" (CPrR: 76). It is the moral law, through its effect on feeling, that drives agents who are doing their duty. This very close connection between

[6]For this decisive point see: Beck (1960: 212) and Broadie and Pybus (1975(66): 63).

[7]"How can a being in the phenomenal world, through his knowledge of the law of the intelligible, control his conduct so that this law does in fact become effective." (Beck 1960: 212).

[8]To cite only a few examples: the law is "the form of an intellectual causality" (CPrR: 73); "respect for the moral law is a feeling that is produced by an intellectual ground [*durch einen intellectuellen Grund gewirkt wird*]" (CPrR: 73); "the cause determining it [respect] lies in pure practical reason; and so this feeling, on account of its origin, cannot be called pathologically effected but must be called *practically effected* [*muß praktisch gewirkt heißen*]" (CPrR: 75); "This feeling [...] is therefore produced solely by reason [*durch Vernunft bewirkt*]" (CPrR: 76); restricting our inclinations "now has an effect on feeling" (CPrR: 78). See also, Kant's claim in the *Groundwork* that respect is "a feeling *self-wrought* [*selbstgewirktes*] by means of a rational concept" (Gr: 401, note; see also, 460).

recognition of the moral law and the feeling of respect as the force driving moral action might explain why Kant sometimes speaks of them as two aspects of one moment and indeed even as identical.

The feeling of respect for the moral law is then, according to this reading, a necessary affective condition of moral agency. This sensible attunement to the rational claims of morality is part of the transcendental makeup of moral agents. No reason could possibly compel us to acquire the capacity to feel respect for the claims of morality. If we lacked it, we would be incapable of moral action. The moral law and reason would exert no practical force upon us.

This feeling of respect for the moral law, or better, the capacity for feeling respect for the law – this *affective attunement to the claims of morality* – is a necessary condition of moral agency. It is not our duty to acquire this capacity – although it is our duty to cultivate it. We are all already sensibly attuned to the demands of morality. Kant does not think any human being is morally insensible. The voice of the moral law "makes even the boldest evildoer tremble and forces him to hide from its sight" (CPrR: 80). But if any rational being were incapable of feeling respect then that being would be incapable of moral action. The significance of this claim cannot be emphasized enough, a sensible attunement to the claims of morality is part of the transcendental makeup of the moral agent. *This is the fundamental affective mood of morality.*

Kant devotes a considerable part of his discussion to a phenomenological (albeit rather general) characterization of this mood. We can see "a priori that the moral law, as the determining ground of the will, must by thwarting all our inclinations produce a feeling that can be called pain" (CPrR: 73). As Kant himself emphasizes, we have here "the first and perhaps the only case in which we can determine a priori from concepts the relation of cognition (here the cognition of a pure practical reason) to the feeling of pleasure or displeasure" (CPrR: 73). Specifically, the moral law is experienced as a limitation of the propensity to make our subjective preferences into grounds of action; more extremely, respect strikes down and humiliates the tendency to make subjective preferences into unconditional principles (CPrR: 73–74).[9]

It is interesting, furthermore, to note that although the topic of discussion is respect *for the moral law*, Kant says that respect always has as its object persons as moral legislators. It therefore differs from feelings that can be directed at inanimate objects such as admiration or amazement in view of lofty mountains or the heavens and from the admiration analogous to respect invoked by other human talents and capacities such as courage, strength and humor. We give way to the feeling of respect only reluctantly and then strive to resist its humbling majesty. However, when we do manage to overcome our self-conceit we feel elevated contemplating the majesty of the law (CPrR: 76–78). Indeed, reflecting upon our subjection to moral laws causes us to feel self-approbation (CPrR: 80–81). As sensible creatures we are always bound by our nature. However, through constant striving for moral perfection, Kant promises, our respect for the law gradually becomes more akin to love (CPrR: 84).

[9]For detailed discussions of these emotional effects see, Reath 2006: 14–17, 23–25.

Finally, it is worth stressing that respect is described in the Incentives chapter as a single undifferentiated feeling. Had Kant had here in mind a detailed conception of our moral duties and of our various moral failings, he might have described the many ways in which the moral law restricts self-love and humiliates self-conceit. The result would be a richer affective depiction of respect. But the moral law always appears in this context in the singular. Kant is thus thinking of the feeling of respect as recognition of the authority of moral laws in general and not of the plethora of affects that respect for the varied claims of morality might take. This point is worth emphasizing because it is partly for this reason that the discussion of respect in the *Critique of Practical Reason* seems to many too abstract and formal to capture the rich texture of our affective moral lives. It is also worth emphasizing, of course, because in the *Metaphysics of Morals*, to which we now turn, the depiction of moral feelings is far richer.

II. Moral Feeling, Conscience, Love of Others and Respect for Oneself

In the previous section we examined the discussion of respect for the moral law in the second *Critique* (1788). According to the reading we followed, Kant claims there that an affective attunement to the claims of morality is a necessary transcendental condition of rational moral agency. Now although Kant claims there that respect for duty "is the only genuinely moral feeling" (CPrR: 85), he introduces in the *Metaphysics of Morals* (1797) a system of four further categories or types of affective conditions of moral agency: "*moral feeling, conscience, love* of one's neighbor, and *respect* for oneself (*self-esteem*)" (MM: 399). Before turning to the characterization of each of these forms of receptivity to morality, it is important to emphasize that they are all similar in character to respect for the moral law, as it is understood by the reading we followed in the previous section: They are all forms of feeling or sensibility; they are all necessarily related to consciousness of a moral law; and they are all subjective yet necessary conditions of moral agency. With regard to them all, Kant says that we cannot have a duty to acquire these forms of sensibility; they are necessary conditions of moral constraint and thus must be part of the makeup of a mind constrained by moral laws. This structural similarity to the feeling of respect notwithstanding, I will claim that none of these forms of moral sensibility or attunement is the feeling of respect for the moral law. Our task then is to answer the following questions: What are the four affective conditions of moral agency that Kant describes in the Introduction to the *Doctrine of Virtue*? What are the connections between them? How do they relate to the feeling of respect for the moral law?

The first notion is ambiguously named moral feeling. In contrast to respect for the moral law that is characterized as painful and humiliating (see, CPrR: 73, 77), moral feeling is a susceptibility to feel displeasure *or pleasure* (MM: 399). Furthermore, moral feeling is not defined as the response to consciousness of the moral law thwarting our inclinations, but to the representation of particular moral actions: "Every representation of choice proceeds *from the representation of a possible action to* the deed through the feeling of pleasure or displeasure, taking an interest in the action or its effect" (MM: 399).

It is a central tenet of Kant conception of action that to view an action as leading to an end we have set is to view the action and the end as a source of pleasure (and to view an action opposed to our end as a cause of displeasure). This does not mean that all action is heteronomous, motivated by a pleasure we hope to gain. Kant says very clearly that not all feeling is pathological. To represent an action as commanded by the moral law is to view it with a *moral feeling* of pleasure. In other words, moral agents do not act because their action will bring them pleasure. Rather, it is because an action is their duty that carrying it out is distinctly pleasurable.[10] Indeed, Kant quotes approvingly the Stoic saying: "'I wish for a friend, not that he might help *me* in poverty, sickness, imprisonment, etc., but rather that I might stand by *him* and rescue a human being'" (MM: 457).

Kant thinks that no human being is "morally dead" (MM: 400; see also: MM: 438). Such a person would be unable to view any action with a moral feeling of pleasure and thus would be incapable of moral action. For such a person duty would be a purely theoretical notion lacking all practical force. Indeed, agents lacking moral feeling would not be able to acquire it. Thus, viewing certain actions as a cause of a moral feeling of pleasure is a necessary precondition of moral agency. It is not our duty to acquire this capacity, although it is our duty to perfect it. We are all already sensibly attuned to morality. The common perception of Kant's moral theory is that moral action must meet certain objective criteria, specified by the moral law, in order to have moral worth. Kant though is claiming here that to act morally is not just to carry out a certain objectively designated course of action. He is claiming that a necessary condition of moral agency is the capacity to view and experience the actions enjoined by the moral law as the source of a distinct affective pleasure. Kant then is offering here a general description of the feeling of pleasure that accompanies and is indeed a condition of any dutiful action. I will suggest below that this type of moral feeling circumscribes a variety of distinctive feelings that accompany and indeed make possible different types of dutiful action, namely, the variety of feelings we experience when we do the right thing in the right way – and it is furthermore the fact that we act with these feelings that enables us to do our duty. These feelings are a further essential component of what I am calling the moral mood.

In the second part of the discussion of the necessary affective receptivity of moral agents Kant says that "conscience is practical reason holding the human being's duty

[10]In the essay "On a Recently Prominent Tone of Superiority in Philosophy" Kant puts the point succinctly: "That *pleasure* (or displeasure) which must necessarily *precede the law*, if the act is to take place, is *pathological*; but that which the *law* must necessarily *precede*, for this to happen, is *moral*" (TSP 8: 395 note). I am grateful to Dennis Schulting for bringing to my attention this pithy formulation.

before him for his acquittal or condemnation in every case that comes under the law" (MM: 400; see also: MM: 437–438). Conscience is a necessary aspect of moral agency, because having a conscience is viewing ourselves as bound by duty and judging ourselves accordingly. As Kant emphasizes, it is not the task of conscience to pronounce the right objective judgment of what law holds in a given situation and what action it commands or forbids. Conscience is the subjective affective response to this objective judgment, that is, the feelings of being condemned or acquitted by this judgment. It is the role of conscience to force us to assume moral responsibility for our plans and actions. Without this subjective response, objective judgments would have no practical import. This affective imputation is clearly a necessary condition of moral agency and another essential aspect of the moral mood.

Conscience, says Kant, has motive force. It pronounces its verdict with "rightful force" (MM: 438). Indeed, conscience is closely allied to the feeling of respect (MM: 438). It warns us before we act; and, after the fact, conscience examines our action and passes its judgment (MM: 440). Conscience, we might say, is the feeling that enables us to harness the force of respect for the moral law and employ it to guide our particular actions. It tries to prevent trespasses and through remorse guides us to try and rectify the wrongs we have done.

The moral phenomenology of conscience, which Kant sketches, is particularly interesting. First, he develops the image of an inner court of law and the necessary internal conflict it tries: "*conscience* is peculiar in that, although its business is a business of a human being with himself, one constrained by his reason sees himself constrained to carry it on as at the bidding *of another person*" (MM: 438). Thus, having a conscience necessarily expresses itself as the representation of an inner "ideal person that reason creates for itself" (MM: 438). Serving as "*defense council* (advocate)" (MM: 440), of course, are our inclinations and more generally the tendency to make happiness our ruling principle.

> Every human being has a conscience and finds himself observed, threatened, and, in general, kept in awe (respect coupled with fear) by an internal judge; and this authority watching over the law in him is not something that he himself (voluntarily) *makes*, but something incorporated in his being. It follows him like his shadow when he plans his escape. He can indeed stun himself or put himself to sleep by pleasures and distractions, but he cannot help coming to himself or waking up from time to time; and when he does, he hears at once its fearful voice. He can at most, in extreme depravity, bring himself to *heed* it no longer, but he still cannot help *hearing* it. (MM: 438)

Kant is circumscribing then the eventful courtroom drama of conscience: the daily toil of self-scrutiny, evasion, denial and the struggle against them, painful moments of honesty, then – condemnation, guilt and determination to mend our ways or, more rarely, self-approbation.

A second aspect of the phenomenology of conscience is its relation to religious thought and feeling. Employing a possible etymological origin for 'religion' in the Latin *religare*, to bind, Kant defines "conscientiousness (which is also called *religio*) as accountability to a holy being (morally lawgiving reason) distinct from us yet present in our inmost being" (MM: 440). The moral representation of an inner "ideal person that reason creates for itself" is also a religious image of our own rational holiness and a feeling of being bound by this moral-religious ideal.

If Kant's discussion of moral feeling and conscience do not seem to be a sufficient defense against charges of complete and utter austerity, the discussion of love of human beings and of self-respect might make it complete. These feelings correspond to the primary division of the system of duties presented in the *Doctrine of Virtue* into duties that have to do with one's own perfection and duties whose object is the happiness of others.

The discussion of love of others is particularly complicated, because Kant is concerned not to be misunderstood as saying that the feeling of love can be the determining ground of moral action. In the last and shortest of the paragraphs of the discussion Kant says in what sense the feeling of love is a necessary condition of morality. The love he calls delight (*amor complacentiae*) is a "pleasure joined immediately to the representation of an object's existence" (MM: 402). The objects Kant is speaking of here are clearly other human beings. In order to perceive the happiness of others as placing moral demands upon us we must be sensibly attuned to them. Kant, I am suggesting, is speaking here of affective moral perception. To view others as the objects of moral duties is not merely to search for objectively specifiable signs of their needs and of their pursuits of happiness, but to view them with affective sensibility as well. This affective sensibility is indeed a condition of perceiving their needs and happiness as placing moral demands upon us. Again, it is not these feelings of love that are the determining grounds of action. They are the necessary sensible and thus subjective conditions of perceiving our objective moral duties.

Like love of human beings, self-respect or self-esteem is "again, something merely subjective, a feeling of a special kind, not a judgment about an object that it would be a duty to bring about or promote" (MM: 402). Moral perceptiveness must be turned inwards to our own moral self as well as towards others.

I am suggesting then that we view respect for the moral law as the basic affective motive force of moral action. The feelings of our conscience make possible and accompany our attempts to overcome our self-seeking resistance to the claims of morality. It does this by comparing the course of action we are setting on (or have undertaken) with the action duty commands. Conscience thus cautions us not to neglect our duty, and through remorse it urges us to mend our ways when we do. It can thus be viewed as a specification of the feeling of respect for the law. It adds to the former a comparison of the duty morality commands and that evokes respect with our own specific plans or actions. Love of others and self-respect, on the one hand, and moral feeling, on the other, are the feelings that accompany, respectively, consideration of the *ends* and *actions* that moral duty prescribes. The first enables us to perceive others and our own selves as demanding active moral attention. The latter arises in view of a particular action that fulfills (or fails to fulfill) a moral duty. Whereas respect, as it is discussed in the second *Critique*, seems to abstract from the situation in which it arises and the particular course of action an agent plans to take (or did take) in view of it – indeed seems not to distinguish between different moral laws – the moral feelings in the *Doctrine of Virtue* are conditions of perceiving our duties and acting morally in concrete situations. The specification of respect into four types of moral affects is thus a direct consequence of the main task of the *Doctrine of Virtue*, namely, presenting a system of moral duties. The *Doctrine of Virtue* presents such a system and thus takes into account the fact that we have two distinct types of moral ends (others and ourselves), that these prescribe certain courses of action, and that setting on actual courses of action to fulfill our ends requires that we ask ourselves whether we are fulfilling our duties. Thus, we have answers to the questions of how Kant comes by the four types of moral affects he presents in the Introduction to the *Doctrine of Virtue* and to how they are related to one another as well as to respect for the moral law.

III. The Variety of Moral Feelings

I have so far argued that Kant's mature moral theory allots a significant role to a varied affective moral mood. What I would like to focus upon in this section are two particularly noteworthy examples of the moral mood, because they reveal just how rich and diverse is the affective life of moral agents for Kant.

In the context of the discussion of the duties of love and respect for others Kant explicitly distinguishes these duties from the feelings that always accompany them. He goes on to give an example of a duty to another which is clearly accompanied both by a feeling of love for another and by a feeling that derives from our own sense of self-respect:

> … we shall acknowledge that we are under obligation to help someone poor; but since the favor we do implies that his well-being depends on our generosity, and this humbles him, it is our duty to behave as if our help is either merely what is due him or but a slight service of love, and to spare him humiliation and maintain his respect for himself. (MM: 448–449)

Knowing what our duty is here is clear and very briefly described, namely, to help someone poor. However, the affective depth of the example is far greater. It is not simply our duty to help the poor in any way that might (if only temporarily) relieve their adversity, say by handing them a sum of money. It is our duty to this *in the right way*. We are to act with great delicacy to make sure that the other feels that our help is no great matter, it is simply what anyone would do for any person in similar circumstances, without further thought. Indeed, Kant is perhaps suggesting (depending on how we understand the notion of love here) that it might be our duty to act as though not duty but pathological love were our motive. For it is perhaps easier to accept help done out of such love than a favor done with the grave thought of duty in mind. Paradoxically, to do our duty might then might sometimes require us to behave as though we are acting unreflectively from love. To see that our duty is to aid the poor – and at the same time spare them humiliation – thus determines the very manner in which we are to give aid; and if we do not act in this manner we might very well fail to do our duty. It is our duty to act as we do when friends are having a hard time making ends meet or make little of what we are doing.[11] Clearly, we have here an example of how the feelings of love and respect for others (deriving from own sense of self-esteem), as well as moral feeling in Kant's narrow sense, are necessary conditions of fulfilling our objectively determined moral duty. It is noteworthy, furthermore, that we are examining a particular duty of beneficence. Thus, the affective shape of the duty to aid the poor gives us greater affective detail than the very general system of duties Kant presents; clearly, helping a student requires different sensibilities.

Another good example of a very particular moral feeling occurs in the discussion of the prohibition against defiling ourselves with lust. The question under discussion is whether a man is "authorized to direct the use of his sexual attributes to mere animal pleasure, without having in view the preservation of the species" (MM: 424).

> That such an unnatural use (and so misuse) of one's sexual attributes is a violation of duty *to oneself*, and indeed one contrary to morality in its highest degree, occurs to everyone immediately, with the thought of it, and stirs up an aversion to this thought to such an extent that it is considered indecent even to call this vice by its proper name. This does not occur with regard to murdering oneself, which one does not hesitate in the least to lay before the world's eyes in all its horror (in a *species facti*). In the case of unnatural vice it is as if the human being in general felt ashamed of being capable of treating his own person in such a way, which debases him beneath the beasts, so that when even the permitted bodily union of the sexes in marriage (a union which is in itself merely an animal union) is to be mentioned in polite society, this occasions and requires much delicacy to throw a veil over it. (MM: 425)

Let me underscore that Kant says explicitly that we first grasp the transgression of the moral prohibition against lust "with the thought of it." This recognition "stirs up an aversion to this thought." Indeed, he characterizes the affective response to this as a distinct sort of shame and contrasts it with the horror to which the thought of suicide gives rise. Though both are violations of perfect duties to ourselves – thus both threaten our self-esteem – thought of these distinct transgressions elicits very different affective responses. Recognition of the prohibition against lust is not associated with shame alone (and clearly this is not the sort of shame we might feel when contemplating a lie). Indeed, even "the permitted bodily union of the sexes in marriage… requires much delicacy to throw a veil over it." It is also worth emphasizing that though strictly speaking Kant seems to be giving us here examples of injuring our feelings of self-respect, contemplating such acts no doubt causes us shame (moral feeling in Kant's narrow sense) and, furthermore, it is quite clear that the guilty conscience of a person who has succumbed to lust will similarly be afflicted with shame.

[11] In a closely related example of the duties of beneficence of a rich man, Kant suggests other ways of fulfilling the duty without humiliating the person in need: "he must show that he is himself put under obligation by the other's acceptance or honored by it" (MM: 453). In another related discussion, Kant says that we must not regard "a kindness received as a burden one would gladly be rid of (since the one so favored stands a step lower than his benefactor, and this wounds his pride)" (MM: 456; see also, MM: 458). The theme of gratitude is of course also pivotal to the discussion of the vice of ingratitude (MM: 459).

What these examples teach us, I suggest, is that the four types of moral feelings that Kant discusses in the Introduction to the *Doctrine of Virtue* are in fact general categories of feelings. These general categories comprise a rich fabric of feelings, indeed as rich as the variety of moral duties that bind us and the diverse actions we undertake to fulfill them. Far from acting with no feeling, the affective life of moral agents, as Kant conceives of it, reveals a highly varied affective mood.

IV. Moral Feelings and Inclinations

Our examination of the *Metaphysics of Morals* has revealed that moral feelings are for Kant necessary conditions of rational moral agency. This must come as a great surprise for those who have taken the caricature sketched by Schiller and Goethe in *The Philosophers* for a portrayal true to Kant's views. But it must also come as something of a surprise to the far more careful readers who defend Kant against the charges of moral asceticism by insisting that it is a grave misunderstanding to depict him as a trenchant and outspoken foe of all inclinations. Recent discussions of the matter often claim that Kant has nothing against the pursuit of happiness – as long as it does not lead to the neglect of duty. The life of moral agents is not the emotionally stunted life of continuously cranking a universalization algorithm and acting automaton-like on its directives. Rather, it is a life in which the human desire for happiness is limited – indeed shaped – by the preponderant pursuit of our moral vocation.

This line of defense is certainly true to the spirit as well as the letter of Kant's moral theory. Yet it still conceives of moral action as accompanied only by the reverent feeling of respect for the law. While respect for the law is a very important part of our moral life, according to Kant, I have argued that he also views a variegated affective mood as a necessary condition of moral agency. This claim is confirmed when we ask why Kant responded favorably to Schiller's *On Grace and Dignity* (1793) and insisted that he cannot admit to too deep a disagreement with him. Indeed, for Schiller the notorious caricature which we examined at the very beginning of this paper (and which is often taken to be his own view) is clearly a caricature of reading Kant the wrong way:

> In Kant's moral philosophy, the idea of *duty* is presented with a severity that repels all graces and might tempt a weak intellect to seek moral perfection by taking the path of a somber and monkish asceticism. However much this great philosopher tried to defend himself against this misinterpretation, which, to his serene and free spirit has to be the most outrageous one, he himself it seems to me, has provided strong grounds for it (although, for his purpose, this was unavoidable), in his strict and harsh opposition of the two principles that have an effect on the human will. (Schiller 2005: 150)[12]

[12] In a later letter to Kant, Schiller conveys his relief that, unlike others, Kant did not misunderstand his *Thalia* essay as expressing opposition to his views, as the reference to the essay in the *Religion* reveals (see, R: 23, note). See, Streitfeld, Erwin and Viktor Žmegnač, eds. 1983. *Schillers Briefe*. Königstein: Athenäum, 252–253 (June 13, 1794).

The reason for this severity of presentation, Schiller elaborates, is the moral state of the times, patent both in the social and political reality and in moral theorizing. The difference between Schiller and Kant is subtle but very important. For Schiller, gracefulness is the state in which inclination and duty move in perfect harmony and feelings guide the moral will with surety. But he also vocally acknowledges the fact that this is an ideal we can never fully attain. The moral life of human beings will always contain conflicts between the call of our nature and the legislation of reason. This is why the notion of dignity is essential to his moral theory. For Kant, in contrast, "the concept of duty includes unconditional necessitation, to which gracefulness stands in direct opposition" (R: 23, note). Indeed, as I have been emphasizing, *rational moral feelings are not inclinations*. They are affective capacities that tie us to the moral ends of reason and make possible moral action and reflection. The "glorious picture of humanity, as portrayed in the figure of virtue, does allow the attendance of the *graces*, who, however, maintain a respectful distance when duty alone is at issue" (R: 23, note). There is to be sure a certain austerity in Kant's vision of the affective mood of morality – it certainly demands grave thoughtfulness, self-possession and an enduring commitment to the moral values that tie us to others and to our own higher vocation. However, it is not at all a life barren of all feeling. Nor indeed is it without joy.

> Now, if we ask, "What is the *aesthetic* constitution, the *temperament* so to speak *of virtue*: is it courageous and hence *joyous*, or weighed down by fear and dejected?" an answer is hardly necessary. The latter slavish frame of mind can never be found without a hidden *hatred* of the law, whereas a heart joyous in the *compliance* with its duty (not just complacency in the *recognition* of it) is the sign of genuineness in virtuous disposition, even where *piety* is concerned, which does not consist in the self-torment of a remorseful sinner (a torment which is very ambiguous, and usually only an inward reproach for having offended against prudence), but in the firm resolve to improve in the future. This resolve, encouraged by good progress, must needs effect a joyous frame of mind, without which one is never certain of having *gained* also *a love* for the good... (R: 23, note)

I have claimed that for Kant, contrary to common perception, an affective attunement to the claims of morality is a necessary condition of rational moral agency. Recognition of a moral duty evokes the feeling of respect for the moral law which drives moral action. Love of others and self-respect and moral feeling are the feelings that accompany and make possible, respectively, consideration of the *ends* and fulfilling the *actions* that moral reason prescribes. The feelings of our conscience accompany and are indeed conditions of the practical efficacy of the judgments we pass over the choices we make. They play a role in trying to overcome the temptations that lead us astray and in trying to mend our ways when our moral resolve fails us.

What can Kant's theory of moral feelings contribute to the philosophical discussion of moods and to the question of the relation of philosophy itself to mood? For Kant, moral feelings are capacities for responding affectively to the demands of morality. It is these affective responses that reveal the practical import of these claims. Kant insists that moral feelings have no cognitive content. If there were morally insensible people they would know everything we know about the world.

However, nothing in their world would place them under moral obligations. Strikingly, it is the affective mood of morality that reveals to us the objective practical import or meaning of moral values. Some moods place me within a subjective space of reasons – reasons for me to view things and to act in distinctive ways. For Kant, *the moral mood places me within the objective space of practical reason*. Finally, the charge of austere intellectualism frequently leveled against Kant's conception of moral agency is a fault many claim to find in his very conception and practice of philosophy. The revelation that for Kant an affective mood is a necessary condition of moral agency should spur us to look at him anew and discover his great sensitivity to our actual moral and intellectual lives.

References

Beck, Lewis White. 1960. *A Commentary on Kant's 'Critique of Practical Reason'*. Chicago: The University of Chicago Press.

Beiser, Frederick. 2005. *Schiller as Philosopher: A re-examination*. Oxford: Clarendon Press.

Broadie, Alexander, and Elizabeth M. Pybus. 1975. "Kant's concept of 'respect'." *Kant-Studien* 66.

Kant, Immanuel. 1996a. *Practical Philosophy*. Trans. and ed. Mary J. Gregor. Cambridge: Cambridge University Press.

Kant, Immanuel. 1996b. *Religion and Rational Theology*. Ed. Allen W. Wood and George di Giovanni, Trans. Mary J. Gregor. Cambridge: Cambridge University Press.

Kant, Immanuel. 2002. *Theoretical Philosophy after 1781*. Ed. Henry Allison and Peter Heath. Cambridge: Cambridge University Press.

Reath, Andrews. 2006. "Kant's Theory of Moral Sensibility: Respect for the Moral Law and the Influence of Inclination." In *Agency and Autonomy in Kant's Moral Theory: Selected Essays*. Oxford: Clarendon Press.

Safranski, Rüdiger. 2004. *Schiller oder Die Erfindung des Deutschen Idealismus*. München: Carl Hanser.

Schiller, Friedrich. 1869. *Schillers Gedichte*. Stuttgart: Verlag der J. G. Cotta'schen Buchhandlung.

Schiller, Friedrich. 2005. *Schiller's 'On Grace and Dignity' in Its Cultural Context: Essays and a New Translation*, ed. Jane V. Curran and Christophe Fricke. Trans. Jane V. Curran. Rochester: Camden House.

The Proto-Ethical Dimension of Moods

Shlomo Cohen

The notion of proto-ethics is missing in ethical discourse. It refers to a domain which is not properly ethical (in a sense to be determined) yet is in some way preparatory for ethics. The general idea is that in order to function meaningfully, ethics needs a shared background of basic intuitions and dispositions regarding the human life form, or in other words, regarding our humanity. Though this idea is at times recognized in different guises, such recognition has not yet begun to crystallize into a distinct conception of proto-ethics. In this short essay I will offer an initial characterization of proto-ethics, suggesting that this virtually unacknowledged category deserves independent philosophical treatment. Specifically, I will stress the role of existential moods and sentiments in this dynamic.

In *Heidegger and the Ground of Ethics*, Frederick Olafson makes a unique reference to proto-ethics. Writing about Heidegger's notion of *Mitsein* (our being in the world together with one another), Olafson says, "My thought was that if that conception could be developed beyond the very brief sketch he gave of it in *Being and Time*, it might be possible to show it has at least a proto-ethical character and that this would be of fundamental importance for any inquiry into the grounds of ethics" (Olafson 1998: 2, n. 2). Olafson's book is an attempt to demonstrate how the ontology of human relations "constitutes the ground of ethical authority" (Olafson 1998: 11). His original discussion is, I believe, an uncommon example of a correct diagnosis of the relation between ethics and phenomenological ontology; it does not, however, dwell on a metaethical analysis of the proto-ethical as such nor deal with the role of moods in that field.

Let us start by asking: What makes an ethical view ethical? This is not an absurd question as "What makes pleasure pleasurable?" nor hyperbolic as "What reasons are there for being rational?" It is an open question, pointing *inter alia* to certain pre-theoretical intuitions we can appeal to regarding what sort of elements we

S. Cohen (✉)
Department of Philosophy, The Hebrew University, Mt Scopus, Jerusalem 91905
e-mail: shlomo_inc@yahoo.com

H. Kenaan and I. Ferber (eds.), *Philosophy's Moods: The Affective Grounds of Thinking*, Contributions To Phenomenology 63, DOI 10.1007/978-94-007-1503-5_12,

expect to find in an ethical doctrine. Surely not anything can sensibly feature in an ethical theory. Recognizing such constraints is the initial lead for the exploration of proto-ethics.

Assuming we agree on the untenability of a strictly formal delineation of the ethical sphere (via, for example, the criteria of universalizability or overridingness),[1] we are then bound to look for some defining content. Schematically speaking, to qualify as "proto-ethical" such content would have to be on the one hand connected to ethics in some essential way, yet on the other hand (sufficiently) distinct from ethics proper. To perceive this, let us first take a step back to consider an argument about pre-requirements of moral thinking, which would lead us towards the object of our inquiry.

Harry Frankfurt claims there are "final ends that to us would be flatly incomprehensible" (Frankfurt 2006: 39). He writes, "Loving death, or incapacity, or isolation, or continuously vacant or distressing experience involves no contradiction. If a person did love those things, however, we would be unable to make sense of his life." Such a person would exhibit "volitional irrationality"; his will would be "defective," and its objects—though not inconceivable—would be "unthinkable." Such constraints on volition *precede* practical rationality, Frankfurt makes clear. "Many philosophers believe that an act is right only if it can be justified to other rational beings. For this to be possible it is not enough that the rationality of the others be merely of the formal variety. Those whom we seek to convince must be volitionally rational as well. If they are not, then their practical reasoning—however formally correct it may be—builds upon a foundation that is in radical opposition to ours." In this respect we can speak of "the volitional necessities from which morality derives" (Frankfurt 2006: 38–47). There are, then, according to this view, certain elements of the human form of life that serve as an essential foundation for the possibility of morality.

Without subscribing to Frankfurt's ethics, I want to further his intuition and look into the idea of experiences that necessarily precede and condition strict practical rationality—the idea that in order to make sense moral reasoning and judgment must be preceded and supported by an acknowledgment of certain givens of human existence. These latter refer to patterns of volition or of the basic aims of human action. Outside of such an initial framework human goals would be "unthinkable," as Frankfurt explicitly says; consequently, ethical judgment would slide into senselessness. Now there is ground to believe that naturalistic accounts of human being cannot ultimately do the job of demarcating the contours of the field of ethics. Firstly, because for any natural fact, its essential connection to ethics is open to doubt; and secondly because there are proto-ethical elements of human intentionality that in all appearances seem to exceed naturalistic accounts (see below).

To overcome those deficiencies toward a sound core conception of proto-ethics we must aim at the essential and most distinctive elements of our "form of life"—those

[1]See for example Warnock (1969). The criticism of ethical formalism as empty goes back to Hegel's *Sittlichkeit* and continues into virtually any contemporary metaethical criticism of Kantian constructivism.

existential certainties presupposed by all meaningful ethical thinking. This suggests an analysis in terms of the existential ontology of humanity. We should inquire how the phenomenology of fundamental elements of our intuitive self-recognition as humans would expose (aspects of) the constitutive grounds of ethics. Basic dispositions involving the consciousness of respect (for self and others), the intrinsic balance between intersubjectivity and individuality, agentic (as opposed to strictly causal) responsibility, and the like are essential, immutable aspects of our understanding of human beings *qua* humans, as well as integral (if sometimes implicit) constituents of the intuitive meaning of our ethical notions in general. Their relation to ethics therefore cannot be explained strictly causally or by means of supervenience. Moreover, as I will discuss, they also exhibit inherent valence. Consequently, they are neither irrelevant nor arbitrary in the constitution of ethics, and for an ethical conception to disregard them would indeed be "unthinkable."[2]

To develop this line of thought we may find assistance in Heidegger. Human Being as "Being-in-the-world" is a constantly concerned engagement, characterized in its deepest nature as one of "care" (Heidegger 1962). The *existentialia* (or "existentials," the essential structures making up this everyday Being-in-the-world) are the basic modes of our existence through which we disclose the world. As ontological elements of human intentionality, they have a transcendental status that goes beyond that of "mere" psychological entities. Of special importance is "state-of-mind" or "affectedness" or "situatedness" (*Befindlichkeit*), variously expressed in moods: modes of "being tuned-in" to the world, that reveal or "make manifest" the world—our world—to us. The nature of moods according to this view, unlike that in many other accounts, supports the possibility of their proto-ethical role. Far from being mere momentary sensations, moods underlie our capacity to be oriented, and in fact express a total orientation to the world (Ballard 1991: 1–2): they generate *interest* in aspects of our surrounding, reflect *interpretations* of ourselves and others,[3] and introduce ways of *mattering*: we could never be affected by anything "if Being-in-the-world, with its state-of-mind, had not already submitted itself to having entities within the world 'matter' to it in a way which its moods have outlined in advance" (Heidegger 1962: 177)—moods supply purposes which set agendas for our actions. Underscoring their crucial role in our general orientation to the world is the fact that we are never mood-free—"in every case Dasein always has some mood." (Heidegger 1962: 173) We always already find ourselves within moods that disclose the world with an already initial meaningfulness. "By way of having a

---

[2] My claim will be that the idea of humanity is already evaluative and serves as a meaning-conferring background for ethical theory. Any ethical consideration of or reliance on the notions of human dignity, respect for persons, love for humankind, etc. (including the ethics that follows from Kant's formulation of "Humanity as End in Itself"), must include an—at least implicit—reference to a philosophical anthropology of humanity, that is, to the basic determinants of human existence. Hence, damage to the image or notion of what it is to be human inevitably entails ethical consequences.

[3] Moreover, these interpretations are not arbitrary: moods express how things have become for one, they embody the history of Dasein and its social milieu.

mood, Dasein 'sees' possibilities in terms of which it is." (Heidegger 1962: 188) Hence practicality is already embedded within this ontological picture. A preliminary evaluative stance is implicit here as attunement establishes "the ability to come across things that are *value-laden*" (Guignon 2003: 186; my emphasis). These characteristics together, making up a practical-evaluative comprehensive orientation to the world, support the ability of moods to function in a proto-ethical capacity.

In moods, the world is disclosed to us with a proto-ethical orientation. Affect (alongside understanding and discourse) is one of the three fundamental elements of (the analytic of) Dasein. Moods, as "the *most complete* affects" (Ballard 1991: 1), are therefore part of the synthetic a priori constitution of the world. With the ontology of Being-in-the-world comes a new sense of transcendentalism, which is not based only on categories of understanding. "A state-of-mind [*Befindlichkeit*] always has its understanding, even if it merely keeps it suppressed. Understanding always has its mood." (Heidegger 1962: 182) The purposefulness of moods allows a sense of transcendentalism not confined to the conditions of possibility of science but rather pertaining also to ethics, as we will see. Moods participate in the constitution of moral thoughts.

The important proto-ethical role of moods is not only suggested by their general transcendental function but more acutely in certain instances where a mood can reveal ontological structures. A prominent example of an "ontological" mood is anxiety (*Angst*). Anxiety is "fundamentally different from fear. We become afraid always in the face of this or that particular being that threatens us in this or that particular respect" (Heidegger 1998: 82–96; 88); but "that in the face of which one has anxiety is not an entity within-the-world." (Heidegger 1962: 231) Indeed, "that which anxiety is anxious about is Being-in-the-world itself." (Heidegger 1962: 232) Having as its object the ontological structure of Being-in-the-world, and not a specific quality or state of affairs *in* the world, makes anxiety "ontological" (in contradistinction to the contingent features of empirical psychology). In anxiety, "Dasein finds itself *face to face* with the 'nothing' of the possible impossibility of its existence." (Heidegger 1962: 310) In disclosing this "thrownness" of Dasein's, "anxiety individualizes Dasein and thus discloses it as '*solus ipse*'." (Heidegger 1962: 233) In that individuation, anxiety brings Dasein before itself as an "authentic ability-to-be-in-the-world." (Heidegger 1962: 232) The disclosure of one's potential for responsible, authentic individuality has proto-ethical meaning. It is admittedly difficult to understand this as a brute description of ontological possibilities devoid of an evaluative dimension. The value of authenticity, we should stress, does not have any alternative ethical justification—rational or otherwise—independent of that basic existential mood.[4] "Anxiety has a unique disclosive role because it reveals to us what it is to be human in the deepest sense," explains Guignon.[5] That which is "human in the deepest (ontological) sense" carries intuitive valence and functions as a ground of

[4]For this point see Golomb (1995: 202).

[5]Guignon (2003: 189).

ethics. Indeed, the avoidance of dehumanization is constitutive of the spirit of ethics and determinative of its purview. Accordingly, the disclosure of our humanity offered by anxiety has a basic proto-ethical nature.

We traced the source of the idea of authenticity to the ontological mood of anxiety. Authenticity has a clear ethical flavor, and its central role in existentialist ethics is well known. Authenticity, however, is *proto*-ethical, for it provides a blank scheme of practical recommendation without offering any positive moral proposition or prescribing anything (indeed, this being its entire *point*). Moreover, an agent may act authentically in ways that would seem morally repulsive to all sane judges. And yet all this does not strip authenticity of its intuitive significance for ethics.[6] While proto-ethical elements function as necessary supportive background for the meaningfulness of our ethical concepts and judgments, they fall short of prescribing action[7] or concretely distinguishing moral right from wrong. Authenticity is one such proto-ethical element constituted by the mood of anxiety.

While working out the progression from proto-ethics to ethics proper clearly surpasses the scope of this paper, it may be beneficial to merely indicate how it works in the case of authenticity. The ethics of integrity is the ethics of living up to the values that make up a personal ideal identity. The ethical value attached to the construction and defense of a personal identity (as an ego-ideal), however, can only be understood against the background provided by existential authenticity. Without the positive valence the phenomenon of anxiety confers on ("authentic") individuality, we would have no ground to regard integrity as superior to other life options (mere internal consistency is not invariably good). The value of integrity as embodying the way a person chooses to express his or her humanity presupposes the value of human individuality as disclosed by anxiety. The ontology of authenticity forms the ground for the quest for personal integrity by providing an ontological sense of true selfhood as a transcendental point of reference, and gives sense to the ethical duty to "become who one is."[8] Moreover, having integrity means living according to one's own conception of the good life, i.e. it implies self-legislation as an expression of freedom. But the very possibility of such freedom is given through anxiety—"Anxiety makes manifest in Dasein…its *Being-free for* the freedom of choosing itself and taking hold of itself." (Heidegger 1962: 232) Personal freedom, which in the ethics of integrity is sought as a goal, is given as an ontological possibility in the phenomenology of anxiety. The autonomy achieved by the person of integrity thus embodies the pursuit of authenticity in the ethical domain.

We are examining the view that proto-ethical elements in the ontology of humanity shape a horizon for ethics. Shame too is a sentiment with distinct ethical aspects, but that nonetheless, as we will see, does not belong in ethics-proper.

---

[6]The question of whether the idea of authenticity in Heidegger's and Sartre's ontologies is not an unlawful transgression into ethics has been a source of controversy. A well-developed idea of proto-ethics may offer an answer by explaining away the dichotomy between ethics and ontology.

[7]In discussing normativity below we will see an important qualification to this.

[8]This, according to Nietzsche, is *what one's conscience commands* (Nietzsche 1974: 270).

It is true that in one embodiment shame is indeed a moral emotion expressing disappointment with oneself for having acted so as to tarnish one's self-conception (as, for example, when one is ashamed of oneself for having preferred personal comfort to being a loyal friend). Moral shame, however, also has a proto-ethical precursor, in the form of *existential* shame. Jean-Paul Sartre offers the ultimate articulation of this essential dimension of shame, which centers on the phenomenon of "the look."[9] The most basic nature of shame, Sartre claims, involves the position of *being seen*. In his analysis this is much more than the trivial experience we all recognize—it is part of human ontology: the fundamental experience where the individual does not engage and transcend the world but rather is engaged and transcended. In this experience, the *subject* assumes the character of an *object*. "I can be ashamed only as my freedom escapes me in order to become a *given* object." (Sartre 1958: 261) The ontological character of shame is manifest in its disclosure of the dynamic between the phenomena of objecthood and subjecthood. Sartre writes, "Pure shame is not the feeling of being this or that guilty object but in general of being *an* object; that is of *recognizing myself* in this degraded, fixed, and dependent being which I am for the Other." (Sartre 1958: 288–9) The transformation of *being-for-itself* into *being-for-others* (a form of *being-in-itself*) is existentially experienced as degradation. "Shame is the feeling of an *original fall,* not because of the fact that I may have committed this or that particular fault but simply that I have 'fallen' into the world in the midst of things and that I need the mediation of the Other in order to be what I am." (ibid.) Such objectification engenders shame because its phenomenal meaning is the loss of independence and control of one's actions: "With the other's look… I am no longer master of the situation." (Sartre 1958: 265) "It is in this sense that we can consider ourselves as 'slaves' in so far as we appear to the Other." (Sartre 1958: 267)

This "fall" in front of the Other is a proto-ethical moment. Existential shame, the conscious expression of a primordial awareness of "falling into objectness," signifies a clear direction of valence: we primordially view agency as positive. This evaluative attitude, however, cannot be directly translated into a moral judgment—there is obviously no moral duty to increase agency per se, at all times or in all circumstances, not even *ceteris paribus*. Rather, exercising agency is inherent in being human, and this has positive valence that forms part of the intuitive understanding of human dignity and so of the background premises of ethical reasoning. Similarly, although existing in the form of *being-for-others* would be miserable as a life plan, it is an integral part of every normal human life. Ethical judgment is necessary to determine when *being-for-others* is unwarranted conformism and when it is in fact the right position to be in. Such ethical reasoning, however, presupposes the proto-ethical level where shame determines the basic valence of agency. As in the case of anxiety and authenticity, here too there is no antecedent

[9]Sartre 1958: esp. part 3, ch. 1, sec. IV.

external factor or reason determining that valence.[10] In anxiety the mood appears vis-à-vis being-in-the-world or "the They" (*das Man*), in shame the proto-ethical dynamic is in front of a concrete other.

The phenomenology of shame is intertwined with that of respect. The idea of respect for persons (self and others) is a foundational ethical notion, but its origin is somewhat obscure. At times we feel great appreciation for a person on account of that person's skills, courage, achievements, and so on. However, the basic attitude of respect for persons clearly goes beyond that level—indeed, we believe it should inform our attitude toward every person, regardless of personal virtues. The phenomenological ontology of shame suggested the awareness of loss of sovereignty as its basic meaning: shame is effected by the Other who, while looking at me, is "an inapprehensible transcendence posited upon me." (Sartre 1958: 270) The Other is in this ontological sense infinitely *distant* from me. Shame expresses the experience of the ultimate distance recognizable in human phenomenology: the distance between the person as object versus as subject. "In the phenomenon of the look," says Sartre, "the Other is on principle that which can not be an object," (Sartre 1958: 268) and this attitude toward a subject *qua* subject is the source of what we call respect for persons.[11] In this way, the existential shame situation, through the ontological dimension of distance, reveals the sentiment of respect as its Siamese counterpart. Only that in front of which I can in principle be ashamed can elicit my respect.

"Respect" designates the primordial attitude toward a subject as such. Heidegger rightly claims that "Dasein's being is not to be deduced from an idea of man" (Heidegger 1962: 226); similarly, we add, the attitude of respect toward a "Dasein" cannot be deduced from the *idea* of dignity. The idea of human dignity is not concretely perceptible; it is an abstract notion and can often be elusive. Dignity rests on a prior existential attitude of respect for humans.[12] The *existential* phenomenon of respect is proto-ethical. This can become clear once we recognize the character of that primordial, pre-moralized attitude of respect. That primary attitude encompasses the widest spectrum of cases of respect, and is connected to phenomena of awe, wonder, or deference. It includes, for example, the respect of a warrior toward a worthy rival whom he in fact attempts to kill. The existential attitude of respect is compatible with forming conceptions of human rights but also with killing a revered enemy. In its pre-moralized origin, respect is thus proto-ethical. Respect is the ontological sentiment that pervades the encounter with a subject as such; it is in this sense inevitable and does not yet determine moral behavior. This sentiment,

[10] Such valence, determined pre-reflectively by affect, can be termed "existential value."

[11] For a thorough discussion of this point see Cohen (2008). A different rendition of an ethical idea of the infinite distance of "the other" (versus the "proximity" of things) is found in Emmanuel Levinas' fundamental distinction between the ontological and the transcendent (Levinas 1969). Kant too recognizes distance as the mark of respect (Kant 1996: 198).

[12] This understanding of respect is of course not from *Being and Time* or *Being and Nothingness*.

however, is constitutive of the special consideration that "humanity" commands, and is thus a presupposition of ethics. It precedes normative moral judgment by being constitutive to its semantic field.

As existential anxiety, shame, and respect show, "humanity" is not evaluatively neutral. It is akin to a "thick concept" whose description *ipso facto* includes evaluation[13]; it is special, however, in being ontological. As a set of *existentialia*, humanity should be thought of in terms of an "existential a priori of philosophical anthropology" (Heidegger 1962: 170). Unlike naturalistic factors, this can indeed set *absolute* criteria for what would become "unthinkable" in ethics (in light of Frankfurt's original observation). In this, the "existential a priori" performs a true proto-ethical function.

According to this picture, the fundamental phenomenology of humanity shapes the horizon of ethics. The existential a priori is distinct from Kant's well-known epistemic kind of a priori (think, for instance, of being-towards-death as existentially but not epistemically a priori). We cannot come up with a theory of morality for "all creatures of reason," for that would violate the existentially a priori elements that make human conduct—ethics first and foremost—sensibly relevant to us.[14] That which in principle does not make sense to us cannot reasonably participate in grounding our rational deliberation and practical judgment. And that which does not involve the deepest existential experiences of humanity cannot be ultimately *important* to us; hence it could not claim the overriding position we (often) ascribe to morality.

The metaethical depth of the proto-ethical status of moods parallels the idea that it goes beyond mere psychological analysis (the latter possibility can still provide some notion of proto-ethics, though that would be just a chapter within a naturalistic metaethical view). This thesis has been supported—albeit very briefly—by three kinds of considerations: (1) logical: the transcendental status of "attunement," (2) ontological: by explaining how certain moods intend ontological structures, and (3) semantically: by the claim that ontological moods are indispensable for the notion of our humanity as we understand it.

A basic metaethical distinction is the one between the normative and the psychological (or social or biological, etc.). Understood as a complementary dichotomy,

---

[13]The view that the "fact" of humanity is constituted via an evaluative stance is not a peculiarly "continental" idea. A similar insight is expressed by Daniel Dennett, who writes that "it is not the case that once we have established the objective fact that something is a person, we treat him or her or it in a certain way, but that our treating him or her or it in this certain way is somehow and to some extent constitutive of its being a person." See Dennett (1978: 270).

[14]Nor does the restriction on the scope of the authority of ethics entail a diminishment in the commanding nature of ethical imperatives—what commands necessarily for any human creature has sufficient, satisfactory authority as a binding imperative. The different senses of categoricity that these distinctions entail deserve separate discussion.

this leaves no place for proto-ethics.[15] In response, we presented the *existential* as a distinct modality: it has preliminary valence but is not yet normative (see below); it refers to human constitution, but is not psychological (ontological moods are "prior to all psychology of moods" (Heidegger 1962: 172)). The dichotomy between the normative and the psychological is usually expressed as that between reasons and causal motivations. Again, the existential modality offers a different picture.[16] Proto-ethical moods are not moral reasons: in moods "Dasein is disclosed to itself *prior* to all cognition" (Heidegger 1962: 175); moods therefore cannot be reasons. But they are not causes either, as familiarity with them is constitutive to the meaningfulness of ethical judgments. In Wittgensteinian terminology, they have "grammatical" status; they function as necessary background for reason-giving in ethics. In this sense we recognize a proto-ethical dimension functioning as a "*material a priori*" for ethics.

"*From the ontological point of view*," says Heidegger, "we must as a general principle leave the primary discovery of the world to 'bare mood'." (Heidegger 1962: 177) Moreover, "the possibilities of disclosure which belong to cognition reach far too short a way compared with the primordial disclosure belonging to moods." (Heidegger 1962: 173) This primary role of moods connects to the notion of *aletheia* as the primary notion of truth: we do not base knowledge and learning on the recognition of transcendent metaphysical truths but on unearthing underlying meanings that belong to the phenomenology of being-in-the-world as are manifest in our lives. The action of mood is part of this "uncovering," challenging the simple dichotomy of cognitive-propositional-objective versus non-cognitive-experiential-non-objective. Accordingly, the dichotomy of normative versus psychological is also broken (as we will further see below). That this disclosure by moods is proto-ethical, as I have explained, means that ethics does not start from strictly theoretical knowledge: "moral knowledge" is contingent on certain basic orientations to the world and to others, which moods provide. That mood is "prior to cognition" entails

---

[15] A parallel difficulty in accepting the notion of proto-ethics concerns its maladjustment to the map of contemporary metaethical approaches. At issue is the idea of the autonomy of ethics. The various strands of reductive naturalism, on the one hand, deny such autonomy, saying there are no peculiarly moral facts, properties, or states of affairs that cannot be reduced to non-moral ones. On the other side of the divide are theories that affirm the autonomy of the moral domain, such as moral intuitionism, Kantian constructivism, non-cognitivism, and arguably non-reductive naturalist realism. The idea of the proto-ethical falls in between those two general approaches: whether the empirical and the ethical completely overlap or whether there is an infinite gap between them—in both cases no unique place is left for preliminaries to ethics. Each of these metaethical theories faces profound theoretical challenges, however; the exploration of the notion of proto-ethics may show a way out of that metaethical impasse.

[16] To state the obvious: the existential-ontological picture does not adopt the Humean philosophical anthropology, as do most metaethical theories (it rests on a conception of persons as "ek-sistents").

that the phenomena of proto-ethics condition the propositional truths of ethics.[17] While this curtails aspirations of moral universalism, it does not spell moral relativism, but, appropriately, means that ethics relies on the most fundamental elements of the human condition. If these changed, morality would lose its grounding intuitions and would accordingly be bound to change along.

The ethical a priori has most often been identified with laws and rationality. Here, however, we find a very different picture, involving pre-reflective dispositions and experiences. Since they involve fundamental elements of the consciousness of being a human subject as well as of being an intersubjective agent, they are *ipso facto* conditions for the possibility of ethical thinking as we normally know it. At the same time, however, they fall short of providing moral judgments. The conjunction of these two features—of constituting necessary evaluative dimensions for the possibility and intelligibility of ethics and of not providing moral judgments—establishes (an initial sense of) proto-ethics. This is indeed the case with the ontological moods and sentiments we have been reviewing, they have certain preliminary "valence" but do not directly determine moral right or wrong.

It is important to relate this ambiguous position of proto-ethics to the general question of normativity. Two basic requirements must be fulfilled for normativity to be present: (1) there must be a standard which is public, and (2) it must be vindicated in some acceptable way that exceeds its mere existence or *de facto* acceptance. We need to examine in what ways proto-ethics does or does not exhibit normativity. Being evaluative and having a clear direction of valence (e.g. agency is positive), implies normative recommendation; how then is the evaluative character of moods different from normativity, if it is, and in what sense? Firstly, the nature of the norms involved is different. Moods as we have seen are "prior to all cognition"; they do not therefore provide laws of conduct or issue norms explicitly. Our common existential makeup disposes us to certain general agreements, but "that is not agreement in opinions but in form of life" (Wittgenstein 1953: §241). The norms embedded in such agreement are not propositional but rather dispositional; they do not dictate, but *orient* our conduct in ways which do not necessarily offer singular solutions. To the extent that we expect ethics to provide rules we can apply to situations, here we can only "retrospectively" retrieve and articulate the norms implicit in our conduct. Our situation in that respect is thus not one of "accepting" a norm in the regular sense but of "being in the grip of a norm" (Gibbard 1990: 60).[18] We are clearly in the grip of powerful norms regarding the evaluative dimensions of shame, authenticity, respect, and so on. This means that we are so constituted as to express those norms in our behavior irrespective of (prior to) judgment, even if upon reflection we find them irrational in a particular case—as, for example, when a person feels shame upon suffering humiliating treatment even though she fully recognizes that the humiliator and not the humiliated is morally blameworthy.

---

[17] The primordial disclosive character of moods stands in stark opposition to the objectivity-thwarting role assigned to them throughout most of the history of philosophy.

[18] While I find Gibbard's terminology helpful, this should not imply any further adoption of his metaethical position.

The mere existence of a norm does not yield normativity unless that norm is vindicated or endorsed in some way that validates its being good or right or just, and so on. Can existential norms claim normative validation? Earlier, we invoked the traditional analytic distinction between the psychological and the normative modalities. The existential modality has a special character in this respect. I said that normativity necessitates transcending the mere existence of a norm—how is that effected? By and large, the answer is: through rational justification. While psychology provides motives, normativity provides reasons or, indeed (if we allow that reasons operate on our factual economy of motivations), justified motives. Now the existential is a descriptive story about moods (and more generally, *existentialia*) that form part of our makeup. In this sense, it resembles psychology, not normativity. The crucial distinction, however, is that we have spoken of the "existential *a priori*." What this means is that, unlike the case with psychology, we cannot sensibly comprehend alternatives to operating according to our *existentialia* (this is the most profound sense given to Frankfurt's category of the "unthinkable"). Since we cannot think sensibly outside of that human condition, we cannot reflectively transcend it in order to endorse it; but—and here is the crux of the matter—instead of ruling out normativity, this actually establishes a unique pre-normative status. An (*a priori*) evaluative norm that cannot be transcended cannot be validated (as every attempt to reflect on it would inevitably presuppose it in order to be meaningful to humans) and therefore cannot be normative in the regular sense; but then it cannot be doubted either. In a "negative" rather than a "positive" mechanism, this leaves us with *an evaluative norm that is beyond dispute*. This offers a special ("negative") sense of normativity which we might want to designate as "pre-normative." The existential then is pre-normative, as befits its status as proto-ethical.

"The normative authority of reason…cannot be what accounts for the normative authority of morality" (Frankfurt 2006: 21). Understanding the reliance of the ethical on the proto-ethical and the dependence of ethical normativity on the binding pre-normative nature of human existential-ontology suggests a novel response to that difficulty. An influential idea in modern ethical theory has been that ethics cannot be justified, for either the justification is in ethical terms, in which case it would already be internal to ethics, or it is in non-ethical terms which would immediately commit the Naturalistic Fallacy. While a search for justification might be misguided, an existential inquiry into the proto-ethical origins of ethics proves to be essential for understanding the meaning and force of ethics. Proto-ethics attests to the fact that ethical normativity is *sui generis*.

With respect to every inquiry of Being, Heidegger says that "the meaning of Being must already be available to us in some way," (Heidegger 1962: 25) which he designates as "pre-ontological." It is true of any general field of investigation that its most basic notions must in some intuitive sense already be available to us (for any understanding must rely on some frame of reference or expectations).[19] In the same vein, the foregoing discussion showed that through ontological moods

[19]Otherwise we find ourselves facing the famous problem of Plato's *Meno*.

meanings of ethical concepts must already be available to us in a proto-ethical way. The *proto-ethical existential experiences of humanity* are the milieu from which the ethical question we posed at the outset of this paper, "What makes an ethical view ethical?" can be asked meaningfully. It is likewise a pre-requisite for the intelligibility of moral skepticism and therefore circumvents it. (Proto-ethics is thus an important buffer against radical moral skepticism.)[20] Morality does not arise with a sudden apparition of a wholly autarchic idea of the good. The moral good is neither a simple nor a primary quality. It is grounded in certain proto-ethical facets of our humanity that endow it with sense. This paper explained the prominent role of ontological moods in that scheme.

References

Ballard, Bruce W. 1991. *The Role of Mood in Heidegger's Ontology*. Lanham: University press of America.

Cohen, Shlomo. 2008. "Fundamental Equality and the Phenomenology of Respect." *Iyyun: The Jerusalem Philosophical Quarterly* 57: 25–53.

Dennett, Daniel. 1978. "Conditions of Personhood." In *Brainstorms: Philosophical Essays on Mind and Psychology*. Cambridge: MIT Press.

Frankfurt, Harry. 2006. *Taking Ourselves Seriously and Getting It Right*. Stanford: Stanford University Press.

Gibbard, Alan. 1990. *Wise Choices, Apt Feelings*. Cambridge: Harvard University Press.

Golomb, Jacob. 1995. *In Search of Authenticity: From Kierkegaard to Camus*. London/New York: Routledge.

Guignon, Charles. 2003. "Moods in Heidegger's *Being and Time*." In *What Is an Emotion?* ed. Robert C. Solomon. New York/Oxford: Oxford University Press.

Heidegger, Martin. 1962. *Being and Time*. Trans. J. Macquarrie and E. Robinson. New York: Harper & Row.

Heidegger, Martin. 1998. "What is Metaphysics?." In *Pathmarks*, ed William McNeill. Trans D.F. Krell. New York: Cambridge University Press.

Kant, Emmanuel. 1996. *The Metaphysics of Morals*. Trans. M. Gregor. Cambridge: Cambridge University Press.

Levinas Emmanuel. 1969. *Totality and Infinity*. Trans. A. Lingis. Pittsburgh: Duquesne University Press.

Nietzsche, Friedrich. 1974. *The Gay Science*. Trans. W. Kaufmann. New York: Random House.

Olafson, Frederick. 1998. *Heidegger and the Ground of Ethics*. Cambridge: Cambridge University Press.

Sartre, Jean-Paul. 1958. *Being and Nothingness*. London: Methuen.

Warnock, G.J. 1969. *Contemporary Moral Philosophy*. New York: St. Martin's Press.

Wittgenstein, Ludwig. 1953. *Philosophical Investigations*. New York: Macmillan.

[20]This fits with the very sensible intuition that we cannot be wholesale wrong about all our moral intuitions (this prevalent conviction underlies, for example, the important idea of "reflective equilibrium" in ethics).

When Reason Is in a Bad Mood: A Fanonian Philosophical Portrait

Lewis R. Gordon

The struggle for reason often left Frantz Fanon, the revolutionary psychiatrist, social-political theorist, and philosopher from Martinique, in a bad mood. As we will see, he was troubled by the discovery that it often took flight whenever he entered white communities. His presence brought color to the environment, which, unfortunately, changed its mood, and given the role of reason in philosophy, one could imagine the plight of a philosopher whose presence changes the mood of philosophy itself. His reflections on these matters are enduring testaments to what I will call the melancholy of reason in the modern age. It is a condition whose leitmotif is often blue, as in blues music, as the trauma of denied humanity attempts to overcome itself. To make this case, some explanation of Fanon's thought should be helpful.

Fanon, who died just after the first half of the twentieth century, is one of the most influential figures in contemporary African Diasporic philosophy and political thought from the Global South. His influence extends, as well, to a variety of disciplines and fields ranging from literary theory to sociology, from cultural anthropology to cultural studies, and his impact in each area is momentous. In philosophy, for instance, his impact is felt in Africana or African Diasporic philosophy, existentialism, phenomenology, philosophical psychoanalysis, and poststructural analyses. In the African Diaspora, he is claimed as a native son in each region (Gordon 2008a).[1]

None of this is, in the end, accidental. Fanon did not write from any one disciplinary standpoint. His thought was such that it required what Calvin O. Schrag calls "radical reflection," which means that he could not lay claim to presupposed foundations, including disciplinary ones (Schrag 1980).[2] I have elsewhere characterized this

[1]For recent, detailed biographies, see Macey (2002) and Cherki (2006).

[2]For more discussion on Fanon's relation to this concept, see Gordon (1995a), especially chapter 3.

L.R. Gordon (✉)
Department of Philosophy, Temple University, Philadelphia, PA 19122, USA
e-mail: gordonl@temple.edu

H. Kenaan and I. Ferber (eds.), *Philosophy's Moods: The Affective Grounds of Thinking*, Contributions To Phenomenology 63, DOI 10.1007/978-94-007-1503-5_13,

way of thinking as a teleological suspension of disciplinarity, which, I argue, transcends disciplinary decadence (Gordon 2006a). That form of decadence has several features. It involves turning away from reality through a deontologizing or absolutizing of either one's discipline or its method. With nowhere to go except through the application of method, purpose, beyond methodological fetishism, dies, and one's disciplinary eyes are turned away from reality. The proverbial error of looking at a pointing finger instead of the object to which it points is the result. The absence of purpose leads to the thesis that reality does not offer resources for growth in the field, which means, in effect, that the methods have collapsed into methodological solipsism. A teleological suspension of disciplinarity brings reality and purpose back into the equation and offers a basis of critical evaluation of discipline and method. In effect, it announces that neither method nor discipline is the proverbial shoe that fits all sizes.

Fanon was not guilty of disciplinary decadence. His work offers a form of teleological suspension of disciplines, and within the philosophical framework, a teleological suspension of philosophy, that offers some of the paradoxes of teleological suspensions articulated by Søren Kierkegaard in his critique of ethics a century and a half ago.[3] As Schrag has also shown in his discussion of Kierkegaard's teleological suspension of the ethical, it does not follow that to transcend ethics, especially where the teleological motive is a leap toward G-d, is to initiate the *un*ethical (Schrag 1994: 27–32). In similar kind, a teleological suspension of philosophy does not entail the elimination of philosophy. It exemplifies the spirit of treating some questions as so valuable that a philosopher may be willing—and in fact, encouraged—to go beyond philosophy for its sake. In the history of philosophy, there are many instances of thinkers who took such a path, the result of which was at times their being rejected or ridiculed by their peers, and found themselves creating *new philosophy* in their efforts to go beyond philosophy. The historical cast of once non-philosophers in the West is familiar: Descartes (the mathematician), John Locke (the physician), David Hume (the lawyer), Rousseau (nearly everything), G.W. F. Hegel (the theologian), Friedrich Nietzsche (the philologist), Gottlob Frege (the mathematician), Edmund Husserl (the mathematician), William James (the psychiatrist), Karl Jaspers (the psychiatrist), Alfred North Whitehead (the mathematician), Bertrand Russell (the mathematician), Ludwig Wittgenstein (the engineer and mathematician), to name several. In the African Diasporic tradition, the situation is similar: Anna Julia Cooper (the mathematician and pedagogue), W.E.B. Du Bois (the historian and sociologist), C.L.R. James (the historian and novelist), and Frantz Fanon (the psychiatrist), to name some. This community of now famous philosophers shares a biography of coming to philosophy through transcending their original disciplines and taking that spirit to the discipline of philosophy itself.

Much of what I will discuss here pertains to these and many other thinkers, many who avowed a philosophical identity. I will focus on these ideas through Fanon as

[3] Problema I: "Is There a Teleological Suspension of the Ethical?," (Kierkegaard 1983: 54–67).

the main spokesperson, however, for reasons of space and uniqueness of argument.[4] Fanon shares much with the others, but he also brought into stark focus some of these themes, especially on the impact of racism on the construction of rational subjects, at the level of thought and lived-experience in his short life of 36 years.[5]

Fanon's work did not retreat into blindness on racial matters. His work demonstrated that racism and rationality are not incompatible, that there is, in other words, a form of racist rationality.[6] He was not afraid to address affective dimensions of the human struggle with reason. He wrote in his introduction to *Black Skin, White Masks*, for instance, of his fiery spirit having been "cooled" from a fiery rage but not extinguished. Such a portrait offers much insight for the question of thought and mood.

Mood is a coextensive phenomenon encompassing emotional states or qualities, affective tones, dispositions or frames of mind. When good, humor and agreeability often reign, and when bad, it is ruled by ill temper and recalcitrance. In English, to say someone is moody means to say she or he is disagreeable. The concept of mood challenges the extent to which philosophy could hope for an alignment with at least one source of its own decadence in the modern age: natural and theoretical science. Enlisted as an ally in the efforts to yoke reason to scientific rationality, philosophy was often subordinated to evaluation in such terms instead of its own and beyond. A feature of some of the modern through recent Western philosophers I have mentioned as attempting to transcend disciplinary decadence is their refusal to subordinate evaluative thought to scientific rationality and expunge the world of affect. Logical consistency and scientific rigor, although important, fall short of the broader problems of evaluation, as Karl Jaspers often argued, especially regarding the character and meaning of social life.[7] And as Alain Locke has argued, the extrication of affect and value fail at the basic human level because, in his words, "Man cannot live in a valueless world" (Locke 1991). The response here is not to justify one's position on life and to provide logical demonstration of the flaws of scientism and logical-centric philosophy—since such a route already offers paradoxes of performative contradictions and an infinite regress of asserted noncontradictions—but to offer a *diagnosis*. Fanon, in this tradition that also goes back to Arthur Schopenhauer by way of Zigmund Freud, Nietzsche, and Jean-Paul Sartre, asks also for the diagnosis of philosophical investments. There, the problem takes the form of repression and internal denial, of what Sartre calls "bad faith" (*mauvaise foi)*, where lying to one's self takes the formal path of a philosophy that may not believe what it claims to believe, and it does so *sincerely*.

An insight from these thinkers is that the modern obsession with the self reveals a profound desire to avoid self-knowledge. Fanon exposes, autobiographically and through engagements with a variety of disciplinary and textual resources, the need for logical consistency, which, if pushed to its logical extreme, makes him look

[4] For more discussion, see Gordon (2006a, 2008b: 304–320).

[5] For more on Fanon's significance in philosophy, see Hope and Nicholls (2010).

[6] See, e.g., the chapter "Racism and Culture" in Fanon (1967a). See also Part II of Gordon (1995b).

[7] See, e.g., Jaspers (1971).

foolish. His initial naïveté was a function of his failure to realize his situation. W.E.B. Du Bois had shown, for instance, that there are people against whom societal prejudices are such that they are often studied as problems instead of people facing social problems. A result of collapsing people into problems is a form of systemic theodicy. Theodicy involves the justification of the consistency of G-d with the presence of evil and injustice. Such circumstances are rationalized as external to the deity because they are either ultimately just or a consequence of human free will. Both formulations exonerate the deity. When secularized, the argument becomes the intrinsic justice of the given system. Should their life and experiences reveal contradictions, those people are blamed for their condition. A member of a problem people seeking acceptance in a system that generates such people as problems, in effect, attempts membership in a club that would, as Groucho Marx once observed, never accept a person like him. The passages of this struggle with reason and mood move, with what appeared to be the recalcitrance of reason, as we will see, from anger to humor and then onward from tears to prayer. Implicit in this discussion will be the thesis of renewal as considerations in an assessment of philosophy's task of paradoxically transcending itself.

I. Reason and Reasoning in a Bad Mood

Fanon was indignant at reason's flight. His response was to write two philosophical masterpieces. The first, *Black Skin, White Masks*, is an extraordinary performance of multiple meanings, ironic reflection, anxiety, and overcoming. After a variety of movements through the limits of language and erotic mirroring and struggles with violence and death to the point of too much seriousness requiring a series of humorous reprieve, Fanon came upon a disappointing aspect of this journey in black in the modern world:

> Reason was confident of victory on every level. I put all the parts back together. But I had to change my tune.
>
> That victory played cat and mouse; it made a fool of me. As the other put it, when I was present, it was not; when it was there, I was no longer. (Fanon 1967b: 119–120)

Fanon, a man of science and by extension an apostle of reason, reached out to reason but was greeted by its concrete manifestation in the form of an insulted object of affection. The candle that he extended with a wick to be ignited by the flame of reason and thereby spread its illuminating effect was rebuffed, and the tone, the mood, the air, was collapsed into the veneer of lived disappointment from an effort to reach out to reason and the reasonable.

Fanon was traumatized: "The psychoanalysts say that nothing is more traumatizing for the young child than his encounters with what is rational. I would say that for a man whose only weapon is reason there is nothing more neurotic than contact with unreason" (Fanon 1967b: 118). The distinction between rationality and reason is not accidental here. Neither is the reference to the child and the man. Recall that rationality demands consistency. It is the proverbial response against the exception: "If everyone did it…." The child's anxiety is straightforward: "But *I* am not everyone." But the child, as we know, wants to have an already eaten cake. When excluded and frustrated, the child asks, after in effect arguing, "But who says I am like everyone else?": "Why wasn't I included, why was I not one of everyone?" Consistency, however, is a terrible demand to meet *consistently*. The misrepresentation, as Freud observed in *Civilization and Its Discontents*, is the notion that out there, in the world, there are grown-ups *who are always consistent* (Freud 1989; Freud 1963: 34–43). The child has, after all, seen things. Out there, in the world of adults, there are people who break rules. There are people who do not do what they say. Even what they say is at times not really what they are saying. Out there, something else is afoot. It is not consistent. And it *evaluates*. Are they, in a word, unreasonable?

At a basic level, reason is broader than rationality, and as such has room for manifestations that exceed the bounds of structured formalities. Although difficult to maintain, rationality is ultimately simple. It boils down to the maintenance of a rule, and in that restriction it is conducive to form. If things appear otherwise, demonstrate that one is ultimately doing what one initially claimed and things should—nay, *must*—turn out right.

At the core of rationality is a distinction between appearance and reality. In reality, rules are maintained. The circularity of being (or Being?) is sufficient here from a principle of identity: That which can generate itself will always be valid, provided, of course, that the thing in question is identical with itself. What is crucial, however, is that being generates being, and that circularity renders things fine in the world. Yet, as we should also have learned from the world of science, especially in physics, sometimes simplicity is not so simple, and it is often even more difficult to achieve. Embedded in such simplicity, especially in our efforts to evaluate it, is the always-more that awaits its emergence in contradictions.

Reason, however, offers no neat distinction between appearance and reality. There is no reason beneath reason. To be unreasonable is to refuse to do something. It is an unwillingness to admit what appears and what lay beneath, which, too, must have appeared in order to be concealed. Unreason, in other words, demands a kind of unseeing or, better yet, referring back to Schopenhauer, Nietzsche, Freud, and Sartre, *repression*.

Fanon's allusion to the child and the man speaks of the modern structure of black to white. As known by African anti-colonial writers, the history of modern colonialism, at least in relation to the people who became known as blacks, is best formulated by Lord Lugard in the late nineteenth century, who counseled a guardianship relationship with the people of Africa (Lugard 1965).[8] The project was the systematic underdevelopment of indigenous Africans into a childlike people whose resources must be managed by grownups, a mature race, or, more formally, the civilized. Children have no weapons against such an assault. But adults suffer an unusual addition: To fight such degradation without the use of reason would legitimate the initial

[8]For commentary see, Mamdani (1996).

subordinating effort. The best way to claim adulthood is to be an adult. Reason thus becomes *the only weapon* against the avowed advancement of a subordinating rationality. As Fanon reflected, "I felt knife blades open within me. I resolved to defend myself" (Fanon 1967b: 18). From what did he want to defend himself?

Colonialism and racism offered Fanon a degraded reflection with seemingly no sanctuary. To point out the contradictory treatments of blacks in a world that espoused universal humanism was to change the celebratory mood of a modernity that saw nothing but progress. To hide from itself, it demanded from black people nothing short of perpetual happiness. Blacks, perversely, are expected to be in a good mood about their plight in the modern world. What could Fanon do when reason, what is expected to be his only weapon, has thus taken flight?

Fanon's response is the language of love. Fanon *loved* reason. Yet such love made him vulnerable. The unreasonableness of reason, the rejection of *his* love, betrayed its source. So the question is posed: Why was reason being unreasonable? Of what was it afraid?

Reason is afraid of love. Or, in Fanon's language, stripped of euphemism, it fears *intimacy*. What occasions such fear?

> The Negro is a human being. That is to say, amended the less firmly convinced, that like us he has his heart on the left side. But on certain points the white man remained intractable. Under no conditions did he wish an intimacy between the races, for it is a truism that [according to Jon Alfred Mjoen] "crossings between widely different races can lower the physical and mental level.... Until we have a more definite knowledge of the effect of race-crossings we shall certainly do best to avoid crossings between widely different races." (Fanon 1967b: 120)

The logic here moves from returned love to amalgamation. What lurk within Fanon's love are intimacy that offers no resistance against sex and, where heterosexual, the possibility of producing offspring. One cannot here say "reproduction," since it is not a separation that is reproduced. In Aristotelian fashion, where like produces like, there is no like in such intimacy. There is not even, properly speaking, the new. For the new would be *sui generis*. There is, instead, the *mixture*. There is no "whole" in this notion of mixture. It is a consolidation of "halves," which should mean, in effect, the logic of never quite enough. But even that does not work since one half has the teleology of higher and the other of lower. In effect, the notion is of attached twins where one has wings and the other has very heavy feet. One half attempts to take flight while the other, although wishing to fly, is weighted down by both feet being stuck on the ground. Perhaps an occasional hop is achieved, to catch a glimpse of what could be.

The black, reaching out to Reason, is calling for intimacy. Mixed offspring await conception. But sex and reason, we have learned, are supposedly incompatible. As we should know, at least from St. Augustine's ruminations in *The City of God*, sexual impulses are at war with reasonable ones (St. Augustine 1950). They are supposedly the product of sin. And more, at least in modern times, their embodied realization is obscene: "Two realms: the intellectual and the sexual. An erection on Rodin's *The Thinker* is a shocking thought. One cannot decently 'have a hard on' everywhere" (Fanon 1967b: 165). How could a fusion of sex and reason be, in a word, reasonable?

Yet Fanon unveils the neurotic situation. He *needs* reason, but its pursuit makes him a lover who brings too much to the relationship. Reason demands that he leaves much behind as a condition of their embrace. But how reasonable is an expectation that requires an impossible performance? How could a black be embraced under the condition that no blacks must be embraced?

Reason's failure to be reasonable elicits a moment's reflection on what to do. Should Fanon, here taking the role of The Black, attempt to *force* his relationship with his beloved? Reason (ironically engendered in the feminine in French—*la raison*) leaves little room for Fanon but rapacious behavior. For the flight of reason from his outstretched arms requires of him that he not molest it into submission. The neurotic thesis is repeated: He faces reason as his main resource against unreason, even where the source of such consternation is Reason itself. But Reason does not want his love. To embrace him is to face "secretions." He admits: "Little by little, putting out pseudopodia here and there, I secreted a race" (Fanon 1967b: 122). He brings things from the past. Most of them are things that Reason does not want to see. His secretions offer the risk of reason becoming "impure." Reason must be clean, firm, or stable. It must not move.

What is the essence of this thing that Fanon supposedly secretes? It is, in a word, "*rhythm*" (Fanon 1967b: 122). His hand reached out to reason. Should reason accept his touch, it would be moved. It would become intimate. It would also dance.

Rational dance is controlled motion. It is movement that does not groove. In dance, there needs to be a flow that exemplifies freedom. Mere unconstrained movement is not sufficient for dance to occur, however. For dance, as with play, the activity must be infused with spirit, in a word, reason. But rhythm, what is manifested in music and dance, is not necessarily melodic or significant enough to manifest higher expressions. In rhythm is the dichotomy between higher and lower. The rhythmic supports what is expressed at the surface. In effect, the rhythmic becomes the subterranean anxiety. It is a tension beneath that enables expression above.

Fanon was thus right to have been concerned by the consignment of rhythm. It locates the Black in the framework of an aesthetic economy of continued servitude. And as in the semiotics of that economy, the rhythmic, requiring repetition, moves through subterranean orders of natural forces. It signifies the blind, the constant, mechanistic possibilities that lurk beneath a dark expansive universe of movement toward that which ultimately makes no difference. For that concern, one must move into existential reflection on the meaning brought to circumstances of objective futility. Stoic resistance relies on the cultivation of meaning as an antidote to despair.

Oddly enough, Fanon did not like the blues. He lamented black music as a symptom of racism. He expected such music to disappear with the elimination of racial malfeasance. Yet, the blues often transcend racism in their lyrical expression of life's contradictions. In the blues, there is an adult sensibility of an unfair and unforgiving world in which one, nevertheless, must take stock and bear responsibility. This theme of looking into the contradictions and absurdity of life, of being born into a world of suffering, is indication of an insight from ancient times that has taken new forms in the modern world. The ancient insight is, as Nietzsche indicated in *The Birth of Tragedy from the Spirit of Music*, a realization that the absence of suffering could only have been achieved from not having been born (Nietzsche 1999).[9] We encounter here, then, the theme of the cathartic realization of life and its relation to suffering. The blues inaugurates a frame of mind, a mood, of openness wherein admission of the contradictory and paradoxical dimensions of life is possible.

The kind of writing Fanon offers is ironically a performance of this blues sensibility. He offers outstretched arms to a world that rejects him, which he responds to at first with humor and then anger and then retreat into a naïve rationalism whose crumbling, at the end of the fifth chapter of *Black Skin, White Masks*, drove him to tears that washed away his investments in completed subjectivity and a neat, consistent rationalism, and prepared him to explore the contradictory, and sometimes paradoxical, world of psychopathological signifiers and symbols. The movements that led to such a cacophonic world are repetitions of the first four chapters through autobiographical admission of loss salvation. In effect, the blues movement of repetition brings the subject's anxieties on reason to bear in an understanding that such subjects require preparation of the self, the inauguration of the proper frame of mind, the right mood, for the dissonance of life.

The self, however, is not here offered as whole, secure or strong. Such a self, Fanon shows, would have to realize how much of what was not itself that enabled it to be itself. There are others out there, who offer themselves even in their acts of rejecting the others around them. The closure of the self, then, invests the self with its exclusions, and that intersubjective process makes recognition a morass of overturned expectations. As Fanon argued, antiblack racism structures a black Self-Other dialectic beneath a white one in which there is an asymmetrical relationship of no-selves below. In effect, The Black, in this schema, does not struggle against otherness but instead struggles *for* otherness in which ethical relations could take place.

This exclusion into a subterranean schema of life beneath the Self-Other dialectic occasions an added anxiety in the modern world. For this world, as Max Weber observed in *The Protestant Work Ethic and the Spirit of Capitalism*, is governed by a shift in self formation from the questioned soul to the salvational one (Weber 1958). The struggle for salvation stimulates an economy of scarcity since not everyone will be saved. Security for one's salvation relies on those who are, in a word, damned.[10]

The word "damned" is from the Latin word *damnum*, which refers to hurt and to loss. We would be remiss to end our etymological excursion here. I have found that ancient Latin words often have foundations in Greek and Kamitian or ancient Egyptian ones, interestingly often also mediated by Hebrew terms. The peculiar connection here with the Hebrew *adamah* (ground), which is also related to the Kamitian/Egyptian *Atum*, which in turn comes from *'dem* (man and clay or ground). Oddly enough, there is a connection between being damned and being put down; one could interpret this as the consequence of what happens when man attempts to

[9]For discussion, see Gordon (2006b: 75–97).

[10]For an updated discussion of this dynamic, see Comaroff and Comaroff (2000: 291–343).

be G-d. Recall that the human being in Western theology is the result of a fall. What, however, happens when a human being falls below humanity?

The Black, as a function of the modern world, has lost something, and, because of its avowed inclusiveness, so has Reason. For many blacks, this has been the historic dignity of their humanity. But the effort to reclaim their humanness raises the question of whose standards are its exemplars. To be *as human as the whites* offers only one counsel: become white. The retreat into the personal quest to find the true self as *the black self* offers frustration as well. How, that is, could such a black stand on his or her own foundations without being its source? The path reveals loss from levels of phylogeny to those of ontogeny. Realization of such loss offers a special kind of despair.

Abdul JanMohamed, the famed postcolonial theorist, has recently explored the modern black as a figure governed by "death-bound subjectivity" (JanMohamed 2005). This subjectivity is conditioned by the rationalization of modernity as best lived without black folk. That judgment offers a moratorium on black subjects that, in its efforts at erasure, constitutes the illegitimate self. That illegitimacy saturates institutions, especially those governed by force, to the effect of destined mortality outside of the sphere of normal expectations. Death, then, is lived not as a horizon that organizes concern, care, or meaning, but one that is as if retroactively foreclosed even in life. "Accident" falls under the weight of "when." "When will I be stopped by the police?" "When will I be beaten by the police?" "When will I be killed by the police?" "When will I cross the path of another black who has foreclosed his existence and has decide to take me with him?" "When will I be imprisoned?" "What will happen to me there?" "Might I die there?" There is, as well, another dimension to this fatalism. As Amy Alexander and Alvin Poussaint have shown, there are many blacks who die from a slow process of suicide (Alexander and Poussaint 2000). High-risk behavior is also a manifestation of self-destruction: The pressures of eventual failure and death become seductive, and freedom becomes the manifestation of tempted fate.

The Black is, however, aware that death-bound subjectivity is not a normative ideal. A dream haunts that existence. It is a dream of anonymity, of *ordinary anonymity* (Gordon 1995a). It is a dream of being able to live, to walk, and to move through the world without having done something wrong by virtue of existence. It is a call against outlawed existence, a demand for legitimate emergence, or, as Fanon preferred to characterize it, for a *Yes* instead of a *No*.

Yet, not all blacks are crushed by the weight of such modes of being. There are blacks for whom there is nothing wrong with being black. The problem is the attitude of the antiblack racist. Such blacks see the limitations of whiteness as a standard of human existence. They also see the danger of demanding of blackness superiority to whiteness, brownness, and any other racial designation. Blackness, in that sense, simply becomes a mode of being among other modes of being with the realization that the wish for the immaculate birth of the self is a misguided one. Begat from negation, the task is not to avoid that history but to understand it as an organization of a social historical emplacement of which The Black is indigenous. This indigeneity calls for an act of living, as well, with knowledge of its limitations.

To fight it is to create a self the repression of whose inner Other and even not-Other governs its existence.

There is, however, the logic of self-defeat. In a word, such positive assertions of blackness appear as contradictions of terms. Are they "really" black? We return to the neurotic relationship with appearance. The logic is as follows. To appear is to be in a semiotic stream of signifiers. But such signifiers *are* the dominant legitimating signs. Those signs are, in their economy of expression, colonizing modes of expression. To transcend them, then, is to not be interpretable by them. In effect, disappearance or invisibility or absence becomes the goal of political resistance. I call this neurotic because of the expectations of its being a *politics*. What could we make of politics without appearance? It has been a truism from the days of Aristotle to reflections by Hannah Arendt that political life is fundamentally about appearance (Arendt 1998). It requires a public realm, a sphere in which one emerges through the words, deeds, and senses of others. It is where glory is acknowledged and power is formed. To abrogate appearance is an assault on politics itself. As Fanon's thought on sociogenesis suggests, implosion of the self into the hidden fails to address the failures of subjects of recognition. The return of the distinction between problem people and people with problems takes on a structural critique of societal forces.

These thoughts on appearance and subject formation raise the question of locations of appearance. There is, after all, appearance that takes on inner narratives of retreat, sadness, and despair. Maurice Natanson, who admired Fanon, offered this reflection from his essay, "From Apprehension to Decay: Robert Burton's 'Equivocations of Melancholy,'"

> What there is must be taken as a faint sign of what permeates our lives: a light despair which nothing can dislodge from memory or consciousness, a time-haunted enchantment of rotted foundations first discovered, the far side of hope, the infections of the body in prayer—the ecstatic davening of the flesh. (Natanson 1989: 134)

The affinities between Natanson and Fanon permeate this passage. Fanon was critical of the notion of neat resolutions of madness and human suffering. The famous encomium at the end of *Black Skin, White Masks*, the prayer to his body to make of him a man who questions, what else is it but "the ecstatic davening of the flesh"? That Natanson is examining this theme as a clue to the kinds of performance stimulated by melancholic investigation, which could also be characterized as pensive reflection or contemplation, stimulated by the subject of melancholia as an object of study raises the question of a correlative Fanonian performance. Writing on Robert Burton, Natanson observes, "For all his discussions and digressions regarding melancholy, I do not think that Burton ever conclusively defines his subject. That is part of his method, no doubt, a clue to the power of typologies of indirection. But if I am correct, attempts to define the meaning of melancholy can at best be entrances to the being of melancholy" (Natanson 1989: 137). In similar kind, Fanon, nearly four decades earlier, had explored such themes without ever conclusively defining his subject. His reasons were explicit: "I shall be derelict. I leave methods to the botanists and the mathematicians. There is a point at which methods devour themselves" (Fanon 1967b: 12). Fanon's response is to offer an exploration that is both psychoanalytical and phenomenological and, as Sara Ahmed and David Fryer have observed and expanded, *queer* (Ahmed 2006 and Fryer 2008).

Acknowledging that the colonization of modern life also happens at the grammatical level by which meaning is produced, Fanon suspends presumption of methodological validity. In doing so, he *performs* the contradictory practice of methodological rejection of method for the sake of its critical assessment, which allows a confession: "If there can be no discussion on a philosophical level—that is, the plane of the basic needs of human reality—I am willing to work on the psychoanalytical level—in other words, the level of the 'failures,'…" (Fanon 1967b: 23).

How does one live with failures? That it is being explored, that reason is being enlisted in such a relationship, suggests that one can do so by understanding it. But such an understanding may require a realization of always falling short of *apprehension*. This theme suggests that something must be given up in a process where something is also possessed, but it is done through a loss. That there are things gained through loss echoes a theme of teleological suspensions, where what was once taken as absolute is transcended for the sake of something else. Recall that engaging reality demands transcending disciplinary deontologism, which I call disciplinary decadence, where reality is subordinated to methods as in modern attempts to subordinate reason to rationality. Fanon understood that disciplinary presumptions lead to an attempt to squeeze reality into categories that could not exceed it. To suspend such presuppositions lead to a continuously humbling relationship with reality. It is decadent because of its implosive retreat; decay begins when disciplines turn away from reality, as is the case when living beings turn away from life. Judith Butler offers insight on this matter in her essay, "Thresholds of Melancholy":

> Melancholy will mark the limits of definition, its indexical elsewhere. As the *in*definite in definition, melancholy will prompt a digression precisely when one might expect something more lexically precise. This digression will not be beside the point, for the very self under question is, as it were, always beside the point, contouring the point, circumnavigating the imprecision that conditions the very definition by which that imprecision is concealed. Melancholic digression means that precisely where one might expect a fine-tuned denotation, a certain circumlocution slowly begins to make its rounds. If it is linguistic meaning that cannot give us being, and if an arrhythmia afflicts the "shift" from meaning to being, then the language that opens the threshold to melancholia will be less than mellifluous. It will stop and start; it will bear the marks of an *essai*, an effort, a trying. (Butler 1995: 5)

Black Skin, White Masks is an ironic, melancholic text. It splits the author into the internal faith of the system and the external critic of its theodicy, which stimulates an ongoing, contemplative gloom. In effect, it offers a struggle by Fanon with Fanon, which is a *tour de force* performance of the fragmented self and the constitutive practices of subjection and loss. Butler could very well have been describing Fanon in the previous passage, and the following is also apropos: "Understood as an anticipatory intentional positing, melancholy might be said to have 'decay' as its object or, better, to apprehend 'decay'—as the constitutive condition of objects in the world. And yet, this horizon of decay intimates the decaying horizon of the apprehending self. This is not the gradual decaying of a self once whole, but a 'decaying' that persists as the permanent ground of the self" (Butler 1995: 5). The realization of there not having been a "whole" black self is what haunts black existence. A response could be narcissistic rage, of erasing the messenger and the message, but the underlying folly reveals itself in what lurks ahead in such performance—namely, as Natanson had observed, "the far side of hope, the inflections of the body in prayer." Recall that *Black Skin, White Masks* ends with a prayer for his body to make of him a man who questions. To become an interrogative, a question, transcends the closed self, the bonds of epistemic closure. The interrogative always holds the possibilities of yes and *no*. Either permutation serves as the specter of the other, which makes even affirmation premised upon its opposition.

Thinking through Freud's thought on melancholia, Butler argues that it would be incorrect to read melancholic activity as an attachment to the absence of the other in the formation of the ego. "Rather," she avers, "the 'ego' might be said to constitute itself and through that continuing identification, to persist in its identity as an attachment to that absent other… In phenomenological terms, the other is sustained not merely as a memory or as an image, but in and as the self in its imaginary dimension" (Butler 1995: 11). The black who sees nothing wrong with blackness appears as pathology in a world of cosmopolitan assimilationism and multi*cultural* diversity. Such a figure loses at both levels. In the former, there is a failure ultimately to become white. In the latter, there is the failure to assimilate into the logic of ethnicity, and even if that were possible, there is the additional failure of zombification. Multiculturalism demands a meeting of culture *as representation*, which means the tallying of "authentic" exemplars. But what is "black culture" to bring to such authenticating processes short of its pathologies? Cultures that are lived by black people do, after all, find themselves in conflicts over *their differences*. As Fanon observed in his chapter on psychopathology in *Black Skin, White Masks*, the notion of systemically well-adjusted blacks is the obscenity of the happy slaves and maladjusted blacks is the systemically produced normativity of abnormality. How can one live beyond this impasse except through first the blues and struggles for social transformation? Part of black melancholia, of the "self in its imaginary dimension," is a healthy black self, of what the blues calls to us as maturation, of that questioned other who has learned to live with understanding but no peace with a reason that always exceeds his grasp. From the "secretion" of a race, perhaps, then, imagined possibilities call for the simultaneous transcending of that onto which we once attempted to hold. "I, the man of color, want only this: That the tool never possess the man," declared Fanon, after which he asked, echoing Martin Buber, "Was my freedom not given to me then in order to build the world of the *You*?" (Fanon 1967b: 232).

It is crucial that Fanon's conclusion was not a conclusion. He announced that it was "by way of" seeking it. His work of a decade later, *The Wretched of the Earth*, was also without a conclusion (Fanon 1963). For the text itself called to the subject that transcended it, as many of his critics have observed, a new man, which should more accurately be understood as humanity itself since, for Fanon, the human being has been inhibited not by a failure to become complete, but by the failed project of completeness. As with Moses, the great patriarch of melancholia, Fanon understood the value of a performance of a love whose subject is always promised but never had.

References

Ahmed, Sara. 2006. *Queer Phenomenology: Orientations, Objects, Others*. Durham: Duke University Press.

Alexander, Amy, and Alvin Poussaint. 2000. *Lay My Burden Down: Unraveling Suicide and the Mental Health Crisis among African-Americans*. Boston: Beacon.

Arendt, Hannah. 1998. *The Human Condition*, 2nd ed. Chicago: University of Chicago Press.

Butler, Judith. 1995. "Thresholds of Melancholy." In *Prism of the Self: Philosophical Essays in Honor of Maurice Natanson*, ed. Crowell Steven Galt. Dordrecht: Kluwer Academic Publishers.

Cherki, Alice. 2006. *Frantz Fanon: A Portrait*. Trans. Nadia Benhabid. Ithaca: Cornell University Press.

Comaroff, Jean, and Comaroff, John. 2000. "Millennial Capitalism: First Thoughts on a Second Coming." *Public Culture* 12(2, Spring): 291–343.

Fanon, Frantz. 1963. *The Wretched of the Earth*. Trans. Constance Farrington, Jean-Paul Sartre (Introduction). New York: Grove Press.

Fanon, Frantz. 1967a. *Toward the African Revolution*. Trans. Haakon Chevalier. New York: Grove Press.

Fanon, Frantz. 1967b. *Black Skin, White Masks*. Trans. Charles Lamm Markmann. New York: Grove Press.

Freud, Sigmund. 1963. "The Relation of the Poet to Day-Dreaming." In *Freud: Character and Culture*. Philip Rieff (Introduction). New York: Collier Books.

Freud, Sigmund. 1989. *Civilization and Its Discontents*. Trans. and ed. James Strachey, Peter Gay (Introduction). New York: W.W. Norton.

Fryer, David. 2008. *Thinking Queerly: Post-Humanist Essays on Ethics and Identity*. Boulder: Paradigm Publishers.

Gordon, Lewis R. 1995a. *Fanon and the Crisis of European Man: An Essay on Philosophy and the Human Sciences*. New York: Routledge.

Gordon, Lewis R. 1995b. *Bad Faith and Antiblack Racism*. Amherst: Humanity Books.

Gordon, Lewis R. 2006a. *Disciplinary Decadence: Living Thought in Trying Times*. Boulder: Paradigm Publishers.

Gordon, Lewis R. 2006b. "Of Tragedy and the Blues in an Age of Decadence: Thoughts on Nietzsche and African America." In *Critical Affinities: Nietzsche and the African American Experience*, ed. Jacqueline Renee Scott and Todd Franklin, Robert Gooding-Williams (Forward). Albany: State University of New York Press.

Gordon, Lewis R. 2008a. *An Introduction to Africana Philosophy*. Cambridge: Cambridge University Press.

Gordon, Lewis R. 2008b. "Reply to My Critics," for special symposium Teleological "Suspensions in Africana Philosophy: Critical Essays on the Work of Lewis R. Gordon." *The C.L.R. James Journal* 13(2, Summer): 304–320.

Hope, Elizabeth A., and Tracey Nicholls (eds.). 2010. *Fanon and the Decolonization of Philosophy*, with a foreword by Mireille Fanon-Mendès-France. Landham: Lexington Books.

JanMohamed, Abdul. 2005. *The Death-Bound-Subject: Richard Wright's Archaeology of Death*. Durham: Duke University Press.

Jaspers, Karl. 1971. *Philosophy of Existence*. Trans. Richard F. Grabau (Introduction). Philadelphia: University of Pennsylvania.

Kierkegaard, Søren. 1983. *Fear and Trembling and Repetition*. Trans. and ed. Howard V. Hong and Edna H. Hong. Princeton: Princeton University Press.

Locke, Alain. 1991. "Values and Imperatives." In *The Philosophy of Alain Locke: Harlem Renaissance and Beyond*, Reprint edition, ed. Leonard Harris. Philadelphia: Temple University Press.

Lugard, Frederick. 1965. *The Dual Mandate in British Tropical Africa*, 5th ed. London: Frank Cass & Co. Ltd.

Macey, David. 2002. *Fanon: A Biography*. New York: Picador.

Mamdani, Mahmood. 1996. *Citizen and Subject*. Princeton: Princeton University Press.

Natanson, Maurice. 1986. *Anonymity: A Study in the Philosophy of Alfred Schutz*. Bloomington: Indiana University Press.
Natanson, Maurice. 1989. "From Apprehension to Decay: Robert Burton's 'Equivocations of Melancholy'." In *The Gettysburg Review 2*.
Nietzsche, Friedrich. 1999. *"The Birth of Tragedy" and Other Writings*. Trans. and ed. Ronald Speirs, Raymond Geuss, and Ronald Speirs. Cambridge: Cambridge University Press.
Schrag, Calvin O. 1980. *Radical Reflection and the Origin of the Human Sciences*. West Lafayette: Purdue University Press.
Schrag, Calvin O. 1994. "Note on Kierkegaard's Teleological Suspension of the Ethical," in his *Collected Papers: Betwixt and Between*. Albany: State University of New York Press.
St. Augustine. 1950. *The City of God*. Trans. Marcus Doas, Thomas Merton (Introduction). New York: Modern Library.
Weber, Max. 1958. *The Protestant Ethic and the Spirit of Capitalism*. Trans. Talcott Parsons, R.H. Tawney (Introduction). New York: Scribner.

Part VI
Epilogue

How Death Deals with Philosophy

Ben-Ami Scharfstein

I've heard that it's hard to evade death. To judge by the energy that philosophers have put into denying that death is final or affirming that it is unimportant, they have taken the possibility of dying seriously. Our individual experience with dying, of others and implicitly of ourselves, is of course quite varied. I was lucky not even to have seen a corpse until I was in my early teens. My reaction was strong. I felt for a while that I would never be happy again. This mood was coupled with the terror (I know now to be usual) of a state the experience of which is incomprehensible because totally opaque to consciousness. My father, tired of a life that had become too painful, died with resignation. His last words were "This is surely the end." In contrast, my father in law, a poet and philosopher, whom I last saw the day before his death, kept repeating "Save me! Save me!" This meant, as I understood it, that he felt his life unfinished as long as he still had poetry to write—the experience of its creation was reason enough for him to insist on continuing to live. If my meager experience is not misleading, it seems that the process of dying, though universal, is reacted to in individual ways.

That leads me to a word on individuality. I have to say it, because by aiming to make plausible generalizations I incur the danger of forgetting how individual philosophers are. Later on, when I discuss Hume and Kant, I will use context and empathy to come closer to the individual. This prospect releases me to make my first generalization, a mere truism: Every philosopher and philosophy is individual. Since I do not know of any individual person or creation that is exempted from affect, that is, emotion or mood, I hazard my second generalization: There is no philosophy devoid of affect.

B.-A. Scharfstein (✉)
Department of Philosophy, Tel-Aviv University,
P.O. Box 39040, Ramat Aviv, Tel-Aviv 69978, Israel
e-mail: sbenami@post.tau.ac.il

H. Kenaan and I. Ferber (eds.), *Philosophy's Moods: The Affective Grounds of Thinking*, Contributions To Phenomenology 63, DOI 10.1007/978-94-007-1503-5_14,

The differing tone, tempo, structure, analytic style, turns of thought, illustrative examples, and similes and metaphors that characterize different philosophies are evidence of the many different ways in which the affect can come to expression.

What is it that most obviously leads to the differences in the forms that philosophies take? The answer is, of course, the philosophers' different natures, from birth itself, and, of course, the difference in their surroundings and development from childhood on, including the effect on them of their teachers. A philosopher-to-be may even inherit philosophy from a philosopher-parent, for example, John Stuart Mill from James Mill, and William James from his father, Henry. But a philosopher's inheritance is surely not of philosophical abstractions alone. Since death is my subject, I recall the effect of illness and death. Descartes feared he had inherited pallor, weak lungs, and a probably early death from his mother. Kant assumed he had inherited a narrow chest and consequent weakness and hypochondria from his mother. William James may have felt his breakdown to be a repetition of his father's. Bertrand Russell tried to imagine the presence of his hardly remembered parents, but he lived parentless, deeply lonely, and thinking often of suicide, from which he was saved, he says, by his interest in mathematics.

Such heritages of fear and absence result in an underlying fear or resentment because the parent, the source and support of life, is felt to be also the source of loneliness, weakness, or death. Nietzsche's life and thought give dramatic evidence. As a little child, he would watch his father at work. When he cried, his father would play the piano for him, and he would sit still and upright in his carriage, his eyes fixed on his beloved father. Unfortunately, the father, a pastor, died of a brain disease when Nietzsche was only 4. Later, in elementary school, Nietzsche became known as "The Little Pastor," no doubt because of his solemnity and his expressive recitation from the Bible. His love for music grew and, like his father, he would improvise movingly on the piano. Once when sick, he wrote to his mother, "When I don't hear music, everything seems dead to me." In the many autobiographical sketches he wrote during his youth, he commemorates his father's virtues and mourns the sudden, bitter catastrophe of his death. For a long time Nietzsche remained afraid that he would die at the same age as his father, 36. His early desire to become a pastor, like his father, changed radically, and he bitterly denounced the Christianity his father had taught. For example, In a passage in *The Antichrist* he speaks of a higher type of man, and then says (1.5) that Christianity has waged deadly war against this higher type, "has sided with all that is weak and base" and "made an ideal of whatever contradicts the instinct of the strong to preserve itself" (Nietzsche 1954 [book 1, sect. 10]: 576) He grew ready to voice open criticism of his father. In *Ecce Homo* ("Why I am So Wise," sect. 3) he again praises his father, attributes to him whatever he has of "privileges"—but adds, "not including life, the great Yes to life" (Nietzsche 1968: 682).

Like Descartes and the other philosophers I've mentioned, every philosopher was once a child whose deeper questions were exacerbated by some fear or loneliness, most profound when caused by the absence or early death of parents. Remember that a mother's moods, the rhythm of her heart, and the modulation of her voice may influence an even unborn child. Remember, too, how the sensitive interchange of information between mother and infant makes each become the other's echo and frame of reference. A helpful, responsive relation with parents breeds trust, a poor, unresponsive one, distrust. Such trust or distrust is expressed in adult life as the willingness or unwillingness to believe in others and, generally, in the world. Because we philosophers often make far-reaching assumptions, maybe you will not disallow the possibility that a mother's insecure arms may be later translated into a world that is insecure, in which the person, like Alice in her hole, falls deeper and deeper. My third generalization is therefore: A child is affected for life by the nature of its parents' presence or absence.

I have committed myself to give relatively developed examples of how affective states color a philosopher's thought. The first example is that of Immanuel Kant's hypochondria; the second is that of David Hume's long depression. The first example leads to another. fourth generalization (restricted to Kant): Kant's hypochondria, considered along with its causes, was a major, perhaps indispensable influence on his theory of the co-presence of universal causation with freedom. The second example, of Hume, leads me to my fifth generalization (restricted to Hume): Hume's depressive period, along with its causes, was a major, perhaps indispensable influence on his belief that there is no necessary connection between causes and effects or between perceptions. Yet Hume believes that human choices and actions, like external events, always have causes. We do experience volitions, he says, but there are always reasons for them. Put as an anti-Kantian maxim, Hume holds that no act is done from a sense of duty alone. His moral theory stresses the role of "sympathy," his term for what is now called empathy, the ability to participate in the pains and pleasures of others.

The evidence to justify my generalization on Kant begins with the effect on him of his parents. They were exceptionally decent, peace-loving, and proper. His father, who taught him above all to avoid lies, died when Kant was 21. Kant loved him, but he adored his pious mother, who had died when he was only 13. She had taught him to identify plants, told him what she knew of the structure of the heavens, and impressed on his mind a reverence for the Creator, opening his heart, as Kant says, to the impressions of nature and exerting a lastingly wholesome influence on his life. He could never forget that it had been her kindness that had literally killed her. This happened when, to persuade a seriously ill neighbor woman to take some medicine, she tasted it first, using a spoon that had been in the ill woman's mouth. What Kant tells about his parents, especially his mother, is easy to associate with the well-known passage in the *Critique of Practical Reason* (at the start of its conclusion):

> Two things fill my mind with ever new and increasing admiration and awe...the starry heavens above me and the moral law within me...I see them before me and I associate them directly with the consciousness of my own existence...The former begins from the place I occupy in the external world of sense...The latter, on the contrary infinitely raises my worth as that of an intelligence by my personality, in which the moral law reveals a life independent of all animality and of the whole world of sense.... (Kant 1949: 258–59)

Despite Kant's view of his parents, he does not see childhood as happy. In his lectures on education he says that our youthful years are the most troublesome because we are under strict discipline, can rarely choose our friends and, still more rarely have our freedom. Yet he does not seem eager to make children's lives any happier. He wants them strictly (though not "slavishly") disciplined and complains that playing with them "like monkeys, singing to them, caressing, kissing, and dancing with them" makes them self-willed and deceitful and shames their parents.

It is clear that Kant distrusts unstructured thought. In the lectures published as *Anthropology from a Pragmatic Point of View*, he states that it is useful to observe in ourselves reflections of the kind that are necessary for logic and metaphysics. He goes on:

> But to try to eavesdrop on ourselves when they occur in our mind unbidden and spontaneously…is to overturn the natural order of the cognitive powers, because then the principles of thinking do not come first.... If it is not already a form of mental illness (hypochondria), it leads to this and to the lunatic asylum. (Kant 1974: 15)

According to Kant, for a scholar, orderly abstract thinking "is a means of nourishment, without which, when he is awake and alone, he cannot live." Philosophical thinking fully interested in the absolute unity that is ultimate goal of reason bears with it a feeling of power that compensates in part "for the bodily weakness of old age by means of the rational appreciation of the value of life" (*The Dispute of the Faculties*, Loewenberg 1953: 307–22).

Sadly for Kant, in spite of all the effort he put into orderly, abstract thinking, he was always, as he says, a natural hypochondriac, a condition he describes in vigorously emotional detail. He tried to master this predisposition by turning his thoughts and actions away from it and ordering his life so rigorously that his health came to be, he thought, a work of art created by himself. But in time, his full fear of death became more and more evident. He talked with great interest about hygiene, diet, and the prolongation of life, and he shared every change of his condition with his friends. He would get the latest mortality statistics from the chief of the Königsberg police and each time recalculate his own life-expectancy, and he memorized and was ready to recite a list of men who had enjoyed a long life. Concerned at the effect of the direction of the wind on his health, he would often take a look at the weathervane and, for caution's sake, would often check the thermometer, barometer, and hygrometer, and open a window for brief moments to test the exact quality of the air. Sweating alarmed him. When he walked outside and felt that he was on the verge of sweating, he would linger in a shadow until the danger had passed. For the sake of his health, he trained himself to breathe through the nose alone. And at night, to avoid what he thought the danger of getting up when thirsty, he would expand his chest to drink in the air instead.

When I describe these ritualistic defenses against death, I wonder if you feel, as I do, a philosopher's sense of insult that so great and so resourceful a philosopher became so imprisoned in his web of irrational beliefs and expedients. How much of the energy that went into the construction of his conceptual edifices may have been derived from his struggle against death? Was there a possible relation between the extreme demands his philosophy sometimes makes, most evident in his ethics, and his growing alienation from others and perhaps himself? Is there a relationship between his compulsions and his unrelenting insistence on the correctness and completeness of his table of categories?

Of all the questions of this sort, I will take up only two, which I join and make an attempt to answer. The first question is on the effect of his parents' views on his doctrines, especially his moral rigorism. The other is on the unpersuasiveness, as I take it to be, of his doctrine of the thing in itself, which is, affectively, as I believe, a defense of this rigorism, that is, of his parents. Before I take up this defense, I should recall that (as I suppose you may know) that Kant in his old age became an embittered misanthrope troubled by dreams in which he was surrounded by thieves and murderers. If it were not immoral, he might take his life, he said (though he still looked forward to the return of the bird that sang near his window and still anticipated his eightieth birthday, which he did not live to celebrate). The contrast of his end with that of David Hume, whose philosophy awakened Kant's, could not be greater.

Kant believed in the unknown, unknowable thing in itself because, he declared, it would be absurd for appearances not to be the appearances of something. Disputes in his own time and later show that Kant might have adopted a more easily defensible view, like that of the Neo-Kantians who held that we can approach more and more closely to the absolute truth that we can never quite attain. Kant, however, needed to keep appearances in diametrical opposition to reality. To do this he fell back on his "principle of the transcendental analytic," by which all occurrences in the world of sense accord with invariable natural law. If freedom is possible, he asks, does every effect in the world arise either from nature or freedom, or simultaneously from both, each in a different relation. But to presuppose the absolute reality of appearances, he says, confuses reason.

> For if appearances are things in themselves, then freedom cannot be saved...If, on the other hand, appearances do not count for any more than they are in fact, namely... only for mere representations connected in accordance with empirical laws, then they themselves must have grounds that are not appearances. Such an intelligible cause, with its causality, is outside the series; its effects, on the contrary, are encountered in the series of empirical conditions. The effect can therefore be regarded as free in regard to its intelligible cause, and yet simultaneously, in regard to appearances, as their result according to the necessity of nature. (Kant 1998: A536/B564)

Of the need, his need, to believe in an unprovable God and an unprovable immortality, Kant says: "Our belief in a God and another world is so interwoven with my moral disposition that I am in as little danger of ever surrendering the former as I am worried that the latter can ever be torn away from me" (Kant 1998: A828/B856).

Such defenses of the thing in itself and of belief in God are not in themselves highly convincing. But they convince Kant because they make it possible for him to pair the phenomena of the world in fact with the hopes conceived by "reason," which make his own ideals plausible and give the memory of his parents, the first source of these ideals, a halo of optimism. Put it this way: If appearances are things in themselves and there is no freedom, then the world in which his mother died of helping a friend and in which her goodness and his father's decency and truthfulness are unrewarded and his own endless thought and endless self-rule consists of no more than brute, intolerable facts. Kant knew that his parents' dignity, which he cherished as his inheritance from them, depended on their freedom to think and act as they thought morally right. From the affective standpoint I have been expressing, Kant was misled by his need to defend his own hopes and his parents' honor. In contrast, Hume's psychophysical struggle did not lead him to philosophical extravagance but to a view of the human mind as a republic made up of different, possibly changing members and rules—a conception that fits contemporary neurobiology relatively well. Furthermore, Hume believed, as Kant could not, that everything in his philosophy was subject to empirical correction.

Who was this Hume, and what do I mean by speaking of his freedom from philosophical extravagance? He suffered the death of his father when he was two. He remembered his mother, who survived until he was 34, as a "woman of singular Merit, who, though young and handsome, devoted herself entirely to the rearing and educating of her children." When she grew ill, he refused for a time to leave her. Her death affected him very deeply.

Hume's life shows how strongly a depressive mood may color the nature of an entire book of philosophy. The book I mean is A Treatise of Human Nature, Hume's first and most famous work. Hume formed it during a period that included some 9 months when he was in the grip of a severe depression. He thought about what was to become the Treatise, he says, before he was 15, planned it before he was 21, and wrote it before he was 25. In a letter he wrote in 1734, when he was 23, to an anonymous physician, he tells of the depression he had fallen into for 9 months, when he was collecting basic materials for many books. He had been "infinitely happy" over his earlier decision to give up law in favor of scholarship and philosophy. "However, about the beginning of September 1729," he goes on, "all my Ardor seemed in a moment to be extinguisht, & I cou'd no longer raise my Mind to that pitch, which formerly gave me such excessive pleasure." He attributes this long "distemper," as he calls it, to the reading of books by writers such as Cicero, Seneca, and Plutarch, filled with moral exhortations. "I was continually fortifying myself," he writes "with Reflections against Death, & Poverty, & Shame, & Pain, & all the other Calamities of Life." He explains that his condition, which resembles that described in the writings of French mystics and some English "fanatics," is "a Coldness & Desertion of the Spirit, which frequently returns." He writes:

> My Disease was a crule Incumbrance on me. I found that I was not able to follow any Train of Thought, by one continued Stretch of View, but by repeated interruptions, & by Refreshing my Eye from Time to Time upon other Objects. Yet with this Inconvenience I have collected the rude Material for many Volumes; but in reducing these to Words, when one must bring the Idea he comprehended in gross, nearer to him...I found impracticable for me, nor were my Spirits equal to so severe an Employment. (Hume 1932 Vol.1: 16).

It is not psychologically surprising that the breaks in Hume's thought, that is, his inability to follow any train of thought for long without distraction, and his repeated feeling of "desertion of the Spirit" (in clinical language, depersonalization) were the background of his doctrine that the mind is not a substance but a series of perceptions whose sequences were often wearying, discouraging, or frightening. It was his sense that his cohesiveness and even reality could be almost extinguished that allowed him to dares to adopt the extreme view that the mind has no uniting principle but "is nothing but a bundle or collection of different perceptions, which succeed one another with an inconceivable rapidity" (1.4.6). Projected on the world outside him, the breaks, the need to "refresh the eyes upon other objects" in order to renew his interest in the subject and in life were the background of his enthusiasm for the similar doctrine (which he found in Malebranche) that it is not inherent necessity but mere habit that links causes with effects. That is, his experience of a world the cohesiveness of which is not constant in perception or emotion encouraged him to accept the view that there is no real, necessary connection between cause and effect, so that the world is not the product of any purpose and is seen and felt as if it had been, so to speak, derealized, deprived of its powers.

To Hume, these observations are the result of careful observation, and his letter comes to the conclusion, to which he always remained faithful, that science and morality must be based on an experientially validated science of psychology. In his own words: "There is no question of importance, whose decision is not compriz'd in the science of man.... And as the science of man is the only solid foundation for the other sciences, so the only solid foundation we can give to this science must be laid on experience and observation" (Hume 1896).

Readers of the *Treatise* may be taken aback by passages in which Hume recalls his fear of the depressive condition of which the book is, at least in part, the hard-won result. He really means it when he says in his conclusion:

> My memory of past errors and perplexities, makes me diffident for the future. The wretched condition, weakness, and disorder of the faculties, I must employ in my enquiries, increase my apprehensions...This...view of my danger strikes me with melancholy; and as 'tis usual for that passion, above all others, to indulge itself; I cannot forbear feeding my despair, with all those desponding reflections, which the present subject furnishes me with in such abundance...I am first affrighted and confounded with that forelorn solitude, in which I am plac'd in my philosophy...I call upon others to join me, in order to make a company apart; but no one will hearken to me. (Hume 1896: 1.4.7).

An Enquiry Concerning Human Understanding, a revised, more urbane version of *The Treatise*, was more appropriate to Hume's later, happier self. His final affectionate, even-tempered disposition turned him into an exemplary philosopher in actions no less than in words. If I were to choose a hero for this essay, it would be Hume. This is because of his enthusiasm for the progress of thought, his insistence on empirical verification, and, as this essay emphasizes, his ability to turn depression into bold, intelligent philosophy. As for death, he wrote in 1776 to a friend, "Death appears to me so little horrible in his Approaches, that I scorn to quote Heroes and Philosophers as Example of Fortitude.... I embrace you, Dear Sir, and probably for the last time."(To Sir John Pringle,13 Aug., 1776, Hume 1932 vol. 2: 356).

I've finished, except to recall a succession of generalizations: that philosophers and philosophies are always individual; that the abstraction native to philosophy is always inseparable from affect; that the character of parents' presence and absence always influences philosophy; and that the philosophies of Kant and of Hume, both of them extraordinarily ambitious and creative, are more fully understood if studied in relation to their different, almost opposite affective lives, ending, in the one case, in misanthropic misery and, in the other, in a relaxed humanism. One sees that, when grasped as complementary angles of vision, philosophy and psychology make our understanding more subtle and realistic. The effect of joining them cannot be predicted, but it can as easily increase as decrease our admiration of a great philosopher.

I've finished, except to say, insight comes from many directions.[1]

[1] The information in the above essay is derived from my book *The Philosophers: Their Lives and the Nature of Their Thought,* London and New York, 1980, where it is more fully developed and documented. In the hope that my essay preserve some of the feeling of freely developing thought, I have refrained from documentation of anything in it beyond direct quotation.

References

Hume, David. 1896. *A Treatise of Human Nature*, ed. L.A. Selby-Bigge. Oxford: Oxford Clarendon Press.
Hume, David. 1932. *The Letters of David Hume*, 2 vols., ed. J.Y.T. Grieg. Oxford: Clarendon Press.
Kant, Immanuel. 1949. *Critique of Practical Reason and Other Writings in Moral Philosophy.* Trans. L.W. Beck. Chicago: Chicago University Press.
Kant, Immanuel. 1974. *Anthropology from a Pragmatic Point of View*. Trans. Mary Gregor. The Hague: Martinus Nijhoff.
Kant, Immanuel. 1998. *Critique of Pure Reason*. Trans. P. Guyer and A.W. Wood. Cambridge: Cambridge University Press.
Loewenberg, R.D. 1953. "From Immanuel Kant's Self-Analysis." *American Imago* 10: 307–322.
Nietzsche, Friedrich. 1954. *The Portable Nietzsche.* Trans. W. Kaufmann. New York: Penguin Books.
Nietzsche, Friedrich. 1968. *Basic Writings of Nietzsche. What Death Does to Philosophy.* Trans. W. Kaufmann. New York: The Modern Library.

Index

H. Kenaan and I. Ferber (eds.), *Philosophy's Moods: The Affective Grounds of Thinking*, Contributions To Phenomenology 63, DOI 10.1007/978-94-007-1503-5,